HANDY GARDENER

Collins

HANDY GARDENER

First published in 2004 by HarperCollins*Publishers*
77–85 Fulham Palace Road, London, W6 8JB

The Collins website address is:
www.collins.co.uk

Based on material from the *Collins Practical Gardener* series, created by Focus Publishing

The majority of the photographs in this book were taken by Tim Sandall. All others were taken by Focus Publishing

Conceived, edited and designed by: Focus Publishing,
11a St Botolph's Road, Sevenoaks, Kent, TN13 3AJ
Project manager: Guy Croton
Editor: Vanessa Townsend
Designer & illustrator: David Etherington
Indexer: Caroline Watson

For HarperCollins
Senior managing editor: Angela Newton
Design manager: Luke Griffin
Editor: Alastair Laing
Production controller: Chris Gurney

A CIP catalogue record for this book is available from the British Library

ISBN 0007172222

Colour reproduction in Singapore by Colourscan
Printed and bound in Spain

Contents

How To Use This Book

***Handy Gardener* is a uniquely user-friendly guide to most aspects of gardening. The book is divided into two distinct parts – the first is a no-nonsense guide to all the essential practical techniques that the gardener needs to know and the second section of the book is a directory of the best garden plants in all principal categories, arranged by Latin names in a convenient A–Z style. Page margin colour coding and a unique system of companion plant cross-referencing combine with detailed indices to make this the ideal handy reference source for every gardener.**

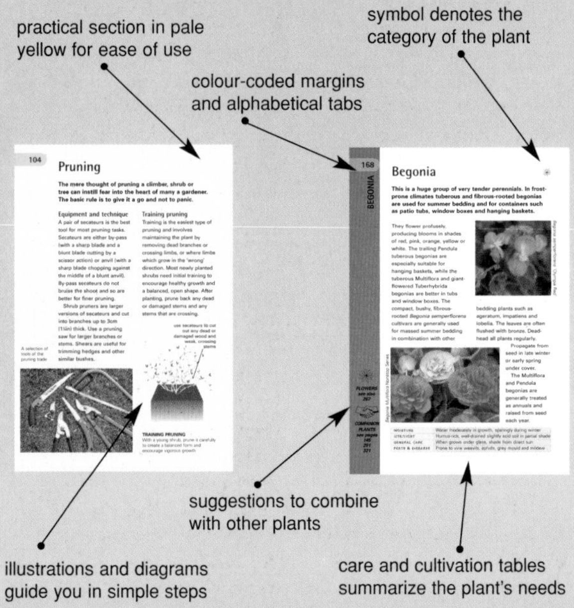

Introduction

Gardening is one of the most consistently popular pastimes of our era. More and more people are taking up this timeless hobby, which offers a unique range of rewards.

In keeping with the demands of its vast and ever-growing band of adherents, there are books on the market that cater for every conceivable aspect of gardening. Some of these purport to tell the reader absolutely everything they need to know about the subject, but these volumes are invariably huge and unwieldy. Other books offer exhaustive lists of plants or masses of practical information – but never enough of both these elements together. Now, however, for the first time, here is a handy guide for every gardener which provides the perfect blend of all-round plant information and practical advice.

Arranged in an easy-to-use, pocket-sized format, *Handy Gardener* is designed for quick dipping-in and out when the user needs instant information about a particular plant or technique. The first part of the book – with the pages coloured pale yellow for ease of use – is a guide to all the essential techniques that any general gardener requires. The second part of the book is a directory of plants from all the principal categories – flowers, shrubs, climbers, architectural plants and trees. The plants are arranged alphabetically by Latin name and a clear symbol beside the plant name denotes to which category the plant in question belongs. This quick-reference organisation is reinforced by colour-coded page margins, each letter of the alphabet being clearly indicated by a different colour.

Detailed descriptions of the A–Z plants are accompanied by care and cultivation notes and tables, colour photographs throughout and a unique system of companion plant cross-referencing, which suggests the best plants to mix with the species you have selected.

Handy Gardener is the perfect quick reference point for any gardener. Tuck it in your pocket, get gardening, and you will soon wonder how you did without it beforehand...

Practical Gardening

This section of the book, with pages coloured pale yellow for ease of use, is a practical guide to all the essential techniques that any general gardener needs.

The practical pages of *Handy Gardener* guide you through all areas of basic gardening, from the first step of assessing your actual site, through the planning stages, knowing your soil, choosing which plants to buy, general care and maintenance and on to propagation techniques. It is an ideal reference for the beginner, as well as the more experienced gardener, which can be kept in your pocket or gardening bag and referred to on site.

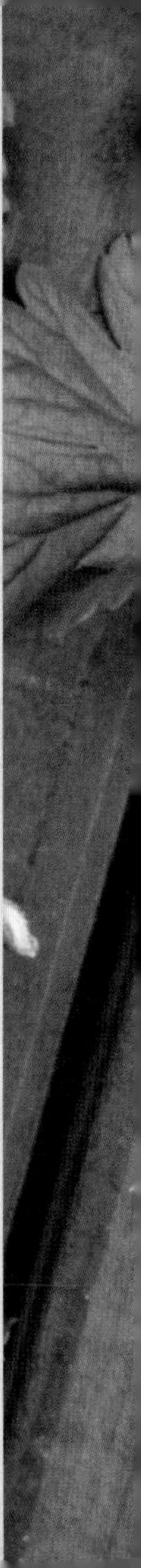

Assessing Your Garden

Understanding your garden will help you in deciding which plants will grow best. Consider factors such as soil type, existing features, and light and shade when assessing the suitability for growing certain plants.

Aspect is an important factor as this will determine which parts of your garden get more sun than other parts, or which are in constant shade. Knowing this will help you choose the right plants – and even the correct species or variety – for specific areas of the garden. It is pointless planting a sun-loving specimen in a spot that never sees the sun!

Digging organic matter into your garden soil will help enrich it

Certain plants can also be damaged by being planted in an open position where the wind whips through. If there are places in your garden where this happens more than elsewhere, either plant wind-resistant specimens or create shelter from the wind if you still want to grow certain plants there.

Syringa vulgaris likes alkaline soils

Soil condition and drainage is another top priority. Is the soil a heavy clay or a light sandy type? Is it alkaline, neutral or acidic? How fertile is it? Soils can always be improved by adding organic matter for a more rich, humus

Hydrangea quercifolia
'Snow Flake' suffers in wind

content, sand or grit for more drainage or even digging in ericaceous soil to affect the pH level.

It is always easier to work with Nature rather than fight against Nature, so in the first instance, look for plants that suit your garden conditions, rather than turning your existing garden on its head!

KEY

This symbol denotes the shadiest parts of a garden

The yellow lines denote sunshine in the garden.

The blue arrows denote the direction of wind.

This green arrow denotes a gradient in the garden floor.

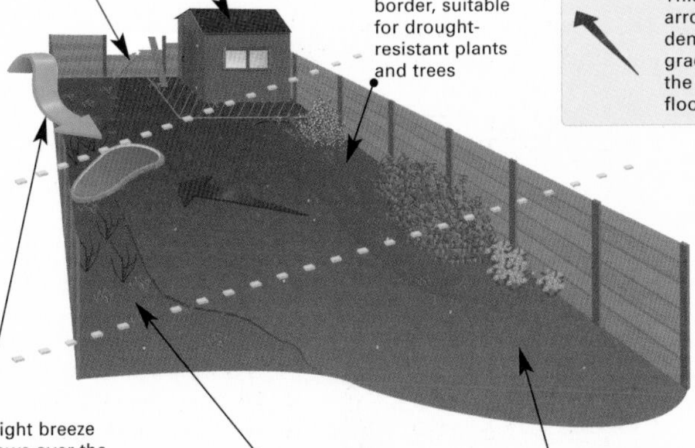
broken old fence; replace with a shrub border or hedging?
sheds and other buildings will cast shadows for some of the day; avoid planting sun-loving plants here
free-draining border, suitable for drought-resistant plants and trees
a light breeze blows over the garden fence. Plants with some wind resistance will do well in this part of the garden
a sunny, free-draining border is the ideal place for having a mixture of sun-loving plants
suitable area for semi-shade-tolerant plants

Planning Your Garden

Once you have familiarized yourself with the growing conditions and the various elements of your garden, the next step is to design a layout, decide what to grow and draw up a planting plan. This can also take into account crop rotation if you want to grow vegetables.

Designing your plot

Permanent planting

You will need to allocate plants to the various areas of your garden. To do this, you should take into consideration the soil, areas of shade or full sun, and permanent fixed structures that you already have in place, such as a shed, greenhouse, fencing or brick walls.

You may have established plants, such as a large specimen tree with a beautiful architectural shape or shrubs used for hedging, already in your garden. The decision is whether to plan around these established features, and use them as the starting point for your design, or dig them up and start again from scratch.

An archway of fruit trees adds interest and structure to a garden

Walkways

Access to your beds and borders is also an important consideration. You do not want to be clambering across a border to get to the plants at the back; even if you manage not to trample the plants at the front, you will end up compacting the soil. If you have pathways already, then make use of them, constructing your beds leading off from the paths.

Otherwise, you may have to lay some type of access to your beds. The paths should be fairly maintenance free, as you do not want to be weeding a path when you could spend the time weeding the garden.

Avoid organic materials, such as chipped bark, and instead choose hard surfaces such as concrete slabs, brick pavers, gravel or stone. Laid in a bed of sand in a herring-bone pattern, pavers look especially decorative yet are extremely practical and hardwearing.

One of the easiest paths to lay is gravel. Laid over a sheet of plastic to deter weeds, gravel gives an instant effect. Lay it deep enough to hide the plastic, yet not so deep that it makes pushing the wheelbarrow difficult.

Brick pavers make an attractive path to give access to your beds

Edging helps to contain the soil and provides a visual separation between the path and the bed. Bricks laid on edge to create a dog-tooth pattern is a popular and attractive form of edging. Other popular edging materials include box, grown as low hedges, which is traditional and attractive but provides a haven for slugs and snails, and low woven hazel or willow hurdles.

Practical elements

Coastal gardens in particular may need protecting from the elements in the form of windbreaks or fencing, so this must be taken into consideration in your planning. Will you need to construct a windbreak or could you achieve this just as easily through planting vigorous, hardy shrubs or several poplars in a row to form a barrier?

Permanent barriers are best made from permeable material such as woven hazel or willow, rather than creating a solid structure, like a fence, which will only increase the wind's ferocity.

A pond makes an attractive focal point in any garden

Water features

An increasingly popular element in today's garden is the water feature and it is vital that this is planned in to your design before you begin planting. You may already have an old or established pond, in which case you need only decide which plants would look good and grow best next to the water. However, if you need to lay tubing or an electric cable from one end of the garden to the other, you do not want to be digging through newly planted shrubs or beds of flowers in bloom to install your water feature.

Vegetable bed designs

Keep the design for a kitchen garden as simple as possible. The aim is to look attractive while making the best use of the space available (see illustration right; the colours correspond with the crop rotation scheme detailed on pages 62–63).

A square plot, for example, works well when divided into either four smaller square beds dissected by a cross-shaped path, or four triangular beds with the paths running from corner to corner. A round plot with three or four wedge-shaped beds is a particularly efficient design, as the space around the edges can be used for fruit, although keep taller fruit trees where they cannot shade the other crops.

Take your time

Planning may seem a tedious exercise, stopping you from getting started with the actual gardening, but it is important. It is all too easy to fall in love with plants you have seen in a garden centre, bring them home, plant them and then realize they really don't suit your established plants, they are too large and are planted in shade rather than sun. Planning is the key to a more enjoyable garden!

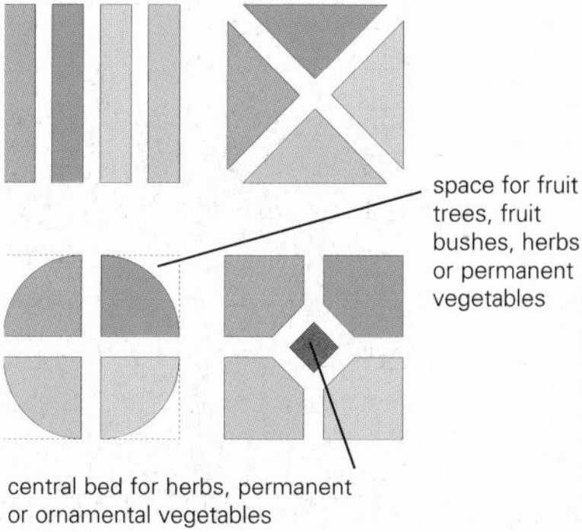

Preparing the Site

After all the planning stages, now is the time for the hard work. This means clearing the area you have chosen for planting and, most importantly, getting rid of any weeds or wild brambles that have taken hold.

Clearing

Having decided upon the ideal site for your plants it is time to prepare the ground for growing. Make sure all preparation takes place over autumn, winter and early spring, so that everything is ready for the main cultivating period in late spring and summer.

If you want to grow plants in an area that has been previously uncultivated for a while, where weeds and wild plants like brambles and nettles have taken hold, a drastic measure may be to spray with a heavy duty herbicide. Once sprayed, cover the area with black polythene and leave for a year.

However, most areas can be cleared simply by pulling up weeds by hand, ensuring you have the entire root, and hoeing through the area to check every weed has been removed.

TIP

Weeding is a whole lot easier if you can remove weeds while they are still young and small, with surface roots.

You should regularly remove perennial weeds from around plants

Dealing with weeds

Unchecked, rampant growers such as bindweed, nettles, couch grass and ground elder can take over an entire garden, so it is vital the whole weed – roots and all – is dealt with.

There are three methods of destroying weeds – mechanical, manual and chemical. The mechanical method is with the help of a rotavator and its assorted attachments. This is excellent if you want to remove annual weeds from a new site and it can save a lot of time and effort. However, this method could cause soil compaction, which would mean the roots on perennial weeds would be chopped up and just distributed more widely.

Manual weeding is simply removing weeds and roots by hand, hoe and fork. This is often easier during dry weather where they can be loosened and left on the surface to dry out. Destroy annual weeds by repeated hoeing. It is important to remove them before they start seeding, thus reducing the chance of them spreading.

Perennial weeds propagate themselves from their roots and stems, as well as from seed. They remain under the ground, making them more difficult to deal with. Even bits of root left undiscovered will quickly gain a foothold, and before you even realise there is a problem, they will have taken over completely.

Weedkillers

If you have a serious weed problem, the third way to control weeds is the chemical method. It is best to avoid chemicals wherever possible, but when clearing a difficult site it may be a useful, one-off method. Use the chemicals before digging over an area, leave them to work, then remove the dead foliage and roots.

Foliage-acting or translocated weedkillers are the best method to use to destroy bindweed, ground elder or other persistent weeds. Spray or paint the chemical onto the leaves; it will then taken down to the roots by the plant. Treated weeds start showing signs of dying after a week or so, but several applications may be needed.

Soil-acting weedkillers are taken in by the weeds' roots, killing them in the process. These chemicals may remain active for a long time, so do not sow in the treated ground until they have dispersed.

Prevention is better than cure, so always try to prevent weeds returning. Mulching with organic material, planting ground cover or using a mulching film all help to suppress weed growth.

TIP

When you are controlling weeds in an established bed, avoid using chemical sprays on windy days where a strong breeze could very easily blow the droplets on to nearby plants. Most weed sprays kill any plant that they touch. This is especially important if you are using a chemical spray anywhere near food crops.

Working With the Soil

The quality of the soil will ultimately decide the success of your garden. On a basic level you need to know whether the soil is heavy, such as clay, or a light soil, such as sand or loam, as well as its chemical characteristics – whether it is acid, alkaline or neutral.

Soil types

An easy way to find out what type of soil you have is by rubbing a handful of moist soil between your fingers. If it feels dry and gritty, and runs through your fingers, then it is sandy. If it stains your hands and can be squeezed into a ball, it is clay.

Clay is sticky when wet and hard when dry, making it a heavy soil, as it is hard work to deal with.

Light or sandy soil needs a regular application of organic material as it is free draining, and so nutrients are quickly washed away by the rain.

Chalk and limestone soils tend to be alkaline, with a shallow depth of topsoil and so are also free draining, needing constant organic matter and fertilizers.

Peaty soil is made up of such a huge amount of organic material that it will be extremely wet and acidic.

Loam is neither too heavy nor too light, so is easy to work without becoming waterlogged or overly dry. It tends to be deep and fertile, with lots of humus (the decayed organic matter which keeps the soil well drained and light).

The range of 'soils' and improvers available can seem vast. As a general rule, use soil-based mixes for perennials and soilless mixes for temporary displays. Soil improvers include; grit for drainage, and blood, fish and bonemeal, as well as organic matter – for providing vital food and nutrients.

Soil-based container mix

Soilless potting mixture

Soil improver – organic matter

Soil improver – grit

Soil improver – blood, fish and bonemeal

Container mix – multi-purpose compost

A

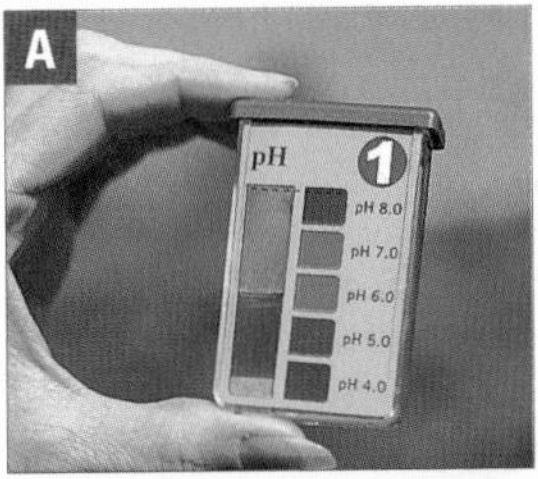

B

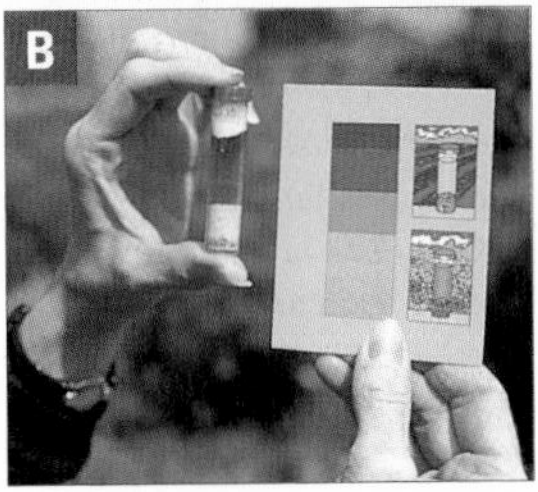

Chemical composition

Now you have worked out what type of soil you have, it is important to decide whether it is acid, alkaline or neutral, as certain plants have specific soil preferences. In general, peat is acid, while chalky and limestone soil tends to be alkaline; sand or clay soils can be either.

Chemical composition is measured on the pH scale, with a reading below pH7 indicating an acid soil, a neutral soil registering as pH7 and anything higher being alkaline.

There are many soil tester kits available today, which you can buy from any nursery or garden centre. The kit shows the various pH levels up the side of the container. A soil sample is added to the tester and shaken. You then match the colour reading to the corresponding colour on the kit which will tell you your soil's pH value [A].

Other tester kits can tell you in more general terms whether your soil is acidic, alkaline or neutral. A sample of soil is added to a test-tube, shaken and matched against a colour chart which shows the varying degrees of acidity or alkalinity of your soil [B].

Bark chip mulches work well but can diminish nitrogen levels

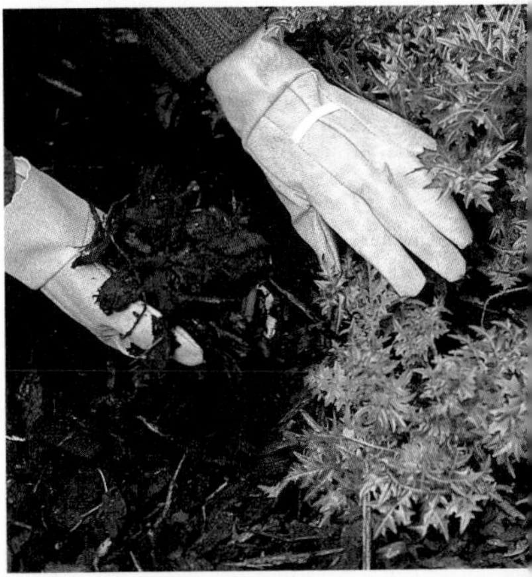

Soil improvers

While the basic soil type cannot be completely changed, we can temporarily alter its pH (by adding lime to make it less acidic or sulphur to make it less alkaline), feed it and improve its structure.

There is a wide choice of manures and fertilizers that you can use to feed and improve your soil.

Compost and manure
Organic household compost, horse, cattle and poultry manure, spent hops and mushroom compost will open up the soil, improve the structure, maintain moisture and feed with nutrients.

A well-rotted compost heap is an essential item for any keen gardener. Grass has begun growing on top of this one!

Organic leaf mould is an invaluable source of nutrients for the soil

Concentrated organic fertilizers
Extract of blood, fish, hoof, horn, bonemeal and seaweed will slowly release nutrients as they break down in the soil.

Green manures Plants, such as alsike clover, comfrey and lupins, are grown to be dug back into the soil to condition it; good for light, sandy or heavy clay soils.

Chemical fertilizers These can be watered into the soil and will feed trees and plants, providing an instant boost. Unlike natural fertilizers, they will not improve the soil, and are generally washed away as soon as it rains.

Digging

Digging over the soil will open up the structure, improve drainage, loosen compacted soil and provide the opportunity of mixing in any organic material.

Do not work heavy clay soil when it is wet or sticky, as digging in these conditions can often make matters worse. The best time to dig the garden is at the start of winter. Leave it open to the elements and over winter because the frost helps break down the clods.

Add sand or grit to improve drainage and open up waterlogged soil.

However, you may only need to fork over lighter, sandy soil and cover with a thick layer of mulch. Otherwise, over-digging may lead to many of the nutrients getting washed away over the winter.

Methods of digging

There are two main methods: single and double digging. Single digging involves turning over the soil to the depth of the spade blade; double digging involves digging down to two spade depths then forking the ground beneath. Double digging is best in areas where the soil is compacted or the drainage is poor.

Digging techniques Mark out a square site, dividing it into two rows of oblong trenches about 30cm (1ft) wide.

Dig to a spade's depth, about 25cm (10in). With double digging, dig to one spit and remove the soil, then dig down a second spit, never mixing soil from the two spits; replace them in the adjacent trench in the correct order.

Dig out the first trench, leaving the soil to one side. Work backwards to avoid compaction, dig out the next trench, filling in the first trench with the soil from this trench. Continue until you reach the final trench, the soil from which should be used to fill the first trench and vice versa.

With single spit digging, turn over the soil to the depth of the spade blade

Choosing and Buying Plants

Plants can be bought at many stages of growth, from dormant seed to flowering plant. Each type offers its own set of benefits.

Seeds

Seeds are the cheapest way for gardeners to obtain new plants. A packet of seeds, promising dozens of new plants, often costs at least fifty per cent less than a single plant ready for planting

out. Not only that, but there is a wider choice of plants and varieties available as seeds.

TIP

Label any seeds that you have saved from the previous season – it may be difficult to tell them apart later on!

Tiny 'sprinkling' seeds Many plants have small or very tiny seeds which are sown by sprinkling them thinly over the compost surface in containers. Seedlings from sprinkled seeds need to be pricked out (transplanted).

Larger seeds Other plants have larger seeds which are easier to handle. In between these two extremes are plants with medium-sized seeds. These are space sown so there is no need for thinning out.

Pelleted seeds Some tiny seeds are available as pelleted seeds to make them easier to handle. There is no need to transplant or thin out.

Bulbs

Bulbs are easy to grow, almost guaranteeing a display of flowers, provided there are no pests or diseases. The term 'bulb' is used rather loosely to include not only true bulbs, but also bulb-like plants such as corms and tubers.

When buying, make sure the bulbs are firm and do not have any soft spots. Ensure they do not have any white or grey fungal growth on them.

Plants

Buying small, young plants for growing on at home is a

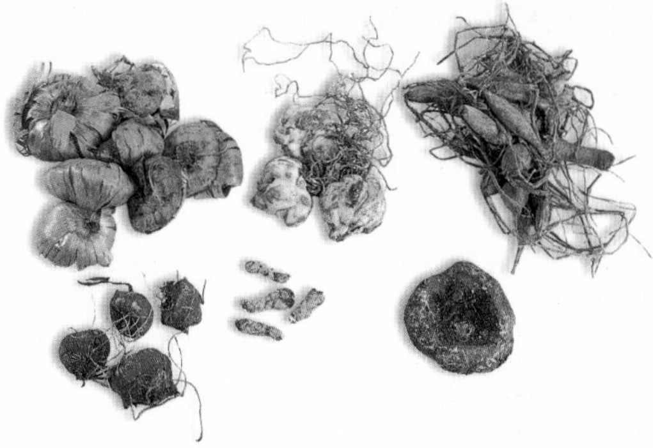

popular way of obtaining bedding plants and other summer-display plants. Make sure they are sturdy, not thin and spindly, and free from pests and diseases.

Seedlings Pots of seedlings need pricking out into trays and growing on in a greenhouse until large enough for planting out.

Plugs Plugs are small plants produced commercially in module trays. The plants are potted up and grown on in a greenhouse until large enough for planting out.

Young plants Larger bedding plants, ready for planting out and almost ready to flower, are widely available.

Mature plants Large potted bedding plants that are coming into flower which is the most expensive way of buying bedding plants.

Prepacked plants Dormant hardy perennials are sold in prepacks in winter and spring. They come in packaging with a picture of the plant.

A tray full of healthy young Viola plants

What is the plant for?

When you are choosing plants there are a number of factors to be taken into consideration. What you have in mind for the plant – ie. where you want to position it, the conditions you have in your garden, how large you want the plant to grow and how much time you can afford to spend looking after it – should determine the type of plant you are seeking.

You can either choose to buy plants by mail order or visit a nursery or garden centre. Visiting a nursery gives you the chance to inspect all the plants on display and buy the one that is in the best condition and which most closely suits your requirements. If it is an instant effect you are after, then a plant smothered with lots of buds is perfect; if, however, the plant is required as part of a long-term planting scheme, then a more critical eye is needed.

Checking for healthy roots

There are several indicators that will tell you instantly whether a plant is in good condition or not and healthy roots are one of the most important. With pot-grown climbers, look for one that sits well in its container; not so tight that it has become pot bound and stunted, or so loose that it comes out of the pot when lifted. The roots should not be growing too far outside the confines of the pot and nor should they be waterlogged and soggy.

Watch out for stems that have not been tied in. Also, reject any plant where the surface of the pot is covered in green moss, indicating that it has been sitting in a damp place for a while.

Check young plants for healthy rootballs

Agaves are generally low maintenance and easy to keep healthy

However, if you cannot wait for plants to mature and want an instant, impressive display, then you will need to pay out for more mature specimens, which will work out to be more expensive due to the time taken for the nursery or garden centre to grow them. Part of the joy of gardening, however, is to watch your plants grow and change with the seasons, doing your best to help Nature fulfil the designs you have created.

Plant *Dicksonia antarctica* to make an instant bold statement

Initial impact

If you prefer to nurture plants from young and watch them grow, then you can save money by choosing tiny seedlings. However, you must then have the patience to wait for your garden to take shape. There is always the temptation to position these small plants too close together, which is fine for a few years, but as the plants establish themselves they will invariably have to be thinned out. Try and plant them with an idea of their eventual size in mind. If you are worried about gaps in the meantime, fill these areas with rocks, bark or woodchippings, or plants in attractive containers.

Selecting your plants

If you are looking for shrubs, the type of flower might be the first thing to consider, even though few shrubs are in flower for more than several weeks at a time. Features such as flowering times, leaves, fruit produced, bark and shape are equally important considerations.

Flowers and fragrance

Most flowering shrubs bear flowers alongside foliage, such as Abelia, Mahonia, Rubus and Weigela. Flowers are highlighted against a backdrop of leaves or shoots.

Others produce blooms which cover up the foliage, such as Ceanothus, Cistus, Rhododendron and Viburnum. These often flower over quite a short period – generally two or three weeks – as opposed to contrasting shrubs which flower for longer periods.

Another floral feature is fragrance. Many flowering shrubs have delightful scents, including Buddleja, Choisya, Lavandula and Sarcococca.

Fruits and foliage

Fruits are usually features for autumn and winter months. Shrubs with showy berry displays include Berberis, Euonymus, Ilex, Leycesteria, Mahonia and Rosa.

Most of the time it is the foliage that creates the colour and visual impact of a shrub. Evergreen foliage has a year-round effect, whereas autumn colour continues to brighten a garden. New foliage colour can have a great impact in spring, such as the golden-yellow *Philadelphus coronarius* 'Aureus', or in red

Buxus harlandii makes a good focal point in the middle of a mixed herbaceous border

flushes through the summer with *Nandina domestica* 'Fire Power'.

Look for varieties with purple foliage which keep a good colour throughout summer, such as *Acer palmatum* var. *dissectum* 'Crimson Queen'. Golden foliage is also attractive, such as *Lonicera nitida* 'Baggesen's Gold', or variegated foliage, such as *Cornus alba* 'Elegantissima'.

BARK

In winter, once the foliage has fallen off and the stems exposed, the bark effect of some shrubs can be impressive. Some, like dogwoods (Cornus), display colourful hues of red, whereas others have stems with a skeletal, chalky-white effect. Unusual shapes or twisted stems are also worth considering.

Magnolia soulangeana 'Lennei'

Designing with shrubs

When planning a shrub bed, consider all the features mentioned, as well as size and form. Prostrate shrubs make good ground cover at the front of a bed, whereas taller plants should be at the back. Contrasting shrubs can look good together, such as spiky and rounded forms. Large, specimen shrubs make an ideal focal point. Ultimately, the choice is endless – and entirely down to you.

Berberis offers varied form and colour, and mixes well

Buying shrubs

You can buy shrubs from various places – garden centres, general and local nurseries, and specialist nurseries.

Garden centres vs. nurseries

Local garden centres will most likely be your first port of call. These outlets sell on plants that are grown elsewhere, and so the range will probably be limited but of a uniform quality. However, they will almost certainly stock the full range of gardening accessories.

General nurseries are more likely to have grown the plants sold in the garden centres, so the range may well be wider and the stock better, but you may need to travel further.

If you are after a particular type of plant or something less common, specialist nurseries are worth a visit. Horticultural societies can help you find specialist nurseries and often provide comprehensive lists.

Check container-grown shrubs over thoroughly before buying

BARE-ROOTED AND ROOTBALLED PLANTS

Bare-rooted plants can have a more extensive root system than container grown plants, even though much of the root system may be left in the nursery soil where it was grown. Rootballed plants have been lifted with the soil still attached and wrapped in a coarse cloth to prevent drying out.

Container grown plants

Shrubs are sold either container grown, bare-rooted or rootballed. When you buy plants grown in containers, you transport them with their root system intact, and so they are more likely to thrive when planted out. They can be planted at any time, although they will need regular watering if planted during the summer until their roots have established. Container grown

Bare-rooted plants weigh much less than container plants

stock is perfect for evergreens, which can dry out if their roots are bare.

Container grown shrubs can become 'pot-bound' if left for too long – shrubs should preferably only spend 18 months in a container before being repotted or planted out. Pot-bound plants have roots that have filled the pot and started to circle around. This would make them unlikely to establish a new root system when planted out in the garden. Pot-bound shrubs often look poor as they have exhausted the nutrients in the compost.

When buying container grown plants:

- ensure roots do not spiral around inside the pot
- watch out for roots through the drainage holes
- top growth should be healthy and soil should not be overgrown with weeds
- check whether the level of compost has dropped below the rim of the pot – container composts break down after a while, so if the level has dropped this is a giveaway that the shrub has been there too long.

Hessian cloth protects rootballed plants, which should be handled with special care

Selecting your trees

Trees are often used in the garden for their form, shape and foliage, as well as for their flowers, fruits and bark.

As there are not many trees in flower or fruit for more than a few weeks, you will need to consider the form of the tree, and the eventual height and spread it will make when mature.

Form Form or shape is an important feature. Unless you enjoy constant trimming, think what shape of tree would be best for the intended spot and the space available, in relation to the other planting.

Most young trees will have upright and narrow crowns (the top part). The dome or rounded crowns only form later as the branches arch out from the main stem. *Populus nigra* 'Italica' retains an upright crown; *Quercus robur* 'Fastigiata' splays out its erect branches as it grows.

Mature trees add shape and prominence

Compost should be near the rim

Avoid pots with weeds on top

Weeping trees can either have all pendulous branches or only side branches that are pendulous. Conifers are found in many forms, from narrow upright to prostrate and spreading, while the Bamboo family provides another range of forms.

Foliage The size and shape of a tree's leaves and whether it is deciduous or evergreen can be a factor in deciding where to position a tree: the

A healthy container-grown tree

larger the leaf, the denser the shade. Yet the large leaves of Paulownia are thin and let light through the leaf, as opposed to the leathery leaves of many evergreens.

Foliage colour is diverse – even with mainly green-leaved trees. There are infinite shades, from the dark, glossy green of Ilex to the blue-greens of many conifers. Foliage can be variegated, red and purple – and that is before autumnal hues are considered. Autumn colour, with leaves turning shades of yellow, russet or red, can give a quite stunning display.

Other features Flowers are obviously delightful on trees and are a real bonus. Catkins are also seen as flowers with a beauty of their own. Certain leaves can also be fragrant, such as *Populus* 'Balsam Spire'. Fruits, as well as bark effects, are usually an autumn to winter characteristic, whether trees have fleshy berries or woody cones.

Designing with trees

Incorporating your chosen tree in a planting scheme is the next stage. Think of the tree not only as a focal point, but maybe as hedging or screening, or to give shade and shelter – or simply to fill unwanted space.

Cupressus leylandii makes fast-growing hedging

Sowing Seeds

As so many flowers, in particular, are grown from seed, it is important to prepare the soil, sow seeds and plant correctly to give your plants the best possible start.

Soil preparation

Soil is initially prepared for flower growing by digging, which allows grit or sand and organic matter to be added, helping to aerate it and prevent compaction. Digging is not needed every year for permanent hardy perennials and bulbs, only before initial planting. The beds or borders only need to be renovated (dug and replanted) every three to four years from then on. Beds devoted to temporary bedding plants and annuals are usually dug over in the autumn to revitalize them and bury annual weeds, normally in between removing summer plants and planting spring bedding.

Clear the soil of perennial weeds (see pp16–17). After this, dig the ground, the best time generally being in autumn ready for spring planting. Usually it is only necessary to dig to the depth of the spade blade, but if there is a bad drainage problem or the lower soil is very compacted, then digging to two depths of the spade blade is advised (see p21).

Before planting, scatter a fertilizer over the dug soil and lightly fork it in, at the same time breaking down any soil lumps. Firm the soil by treading with your heels and then use a fork or rake to create a smooth, level surface.

Seed sowing

Many flowering plant seeds are sown in the open ground. Hardy annuals are sown in beds and borders in spring (or autumn for some) where they are to flower. Many of the easier hardy perennials such as lupins, delphiniums and columbines (Aquilegia) can be sown in a nursery bed in early summer and later transplanted to their flowering positions. Hardy biennials such as wallflowers (Erysimum), foxgloves (Digitalis) and forget-me-nots (Myosotis) are raised in the same way. Seeds of slow-germinating hardy bulbs, alpines and various hardy perennials are sown in pots outdoors or in a cold frame as soon as they are ripe.

Seed-bed preparation For seed sowing outdoors the soil surface needs to be smooth and level. Carry out all preparation when the soil is dry or only slightly moist on the surface, never when wet.

Once the area is free from large lumps of soil and debris, systematically tread in with the heel and then lightly rake it level. Next, spread a general-purpose fertilizer over the surface [A] (read packet instructions for amount) and then thoroughly rake it in [B], ensuring the surface remains level at the end.

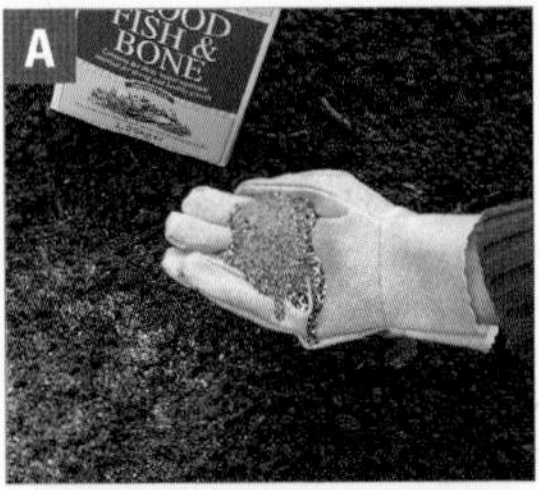

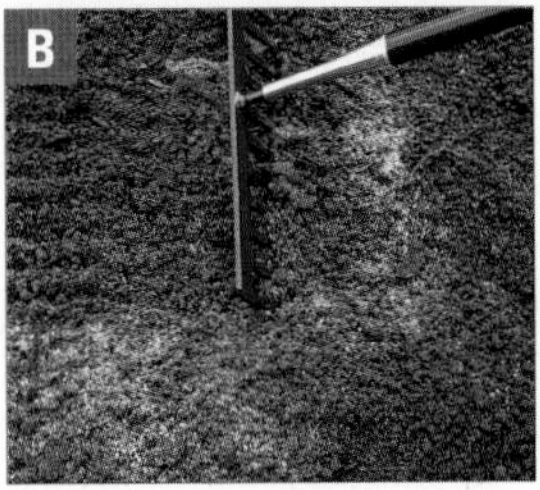

Sowing in rows The usual way to sow seeds outdoors is in straight rows, in shallow furrows known as drills. It makes subsequent care of seedlings, such as thinning and weeding, much easier. This is certainly the best way when sowing seeds of plants such as hardy biennials and perennials in nursery beds.

Hardy annuals sown in their flowering positions can also be sown in rows. Generally, each annual is grown in a bold, informal group in a border. Before sowing, the groups can be marked out with a trickle of dry sand. Within each group the seeds are sown in straight drills, spaced according to the size of the particular plant, but about 15–30cm (6–12in) apart. As the plants grow and close up, it will become less and less obvious that they have been sown in straight rows.

To make drills you will need a garden line (at its simplest, a length of string with each end tied to a short cane), a draw

hoe or a pointed stick. Stretch the line tightly where you want the drill. Then, using the line as a guide, use the corner of the hoe or stick to create a shallow furrow [C]. The depth will depend on the size of the seeds, but should be sown to about twice the seeds' depth. On average drills are about 6mm (¼in) deep.

Sow seeds straight from the packet or take a pinch of seeds between finger and thumb. Sprinkle them thinly and evenly along the drill [D]. Cover them by gently raking fine soil into the drill [E]. Water the seed bed if the soil is dry, using a garden sprinkler or watering can fitted with a fine rose. Thereafter, keep the soil moist to encourage germination.

Using seed tapes Seed tapes are laid along slightly wider drills, following the packet information regarding depth. Before covering with fine soil as above, moisten the tape using a watering can fitted with a fine rose.

Broadcast sowing Another way of sowing is to broadcast or scatter them thinly over the soil surface. This technique is not often used for flowers, but is the normal method of sowing lawn grass seed and wildflower meadows. Broadcast sowing can be used for hardy annuals, but bear in mind that thinning and weeding will be more difficult.

The soil surface should be prepared by raking shallowly in one direction to create a series of closely spaced mini furrows. Scatter the seeds thinly and evenly all over the surface and cover them by gently raking across the furrows to fill them in.

Thinning seedlings Even if seeds have been sown thinly, seedlings will still need to be thinned out to the correct distance apart. To avoid overcrowding, resulting in weak, spindly seedlings, thin out as soon as they can be handled. This can be done in two stages: an initial thinning to give them more room to grow and a second thinning to the correct distance apart when they are a bit larger.

The soil should be moist at the time of thinning. Most people prefer to use their fingers to remove surplus seedlings. Place a finger on the soil surface on each side of the seedling that is to remain, then gently pull out surplus seedlings on either side. Work along the row in this way.

When thinning seedlings, pull out any weeds. After thinning, hoe between the rows to kill remaining weeds.

Sowing in pots outdoors
Seeds of hardy bulbs, alpines and slow-germinating hardy perennials such as hellebores, anemones and primulas, are usually sown in pots as soon as they are ripe and placed outdoors or in a cold frame. After a cold period during the following winter they should germinate in the spring.

Use a soil-based seed compost and cover the seeds with a thin layer of compost followed by a thin layer of coarse sand or fine grit to prevent disturbance from rain and to deter moss growth. Sink the pots up to their rims in a bed of grit or coarse sand to prevent drying out and excessive freezing.

Use good quality terracotta pots for planting

Basic Planting Techniques

Planting out needs to be done with a great amount of care, as the correct planting technique makes all the difference to subsequent growth and flowering. Poorly planted specimens may never become properly established and will fail to perform well.

Having sown your seeds and watched them germinate and become strong, healthy seedlings, it is now time to plant them out in their flowering positions.

Hardening off

Young plants that have been raised and grown on in a heated greenhouse, such as summer bedding plants, and including all those purchased plugs, and larger young plants, must be gradually acclimatized to outdoor conditions before they are planted out. If they are not allowed to do this, then their growth may be severely hampered. This technique, known as hardening off, is carried out in a cold frame.

Hardening off needs to start at least three weeks before planting out. Remember that frost-tender plants must not be planted out until the danger of frost is over.

After putting the young plants in the cold frame, give them a little ventilation for the first few days by opening the covers slightly, but close the frame at night. Over the next few weeks open the frame daily, gradually increasing the ventilation by opening the covers wider and wider until fully open. Again, close the frame at night. A few days before planting out, the covers should now be left fully open at night, provided there is no risk of frost. Following this procedure will give the plants the best chance of survival and success in the future.

Harden off potted plants before planting out

TIP

If you have planted out all your carefully grown young plants, thinking that frosts are over, but the weather takes a turn for the worse, cover the plants with horticultural fleece to protect them. Another option is to protect them with sheets of newspaper or polythene. Take the cover off only when temperatures rise.

Planting out

When plants are fully hardened off they can be safely planted out. Let us first consider young plants in pots, seed trays, large-cell module trays and flexible-plastic or rigid polystyrene strips. The plants should be watered the evening before planting so that the compost is moist when they are planted out.

There are various techniques for removing plants from their containers, but it must always be done carefully to avoid root disturbance as much as possible. Plants can be removed from pots by inverting the pot, placing one hand over the compost surface and tapping the pot rim on a hard surface, such as the edge of a bench. The rootball should slide out.

To remove plants from an ordinary seed tray, first tap the lower ends and sides on a hard surface to loosen the compost and, holding the tray close to the ground, gently tip the contents out. The compost should remain intact. Then the plants can be gently teased apart with your fingers. There will be some root disturbance but this is inevitable. You can do the same with plants growing in strips.

Plants can be removed from module trays by pushing a pencil through the drainage hole in the base. This will loosen the plant, which can then be lifted out.

Put in the ground immediately after removing plants from their containers to prevent the roots from drying out. Arrange the plants as

Once plants have hardened off, it is safe to plant them out

Correct planting techniques can lead to healthy bedding plants

required in the bed or border. Planting holes can be made with a hand trowel. Each hole should be large enough to take the rootball without squashing it, and should be of such a depth that after planting the compost surface is only slightly below soil level. Fill in around the plant with fine soil, making sure it is in close contact with the rootball and there are no air pockets, and firm it with your fingers. To check whether it is firm enough, lightly tug the top of the plant – it should remain firm in the soil. The top of the rootball should be lightly covered with soil.

After planting, brush the soil with a fork to remove any footprints. Water in the plants if the soil is dry, ideally with a garden sprinkler or a watering can fitted with a rose.

Larger plants, such as herbaceous perennials bought in 12.5–15cm (5–6in) pots from the local garden centre, are planted in the same way as smaller potted plants. Some gardeners like to carefully tease out the outer roots before planting to help them establish quickly in the new soil. Just carefully pull out the roots with your fingers so that they are not growing in a circle around the soil ball. Again, set the plants so that the top of the rootball is only just below soil level.

You may also have larger plants of your own to plant, such as divisions of hardy perennials – large clumps of plants that you have divided or split into smaller portions for replanting. It is important to dig deep enough holes for these so that the roots are able to hang straight down without turning up at the ends. Work fine soil between and around the roots and firm it well with your fingers.

It is equally important to plant them at the same depth that they were positioned in originally. That is, with the crown of the plant, where the growth buds are situated, at soil level. The buds must not be covered with soil, otherwise the crown may rot.

If you are planting divisions of bearded irises, which produce thick rhizomes (swollen stems which grow above the soil), the rhizomes should sit on the soil surface, but the fibrous roots below should, of course, be under the soil.

Transplanting seedlings

Seedlings raised in a nursery bed, such as hardy biennials and perennials, need to be transplanted to another nursery bed to grow on to a larger size before planting in their flowering positions.

As soon as they are about 5–8cm (2–3in) high and easily handled, carefully lift them with a hand fork, a few at a time to prevent the roots from drying out. They are replanted in rows spaced about 30cm (12in) apart, setting the plants about 15cm (6in) apart within the rows. Dig deep enough holes to allow the roots to dangle straight down, then return fine soil around them

Carefully nurtured bulbs will ultimately reward with stunning displays

and firm it with your fingers. Plant them to the same depth that they were positioned in originally. After planting, water in thoroughly with a garden sprinkler or watering can fitted with a rose.

By the autumn of the same year you will have sizeable young plants for setting out in their flowering positions. The biennials will flower in the following spring or summer, and some of the perennials may also flower, but others may need to grow a bit larger before they bloom. Lift and plant in the same way as seedlings, setting the plants at the correct distance apart.

For perennials and alpines raised in pots there are two options. Either pot up the seedlings individually as soon as they are large enough to handle and grow on outdoors or in an open cold frame, or line them out in nursery beds to grow on, as for biennials. If potting, start them off in 8cm (3in) pots and use well drained, gritty, soil-based potting compost.

Leave seedling bulbs in their pots for a further year to grow larger before transplanting them. In the second year, while they are dormant, pot them to twice their own depth – say six to eight per 12.5cm (5in) pot – using gritty soil-based potting compost [A & B]. Place in a sheltered spot outside or in an open cold frame and grow on for another year [C] before planting out when dormant.

Transplanting

Moving established plants can be an alternative to digging up and discarding unwanted plants which look out of place in your new garden design.

It is fairly straightforward to move small plants that are less than 1m (3ft) by digging and lifting up with a spade and moving it bare root, as the rootball will not be sufficiently established. Move larger specimens that are at least 2m (6ft) in height with their rootball.

The best time to transplant is during the dormant season from late autumn to early spring, although evergreens prefer to be moved when the soil is still warm in early autumn.

Care is needed to retain the rootball when transplanting a mature tree or shrub. To begin with, make a guideline around the plant and dig a vertical slit no nearer than 30cm (12in) from the stem (double the distance for trees and shrubs 3–4m [10–13ft] high). Dig a spadeful of soil from outside the line, and make a trench around the plant roughly 30–50cm (12–20in) deep.

Take the spade and push in, right under the tree or shrub, from the base of the trench. Once the plant is free, carefully rock to one side and push a sheet of polythene or hessian cloth beneath the rootball. Gently manoeuvring the plant, pull the sheet out at the far side. Then either lift or drag the plant to its new position. Replant as for a new rootballed plant. If the rootball has stayed intact then it should not need staking.

Dig well under the rootball when transplanting a hydrangea or any other shrub

Planting Bulbs

Bulbs, corms and tubers are generally planted when dormant, but should be planted immediately if bought in pots when in growth, just like pot-grown perennials.

Bulbs which are bought 'in the green' after flowering, such as snowdrops (Galanthus), should be planted immediately. If they have been lifted from the open ground, plant them to the depth that they were growing originally (soil level is indicated by the change from white to green at the base of the leaves).

The time of planting depends on the flowering period of the particular bulb. Winter- and spring-flowering bulbs are planted in the autumn. Summer-flowerers are planted in spring. Those that flower in autumn are planted in late summer.

There can be confusion among gardeners about how deep to plant bulbs. The correct depth is governed by the size of the bulb. A good guide is to plant a bulb two to three times deeper than its length (measured from tip to base). In other words, the bulb should be covered with a depth of soil equal to two or three times its own depth.

Planting should be deeper in light soils – such as sandy types – than in heavy soils such as clay. Space between bulbs should equal two to three times their own width.

In mixed borders

Bulbs are generally planted in informal groups or drifts in mixed borders to look more natural. There are two ways to plant them, the easiest being to put them in a large, flat-bottomed hole. Space the bulbs at random, as this looks more natural. After setting them all, cover with fine soil. Use your hands to avoid disturbing the bulbs, then firm the soil slightly by pressing it down with the back of a rake.

Alternatively, you can plant the bulbs individually, using a trowel or bulb planter to make the hole. A bulb planter takes out a core of soil, which is then replaced over the bulb when it has been planted. When planting in individual holes, make sure that the base of the bulb is on the soil in the bottom of the hole. If there is an air space the bulb will not produce roots and consequently will not grow.

In spring bedding schemes

Bulbs such as tulips are often planted among other plants, such as forget-me-nots (Myosotis) in spring bedding schemes. The easiest way is to plant the bulbs first, followed by the other plants. This does not harm the bulbs as the other plants are planted to a more shallow depth. If you are unsure about this, plant the other plants first, then plant the bulbs between them.

In grass

Bulbs are planted in informal drifts in grass to create a natural appearance. The best way is to scatter handfuls of bulbs over the area and plant them where they fall, filling in large gaps with more bulbs.

Remove the turf where you want to plant them. This can be done with a spade, lifting the turf with about 2.5cm (1in) of soil attached. Scatter the bulbs and plant them with a trowel. Then return the turf and firm it. Alternatively, plant bulbs individually in the turf, using a bulb planter, especially with large bulbs.

Wonderful springtime effects can be achieved by scatter-planting bulbs in grass

Planting in Containers

Growing flowering plants in containers, such as patio tubs, window boxes and hanging baskets, has never been more popular. They allow colour to be added easily to paved areas and the walls of the building.

Window boxes

When planting, it is best to use soilless potting compost to reduce the amount of weight in the window box. Do make sure that window boxes are firmly secured to the windowsills with metal brackets – never rely on weight alone to hold them in position.

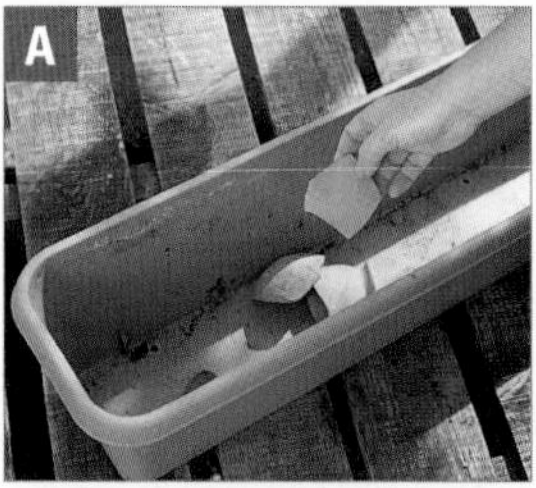

Cover drainage holes with broken clay pots [A] and add a 2.5–5cm (1–2in) layer of gravel for drainage. There are two methods of planting: either fill with compost and make planting holes; or partially fill the container, stand the plants on the compost and fill in around them [B]. If you are planting bulbs with other plants, the latter technique is the best to use. To allow room for watering, fill the compost to within 2.5cm (1in) of the top.

There are various ways of arranging the plants. For instance, try a triangular arrangement, with tall plants in the centre, shorter plants

TIP

Avoid time-consuming watering chores by installing drip irrigation, with evenly spaced outlets.

on either side, then some still shorter subjects out towards the edges of the box. Trailing plants can be set at the ends of the window box and along the front edge [C].

Alternatively, position some tall plants at one end, grading down the length of the window box to shorter plants at the other end. Again, make use of trailing plants, to add variety to the arrangement and to hang down over the sides of the window box, enhancing the display.

Patio tubs and pots

Containers should be large in size to avoid rapid drying out and to enable effective displays to be created. The depth of containers should ideally be no less than 30cm (12in), and the width from 30–60cm (12–24in).

Patio tubs and pots are prepared and planted in the same way as window boxes. Plants are generally set close together in containers to create an instant effect, so ignore the usual plant spacings. They need to be arranged attractively and to make best use of the limited space. Generally, set a tall plant in the centre to create height and arrange the main plants around this. Finally, trailing plants can be set around the edge.

When you plant up containers, ensure that the arrangement is well balanced

Hanging baskets

Hanging baskets are invaluable for adding colour to the walls of the house, say in the vicinity of the patio or around the front door.

To plant a wire hanging basket, firmly line the entire basket with a generous layer of sphagnum moss [A]. Next, pour a layer of lightweight soilless potting compost into the bottom of the basket and lightly firm it. Then arrange a circle of plants in the side of the basket by pushing the roots through the liner from the outside and laying them on the compost surface [B]. Cover the roots of the plants with a layer of compost and then add another circle of plants and cover their roots with compost. Of course, you will have to make holes in the liner to insert the plants. Then add plants at the top by standing them on the compost and filling in around them with more compost, leaving space at the top for watering [C].

Hanging baskets provide instant, portable colour

TIP

You can pot plants in virtually any size or shape of container, from an ordinary terracotta pot to an old wooden barrel, as long as there are drainage holes in them. However, bear in mind that terracotta could well crack in freezing weather, so make sure you can protect them or bring them inside if severe frosts are forecast.

Patio containers

When it comes to growing a plant that will be kept in a pot or container on the patio or in a courtyard garden for a long time, then planting it in the correct soil mix is very important for its continued, healthy growth. One of the best potting composts to use is John Innes No. 3, plus 50% extra grit. This compost is loam-based and aims to provide balanced nutrients to the plant over a long period. The addition of grit means it is also free-draining, which eliminates the need for broken crockery pots to line the base.

Tree ferns require a peat-based or peat-substitute compost, plus added leaf mould if possible.

Pictured below is a *Yucca floribunda* replanted into a pot. Hold the plant in place in the pot or container and scoop in John Innes No. 3 with added grit [A]. Fill the compost to just below the rim [B] and then finish off with a layer of gravel on the top to prevent the soil losing moisture and drying out [C].

A

B

C

Planting Trees and Shrubs

As with any plants, preparing the site is half the battle when planting trees or shrubs to ensure the condition of the soil is the best it can be.

Preparing the site

Instead of taking a half-hearted guess at where you think your trees and shrubs would look nice, you really need to know beforehand where you are going to place each plant. At this point, three main aspects of the soil should be considered, namely compaction, waterlogging and weeds (see also pp16–21).

Remove weeds from around shrubs to reduce competition for the nutrients in the soil

Compacted soil Due to several factors, trees and shrubs cannot grow in compacted soil. Water is not able to drain away if the soil's structure is not adequately porous, which will lead to waterlogging (see opposite). This means that air cannot percolate, so the plant's roots cannot obtain oxygen for respiration. Because of the compacted soil's density, newly planted shrubs will find it nearly impossible to take hold, as the roots will not be able to penetrate the soil.

Compaction is more likely to be a serious problem with new houses, as builders' heavy machinery would have compacted the soil in the garden when the house was being built. Unfortunately, the only answer is hard graft... Remove about two fork depths of soil, then, with a pickaxe, break up the subsoil underneath and replace the topsoil. Rotavators are not much help as they only scratch the surface, unfortunately.

TIP

There are various materials to help improve your soil's quality and drainage, including coarse sand, rich and crumbly garden compost, gypsum (or sulphate of lime), leaf mould, shredded bark or woodchippings, well-rotted manure and shells or other organic mulch. Ensure they are all well dug in to the soil.

Waterlogging

Soil is said to be waterlogged when the amount of water entering the soil exceeds that which drains out of it. Heavy, clay soils often tend to have poor drainage.

Roots are unable to function effectively in waterlogged soil, as the roots get drowned. Some trees and shrubs can grow with their roots under water (including Alnus, Salix and Taxodium, but even these will do better in soils with good drainage). However, many tolerate short periods of waterlogging in the dormant season, as the fine – and more susceptible – roots that absorb water from the soil are not produced during the dormant season. The plant relies upon the older roots.

Apart from compaction, waterlogging is caused by poorly draining soils, such as clay. Digging in organic matter and applying a layer of organic mulch will help crumble the soil and improve drainage, as well as increasing soil fertility. If the soil is severely waterlogged, rather than taking the drastic measure of building a complicated drainage system, try making a series of mounds with the soil and plant the trees or shrubs into the mounds. These plants still need to be tolerant of damp conditions, however.

A well planted tree (here, *Paulownia tomentosa*) will reward you with healthy growth

Planting methods

Trees or shrubs do not like to be put in the ground any deeper than they have been growing. Always try and plant them where the soil left a mark on the stem when it was in the nursery soil, or the level of the container soil.

Because trees and shrubs will generally remain in the same location – and will, hopefully, last a long time – it is essential that the ground is prepared before planting. If you have dealt with poor drainage and compaction by thoroughly digging over the soil (see p21), then excavate a hole slightly larger than the width and to the correct depth to accommodate the roots.

If not, then the 'two holes' method will give your plant the best possible start. Firstly, dig a hole at least 15cm (6in) larger than needed. Fill the earth back in to the hole.

Next, from the same hole you have just filled in, dig another one the exact same size. Although this might seem as if you are making more work than is necessary, by digging two holes you are breaking up the soil in which the plant is sitting so that the roots can freely extend out.

TIP

Do not forget to spend time in preparing the planting site, as this will save you time – and effort – much later on.

Container plants Once you have selected and bought a healthy young tree or shrub (see pp28–9), soak the plant with its compost in a bucket of water for an hour or so, but no longer, as the fine roots will be drowned and die. Cut away any damaged top parts of the plant to good shoots.

If you are planting container-grown trees and shrubs during the summer (as they can usually be planted at any time of the year), make sure they are given regular watering.

As mentioned before, dig a hole of the right depth but at least 5cm (2in) wider than the container [A]. Take the plant from its pot and tease out the roots so that they are spread out in the hole as much as possible, and place the rootball in the hole [B]. If you happen to have a slightly pot-bound plant with congested and fairly circular roots, trim a few of the woody ones with secateurs at three points around the root system. New roots will then have the space to form and spread out. Replace the soil in layers no more than 10–15cm (4–6in) thick, firming as you go [C]. Do not tread too heavily as you will compact the soil again. The aim is to firm the plant in and get rid of air pockets in the roots. Give the plant a thorough watering [D].

TIP

When you are planting a large shrub or tree as part of a wall border filled with perennials and lower flowering shrubs, make sure that you plan your design beforehand, leaving ample space for your newly planted small tree or shrub to mature. You do not want the young plant to look cramped when fully grown.

Planting a wall shrub

Shrubs are most often grown up against a sunny wall for protection against wind and frost, as well as giving climbers some sort of natural support. Excavate a planting hole 30–50cm (12–20in) out from the wall, as the soil right beside a wall is often drier due to the overhang of the roof. Before planting, make sure you have affixed trellis or hooks and twine into the wall as an anchor for plants to attach themselves. Put the plant in at an angle towards the wall, using a cane as a temporary stake.

It is important to train all wall shrubs from an early stage through tieing in and pruning so that they maintain a good shape and appearance, and produce plenty of flowering shoots.

Place the plant carefully in the hole [A]. Netting or regularly spaced wires should be attached to the wall using 'eyes'. Another option is to use wooden battens or trellis to support the wires [B]. Start the wires roughly 30cm (12in) above ground level.

Make sure that the wires or ties you use are garden twine and will not cause damage by completely restricting the growth of the stems [C].

To train the shrub in the beginning, remove branches which grow in the 'wrong' direction and keep those which fit neatly against the wall.

Bare-rooted plants

Only plant bare-rooted trees and shrubs when the plant is dormant, normally in late autumn and early spring. If the plant is in leaf it is unlikely to survive being transplanted out.

Soak the roots in a bucket of water for up to 12 hours. Any broken or damaged roots should be removed using a sharp knife or secateurs. Ensure the roots are spread evenly in all directions.

Rootballed plants

Rootballed trees and shrubs are lifted from the ground

with their roots and the surrounding soil attached. This is wrapped in a hessian-type cloth to stop the roots from drying out. Avoid planting from late spring to early autumn.

It is generally safer, even if the soil around the roots is fairly dry, to put the rootballed tree or shrub in place and water them in thoroughly after planting. As with bare-rooted plants, trim any damaged top portions back to good shoots.

Planting a bare-rooted tree or shrub

Dig the hole slightly larger than its dimensions, ensuring that the roots will have sufficient room. Make sure that the depth of the hole is even and that it is no deeper than the level it was planted in the nursery by laying a straight stick across [A].

If any roots look as if they are bent into the centre of the tree or shrub, bend them back so they are spreading outwards. If they refuse to be twisted back then prune them off, otherwise the bent roots will wind around the other well-established roots and cause the tree or shrub to become unstable and blow over in the future.

Put the soil back around the roots [B], firming as you go but making sure you do not compact the soil [C]. Tie the main stem or trunk to a stake if necessary (see p55).

Planting a rootballed tree or shrub

Rootballed trees and shrubs are those lifted from the ground with their roots and the surrounding soil attached. The root system is wrapped in a cloth to stop the roots from drying out. Avoid planting from late spring to early autumn.

As with bare-rooted plants, dig the hole slightly larger than its dimensions to allow for the roots.

Place the plant in the centre of the hole and cut or strip back the material surrounding the ball (below). Just spread the material in the bottom of the hole around the plant, as it can be safely left to rot down. As with bare-rooted plants, tease out any roots that are protruding from the soil of the rootball and bend back or remove those that are girdling or circling.

Backfill with soil in layers of 10–15cm (4–6in) thick, firming as you go but ensuring that you do not compact the soil. The next step is to stake the tree or shrub if necessary.

Once the rootballed tree is in place, untie or cut its wrapping and leave to rot down in the hole

Staking

To help establish newly planted trees and shrubs, a stake is needed. The reason for a stake is to hold the roots firm so that the feeder roots are not damaged by the plant swaying in the wind. Its purpose is not to hold the stem rigid. The stake itself should be driven in the ground (roughly 60cm [24in] below soil level) before the tree or shrub has been planted. The tie should not be positioned right at the top of the stake, as the stem of the tree is likely to rub against the stake in windy weather, damaging the tree.

When the fine roots have become woody and established, the tree or shrub need not be staked any

Staked too high

Correctly staked

Another staking method (below) is to place the stake diagonally to the tree

longer. As stems of trees and shrubs are designed to have a certain amount of flex in the wind, holding the stem rigid confuses the plant, as it determines its wood growth by the flexing of the stem. Rigidly staked trees – and those staked too high – can be thicker at the top and thinner near the stake.

For smaller plants, a thin batten such as a bamboo cane would allow for more flexibility. Tie in the cane with tape rather than twine, which will cut into the stem.

A shrub ought not to be staked for more than a year and a larger tree for up to two years. After then, if it still needs staking, it may have been planted too deep, in which case, trim it back and allow it to firm itself rather than continue staking it.

Planting Climbers

There is no end to the choice of supports available for climbers, such as trellises or various shaped frameworks, which can all be bought readymade or home designed.

Climbers in containers

A climber in a container can either be positioned against a wall with trellis or other support for it to clamber up, or else given its own support to climb within the pot. If this is the case, the climber can be placed wherever in the garden and need not be confined to a wall area or fixed structure.

The ideal growing aid to use in a container is a tripod, as a climbing plant can be easily trained to grow up within and around the vertical struts that form the structure.

If you are transplanting a climber from its shop-bought pot into a permanent home in a container, put pieces of broken pot into the base for drainage. Transfer the plant into the new pot and tease out its root system gently. Fill in around it with compost and carefully firm in. Only once the plant is in its new home, place the tripod or cane structure around the climber. Ease the stems through, then tie up with loose twine.

Planting against a post

As well as readymade structures, such as tripods, bought directly from the garden centre or put together at home for the gardener's particular individual purpose, an easy support solution is to use a structure that is already in your garden.

In the example shown, a fixed post is used as the support, which is an ideal way of brightening up what is, to be honest, a rather dull element in the garden!

First, if you have laid down a mulching sheet to discourage weeds, cut out the shape of the hole to be dug through the sheet [A] – roughly double the size of the

climber's root system. Then dig the hole around the post [B]. With clematis, the rule is the deeper the hole, the better. But in general, keep it to around the same depth as it was in the pot or container. Test the depth as you are digging to see if you have dug deep enough [C].

Gently remove the plant from its pot – leaving any cane supports which it came with in place – and carefully tease out the roots so they have an easier time establishing themselves in the new home. Place the plant in position, leaving a gap of about 10cm (4in) away from the post and angle the plant back towards the support. Backfill the hole, firming it in place by lightly pressing with your feet [D]. Do not position the plant directly up against the post.

Cover with a layer of mulch, bark or woodchippings around the climber if desired and water in well [E]. A mulch layer is a good idea of retaining moisture, even though you will have to keep watering regularly until the plant is established.

Planting Vegetables and Herbs

Even though you can easily buy vegetable and herb seedlings ready for planting from nurseries and, occasionally, garden centres, this works out quite expensive. What could be better than growing seedlings that you have raised yourself? Follow the steps here and prepare for bumper crops.

Sowing outdoors

You can sow most vegetables and herbs directly into the ground where they will grow, but this must be done at the right time and with the weather conditions perfect for germinating as many seeds as possible. The average temperature during the day must be above 6°C (43°F) or the seedlings will simply die. Make sure the soil is well prepared (see pp16–21) and that you follow the guidelines on the packaging or within a leaflet for the planting depth and distance.

The ground must be the correct temperature for the seeds to germinate, as well as being neither too dry nor too wet. If the soil becomes too wet, then the seeds will just rot and if it is too dry they will shrivel up. You can lend nature a hand in warming up the soil by placing cloches on the ground where the seeds are to be sown (see pp71–2) or putting a layer of horticultural fleece over it.

TIP

Sow crops in succession. For example, plant carrots outdoors every two weeks until late summer and sow lettuces every fortnight outdoors between early spring and late summer. You will then have successive crops for a longer period, rather than an enormous amount all at once which will just be wasted.

Healthy young cauliflowers in a row

To sow outdoors

The first thing to do is prepare your seedbed. This area must be weed free and dressed with a general fertilizer, then raked until it is covered with a fine tilth. You then need to mark out a straight line with a taut piece of string and an old nail at the end [A]. Using a dibber, mark out a drill with a uniform depth along the piece of string [B]. Check the seed packet for the correct depth.

During dry spells, water the drill before sowing the seeds. Sprinkle small seeds sparingly and evenly [C];

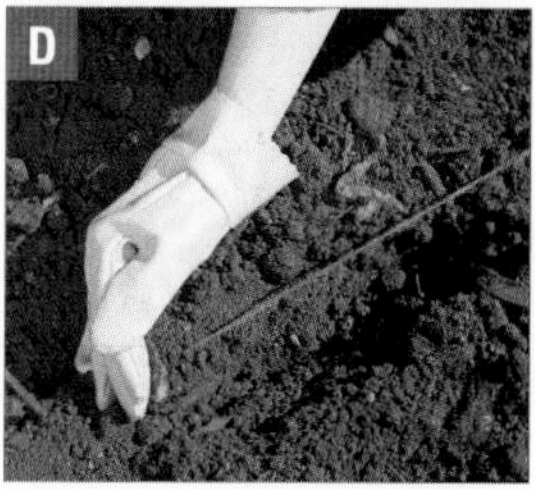

place larger seeds individually. Finish by lightly covering the seeds with soil [D]. Gently firm down and water.

When the seedlings come through, to prevent them becoming cramped for space, they need to be thinned out. Once there are a few leaves, gently pull out the weaker seedlings and either transplant or discard them.

Grow some vegetables, such as peas and 'cut-and-come-again' salad crops in more spacier drills of perhaps 23cm (10in) wide, as they need more space to mature.

Sowing indoors

Some plants are more tender than others and need the extra heat and protection of being planted indoors to get them off to a good start. This way, only the strongest and best plants make it into the kitchen garden.

Sow certain half hardy vegetables and tender herbs later, then protect them from frost. These include French and runner beans, courgettes, cucumbers, peppers, squashes, sweetcorn and tomatoes.

To sow indoors

Put a good multi-purpose or seed compost in a clean seed tray to within 1cm (½in) of the top. Tap the tray to help settle the compost, gently firm the compost then sprinkle with water. Thinly and evenly sow the seeds, placing large seeds individually with a dibber [A], and sieve a fine layer of compost on top.

Water lightly and cover with a sheet of glass or polythene. To protect the seeds from condensation or excess sunlight, lay a sheet of newspaper on top as well. Put the tray in a warm, well-lit, draught-free place. Check each day to see if the seeds have germinated and wipe off excess condensation. When seedlings begin to come through, remove the glass and place the seed tray on a window-sill.

Once the first leaves have developed, they are ready for pricking out. Fill a seed tray or modules with potting compost and water. Put holes in the compost with a pencil 2.5–5cm (1–2in) apart and gently prise out the individual seedlings. To avoid damaging their tiny roots, hold them carefully by the leaves, not the stems.

Place in the holes, firm gently then water lightly. Put the seed tray in a bright position not in direct sunlight, as this dries out the compost and burns the seedlings. Leave there for a few days before moving to a sunnier position and water daily.

TIP

If your kitchen garden is designed with vegetables growing in blocks, then you will probably find it easier to broadcast – or randomly scatter – the seed. Prepare the area by carefully raking it over in one direction. Scatter the seed thinly, then rake the soil at right angles to cover the seed.

If the seedlings get too big for the tray before planting them out, move them into individual pots. Gently take them from the tray, so as not to damage the root systems, and replant them in pots with compost [B]. Water daily to maintain the moisture.

Hardening off and transplanting

Before planting out, the seedlings must be gradually acclimatised to their new conditions. To date they have had even temperatures, no wind and constant watering, so without a hardening off period the sudden change in conditions could kill them.

On fine days, put the seed tray or pots outside in a sheltered spot, but bring them back in at night. After a week to ten days, depending on the weather, the seedlings are safe to be left out, giving them protection if the weather turns harsh.

Cold frame or cloches are excellent for hardening off. Gradually open the lids or remove the cloches for longer periods (see pp70–2).

Once the seedlings have hardened off, it is time to plant them out. The planting hole must be slightly deeper than the depth which the seedling was sitting in the seed tray or pot. When prising it out of the compost, be careful not to damage its rootball [C]. Place it in its new home, firm in and water well.

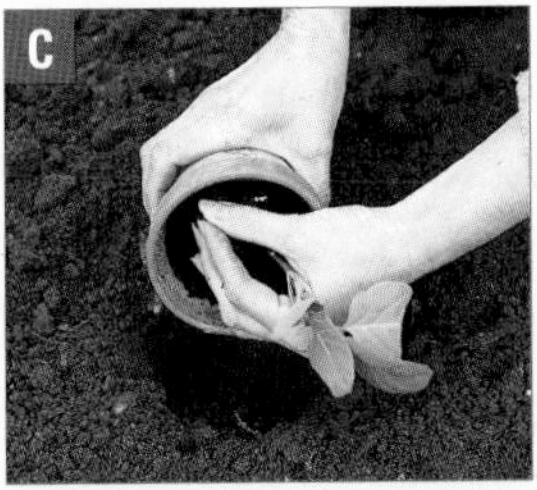

Crop Rotation

Crop rotation is a system of growing different types of vegetables, alternating between different areas of the kitchen garden over three or four consecutive years.

Although it might appear that crop rotation plans are just complicated schemes drawn up by professional gardeners to alienate the amateur vegetable grower, there are scientific principles behind the method. By taking the trouble of drawing up a plan and actually applying it to your vegetable garden, you will discover that your crops are healthier and less troubled by pests and diseases, and, in addition, your actual yields are up.

The theory behind it is that each crop, or each family of plants, is prone to specific diseases, with particular pests that prey on that group of crop. If that same crop is grown there year after year, then those pests and diseases increase rapidly, making cultivation of that crop practically impossible. If you move the crops from bed to bed you make sure that these pests and diseases do not get the chance to establish a strong foothold, as they gradually disappear without their 'host' crop.

Another advantage is that nutrients in the soil get a chance to replenish themselves. By dividing

A FOUR-YEAR CROP ROTATION PLAN

Year 1: Plant your four beds out in designated groups, as described opposite on p63	1	2	3	4
Year 2: Rotate the contents of the four beds in the sequence shown	4	1	2	3
Year 3: Once again, rotate the contents of the four separate beds, as shown	3	4	1	2
Year 4: In the final year, rotate the positions of the plant groups one last time	2	3	4	1

vegetables up into groups, it will be easier to put crops with similar soil requirements together. Some vegetables, such as cabbages, prefer rich ground while others, such as carrots, like poorer soil. It is more logical, then, to site these plants in beds with the right soil conditions to cater for the right crops.

Divide vegetables into three or four main groups, according to the design of your kitchen garden. The simplest way of grouping is to choose a plan which works over the same number of years as you have beds. So if you have a four-bed kitchen garden, the plan should run for four years before repeating, and so on.

Before the start of each season, prepare the beds for the specific crops. At the end of the growing year, turn over all beds, prepare the soil again, then move the crops round to the next bed.

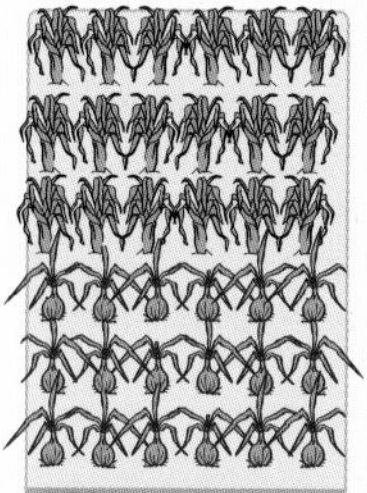

BED 1: ALLIUMS

Vegetables:
Bulb onion; shallot; garlic; spring onion; pickling onion; leek; Japanese bunching onion

Care:
Double digging; mixing manure in soil; application of blood, fish and bonemeal

BED 2: BRASSICAS

Vegetables:
Cabbage; Chinese cabbage; Brussels sprout; cauliflower; kale; calabrese; broccoli

Care:
Single digging; mixing manure in soil; application of blood, fish and bonemeal

BED 3: LEGUMES

Vegetables:
Broad bean; French bean; Lima bean; pea; runner beans; yard long bean; asparagus pea

Care:
Single digging; mixing lime in soil; application of blood, fish and bonemeal

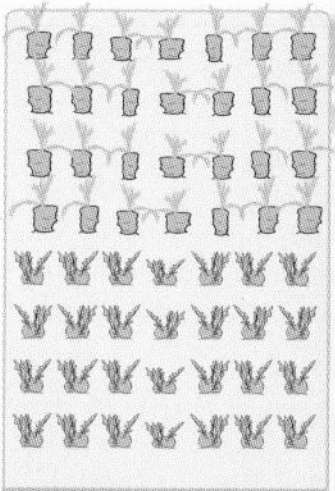

BED 4: ROOTS & TUBERONS

Vegetables:
Beetroot; carrot; parsnip; potatoes; salsify; scorzonera; swede; turnip; sweet potato

Care:
Double digging; liberal application of blood, fish and bonemeal before planting

Planting Tree Fruit

There are several factors to be taken into consideration when deciding which variety of fruit tree to choose. These include local conditions, space and pollination.

Local conditions to consider include weather, average temperature and soil type. You then need to decide where the tree is to be grown, how much space is available, and whether the tree is bush, standard or decorative. Finally, there is the question of pollination. If you do not get this right, the tree simply will not bear any fruit.

The rootstock grafting point of an Apple 'Lord Lambourne' variety

Pollination groups

Most fruit trees need to be cross-pollinated to bear fruit, although some are self-fertile, so buy at least two cultivars of the same tree.

For trees to cross-pollinate there must be another tree in bloom nearby. Nurseries and growers divide fruit trees and their varieties into pollination groups, usually indicated by numbers. These tell you when in the season a tree flowers, so you can buy another tree in the same group and ensure cross-pollination.

Rootstocks

When you buy fruit trees, most are grafted on to rootstocks which determine their size and speed of growth. If the growing conditions in your garden are not ideal, choose a more vigorous rootstock to compensate.

Buying a tree

Having chosen what type of fruit you want to grow, selected a rootstock and variety, then you will need to decide whether to buy container-grown or bare-rooted trees.

Bare-rooted trees are usually cheaper than container-grown trees and are less likely to have been sitting in a nursery or garden centre. However, bear in mind that you are restricted to planting bare-rooted trees only when the roots are dormant, while container-grown trees can be planted all year round (see pp50–2).

You can buy fruit trees at various stages of maturity, from maiden whip trees with a single leader to two- and three-year-old trees. Two-year-old trees are often the best, as they fruit faster and can be trained more easily than maiden trees. It is harder to establish three-year-old trees and they are normally much more expensive.

It is vital to buy a healthy specimen. On bare-rooted trees, the main stem must be straight, with three to five evenly spaced branches, the root system should grow in all directions and the root graft should be clean.

Check container-grown trees for any signs of pests and diseases; the roots

Apple trees can be trained into useful shapes to aid harvesting

TIP

Proper planting is essential to get your tree off to a good start. Make sure the soil preparation is complete – adding in additional mulch or compost if necessary – and all the weeds have been removed at least two weeks before planting. This allows the soil to settle before you come to plant the tree.

should not be growing through the base, the surface of the compost should be weed-free and the rootball should be firm when you lift the tree.

Planting fruit trees

The ideal site for your fruit trees should be sunny and sheltered, with well drained, slightly acidic, fertile soil. Trees can be trained against walls or along wires – free-standing trees is not the only option.

Prevent the roots from drying out and protect them from frost damage before planting. If you are not planting them straight away, heel in the tree. This means planting it temporarily in a trench at a 45° angle to protect the trunk, and covering it with moist, light soil.

Make sure it is well watered before planting – if necessary left in a bucket of water for a few hours. With container-grown trees the roots may be growing in a spiral around the rootball. If so, then gently tease them out and cut back any damaged ones to about 30cm (1ft).

To plant a fruit tree

Dig over the ground and incorporate plenty of well-rotted organic material and fertilizer, such as bonemeal, into the soil (see p20).

The hole should give the roots plenty of space widthways; the graft point should be 5–8cm (2–3in) above the soil level. Splay out the roots and check that the hole's depth is level.

Fill around the roots with compost and fertilizer, then backfill with earth. Firm the tree in and build the soil up to form a slight basin around the trunk to help retain water. Secure to a short stake with a collar-type tree tie.

Prune branches of bush and half-standard trees back by a third of the previous season's growth.

Give a good watering, then water daily during any dry periods. Keep the area around the tree weed free.

Planting Soft Fruit

Most cultivated soft fruits are usually divided into bush or cane fruits, with the exception of strawberries, which are herbaceous perennials.

Cane fruit includes blackberries, raspberries and hybrid berries, such as loganberries and tayberries. Bush fruit consists of gooseberries and black, red and white currants. All soft fruit should be sheltered from strong winds, in full sunshine – or light shade – with fertile, well-drained, but not dry, soil.

As virtually all soft fruit is self-fertile, pollination is not a concern. However, soft fruit demands more effort with feeding and pruning to achieve a good harvest. Soft fruit bushes should last for a good ten years, though, and provide as many harvests.

Planting soft fruit and canes

Visit a reputable nursery or garden centre, and look for healthy plants with a well developed root system. Check container-grown plants are not pot-bound; if they lift out of the pot when you pick them up by the stem, they must have been allowed to dry out.

Plant in the same way as fruit trees, but mulch around the base of the plants to minimize evaporation. Make sure the mulch is 5cm (2in) deep and 1m (3ft) all around the stems (do not let it touch the stem, as mulch can rot it).

Planting times are between autumn and winter, but check with each individual plant. Again, strawberries are the exception, as they should be planted in the summer.

A good harvest of colourful berries is hard to beat

Growing Under Cover

There are many advantages of growing plants under cover, be it under glass or plastic. The warmer, more stable, conditions allow not only the extent of fruit and vegetables or other tender plants that can be grown, but also the length of the growing season.

You are more likely to achieve higher yields under cover and the quality of the crops are generally far better. There is no need to worry about wind and storms, and pests, such as rabbits, birds, cabbage root fly and carrot fly, can be easily excluded, while others such as whitefly and red spider mite can be dealt with more effectively.

Lemon trees are excellent grown in a container under cover

Although a greenhouse is the obvious solution, there are many other options available, especially where space is a problem. These include low mini polytunnels, cold frames, lantern lights and cloches – even plastic bottles sliced in half and placed over seedlings. These methods are obviously on a much smaller scale compared to a greenhouse, but they are able to fulfil the criteria of a greenhouse, which is to heat up the soil, offer light and warmth, as well as offering protection from extremes of weather and many pests.

Greenhouses

Choosing a greenhouse

The starting point when it comes to choosing a greenhouse must be size. As there is such a bewildering array of greenhouses on the market, decide how much space you have and how much you want to grow.

The next choice is the material for the frame. The choices are basically wood or aluminium, with pros and cons for each option. A wooden frame certainly looks nicer, there will be fewer problems with condensation and it does hold the heat well; on the other hand, the frame is bulkier than aluminium, which will lead to less light, and, most importantly of all, it will need to be regularly maintained.

Aluminium is less attractive to look at and it can get quite cold, creating damp problems; however, it is relatively maintenance free, making it a popular choice for most amateur gardeners. Whatever material you choose, make sure the greenhouse has adequate ventilation to prevent damp, which is exactly the sort of environment that encourages all types of pests and diseases to breed.

TIP

You should think carefully about how to organize the contents of your greenhouse. Some crops will require more shade than others, and there will be those that need better ventilation. Many fruits and vegetables will also have different watering requirements. Much depends on the time of year, but a greenhouse will need consistent management.

Heating the greenhouse

You may decide that you want simply to rely on the sun's heat, which would be absolutely fine for basic crops, such as salad and carrots. On the other hand, you could opt for maintaining a hot greenhouse, which would require extra heating supplied from the house to the greenhouse. A hot greenhouse is one where the temperature in winter stays above 16°C (61°F). However, bear in mind that the expense of maintaining such heat could be prohibitive.

By far the best option would be to go for a warm, rather than a hot, greenhouse. In a warm greenhouse the minimum night temperature in winter should not fall below 8°C (45°F). This can be achieved by installing electric or oil heaters. The portable paraffin oil heaters are the cheapest option. A frost alarm would also be useful. Insulating the greenhouse with bubble plastic wrap securely attached to the framework will also help.

Optional extras include blinds, automatic ventilators and an irrigation system.

Planning the space

To make the best use of space in a greenhouse, plan the layout beforehand. The classic layout consists of two beds and a path running between them, with some staging or shelves running along one or both sides. These should be at bench height for ease of working and near the light to promote growth. They are ideal for trays of seedlings. As well as providing extra storage space, if you have it just on one side, it allows you to grow taller crops on the other side.

What to grow

A huge variety of crops and tender plants can be grown in a greenhouse, as the warmer conditions provide the opportunity to grow more tender genera of fruit, herbs and vegetables, as well as plants more accustomed to warmer climes. Good salad crops and vegetables include asparagus, beans, carrots, cauliflower, chicory, peas, potatoes, radishes, rhubarb and tomatoes.

Polytunnels

Where aesthetic appearance is not important, plastic polytunnels may be the answer in the vegetable plot. They are basically a tunnel-shaped frame covered with transparent plastic sheeting. They are a fraction of the price of a greenhouse, and can be put up in a few hours and then taken down when not required.

If you have the space then they will enable you to produce crops at least six weeks ahead of those grown in the open, so you can raise two crops a year instead of one. Low polytunnels are particularly useful in protecting crops against flying pests, birds and carrot flies. You can make them yourself with a length of tough polythene, galvanised wire hoops, some twine and posts.

Cold frames

A cold frame is basically a box shape with wooden or

Cold frames are ideal for hardening off young plants or raising seedlings

brick sides, and covered over with a glass or plastic lid, which is often sloping downwards towards the front. A simple way to construct a cold frame yourself is by fixing a sheet of plastic over a wooden box.

Cold frames are a good way of hardening off greenhouse-grown plants and raising seedlings. They can also be used for growing tender crops, such as aubergines, peppers, melons and cucumbers, as well as giving protection to hardier crops.

They should be sited in a warm, sheltered position where they can get maximum exposure to the sun. On really hot days, prop the lid open to prevent the plants inside from overheating or drying out. During cold, frosty spells you may need to insulate the cold frame with old carpet, sacking or newspaper over the top.

Cloches and lights

Cloches and lantern lights are plastic or glass tents, which are somewhat smaller and much easier to move around than cold frames. They are used to protect plants that have been grown out and need a little extra warmth early in the season. A glass cloche holds the heat better than a plastic one and as it is heavier, is less prone to being blown away.

You can use cloches and lights for drying out and warming soil before planting, as well as protecting seedlings and hastening their growth. They are also good for hardening off greenhouse-grown plants and, for older specimens, offer protection against pests, speed up the ripening process and extend the growing season. You can even use them to protect some crops during winter.

Remember, however, when you start crops off under cloches they will be more delicate than other seedlings raised into the ground without protection, so if you suddenly take off the cloche without acclimatizing the plants, it will cause them quite a shock. Instead, only remove the cloche during the daytime and put it back again at night.

A modern cloche protects this young cauliflower plant

Conservatories

Building a conservatory on your house has become very fashionable over the past few decades. Yet many modern conservatories are rarely used for what they were intended over 100 years ago or more. Conservatories today often tend to be little more than an additional room where you can sit inside but feel you are closer to the garden. Unless the owner has invested in blinds, heating or a method of air conditioning, these rooms scarcely have any ventilation,

Conservatories are ideal for growing all kinds of tender fruit and exotic vegetables

which makes them hot in the summer and cold in the winter – generally unsuitable for growing many plants.

The conservatories of yester-year would have had a range of windows that could easily be opened in various combinations to bring air into every corner. The floor would have been tiled and there would have been channels and drains, allowing the whole place to be sprayed and washed down.

Yet modern conservatories are great for growing vines, figs and citrus fruit, as long as the temperature and humidity is controlled. Grow vines with their roots planted outside the building and their foliage trained inside. Citrus fruit are best grown in containers that can be moved outside in the summer.

Watering Plants

There is no hard and fast rule when it comes to watering plants. The amount and frequency depends on various factors, including the weather and soil conditions.

Never allow plants to become stressed due to lack of water, as they will not grow as well. Aim to keep the soil, or container compost, steadily moist. Do not allow it to completely dry out and then apply water as by this time plants will be suffering.

In the first instance, any plant transplanted from a pot should be given a good soaking before being planted. They then need watering in as soon as planted if the soil is dry. Thereafter, check beds and borders several times a week during the growing season. A plant's water requirement is quite low during the dormant growing season, usually the winter.

Containers such as tubs, window boxes and hanging baskets need more watering and should be checked daily for water requirements from spring to autumn. Unlike those planted in the ground, these plants are unable to draw upon water reserves in the soil. Apply water as soon as the soil or compost has become dry on the surface.

Watering is obviously a necessity in hot weather, but even during winter, if it hasn't rained for a few weeks, then newly planted shrubs, trees and bamboos will still need to be watered.

Working out quantities (1)

Always apply sufficient water each time to soak the soil to a good depth. For example, to moisten the soil to a depth of 15cm (6in) you need to apply the equivalent of about 2.5cm (1in) of rain. This is about 18 litres per sq m (4 gal per sq yd). With containers, fill the gap between the compost

TIP

Apart from not watering your plants, the next worst thing you can do is to provide regular watering in small quantities. This results in most of the water evaporating and failing to reach the roots. Most plants, particularly newly planted trees, shrubs and bamboos, need a good drenching followed by several days of nothing.

surface and the rim of the container (usually about 2.5cm/1in) with water to ensure the full depth of compost is moistened. It should run out of the bottom.

Another major factor depends on the structure of your soil. Heavy clays can hold on to too much water and so the ground becomes waterlogged, whereas chalky soil holds on to far less moisture, and so the soil dries out very quickly (see p18).

There are, of course, drought-resistant plants. However, this generally only applies after the plant has become established. For the first few seasons they will still need regular watering during dry weather.

If a plant comes with any special watering requirements, these will be indicated in the plant directory. However, experience and observation is the best way of getting to know your plants and their particular needs, so watch as they grow to find out what they prefer or dislike.

Watering systems

Watering cans, hand-held hoses and sprinkler systems are cheap and easy to use, but quite a large amount of water is lost to evaporation and it is easy to apply too much.

Automatic watering of beds, borders and containers saves a great deal of time. A watering system attached to a tap only needs the turn of a tap when water is required. But to be fully automatic, timing devices that switch the water on and off are widely available.

A more efficient, but expensive, alternative is to install a network of pipes or buried hoses, which can be supplied as fully automatic

An automatic irrigation system makes watering plants less of a chore

systems complete with pop-up sprinklers. A seep hose watering system is a cheaper option and is ideal for beds and borders. This is a porous pipe which releases water steadily but gently through its pores, oozing out into the soil. The pipe is laid among plants just below the soil surface, or it can be covered with mulching material.

With these systems virtually no water is lost through evaporation, but it is hard to measure how much is being applied, as well as the fact that seep hoses, in particular, are liable to become blocked after a year or two.

Large numbers of containers, such as patio tubs, window boxes and hanging baskets, can be watered by means of a drip or trickle watering system, consisting of thin tubes sprouting from the main pipe. Each container is supplied with one or more tubes.

Hand watering

Using a watering can is the most time-consuming method of watering but is recommended for small numbers of plants. Water plants individually, applying water to the soil around the stems rather than sprinkling the plants from above. A rose fitted to the can will give a slower delivery rate and so ensure most of the water

penetrates the soil instead of running off. A can is also the best method of watering a small number of containers.

Working out quantities (2)

As plants can easily be drowned, it is vital to know that the plant has adequate water, and yet is not swimming in it.

With shrubs, in particular, there will be differences between the amount the plant needs in its first year after planting, where watering is needed to give quick establishment, and later years when water may be needed to promote healthy and balanced growth.

The amount of water needed during the summer increases with the strength of the sun. As a guide, in average temperate climates, the sun's strength in mid-spring and early autumn will evaporate roughly 1.5cm (½in) of water per week. In late spring and late summer this increases to 2cm (¾in) each week, and in high summer roughly 2.5cm (1in) per week will be lost to evaporation. To find out exactly how much you need to water, take a measurement by leaving out a

Young trees need a good drenching, then a few days of no water at all

rain gauge [A], which will tell you how much rainfall has fallen during the past week [B], then simply apply the amounts described in 'Working out quantities (1)', less the rainfall.

As mentioned on previous pages, you will also need to factor in the water-holding capacity of your particular soil type. Well-drained fertile soils, such as loams, hold nearly three times as much water as sandy soils. With good loam soils, high rainfall and few drought periods, you will generally only need to water new plantings to establish them. Drier regions with light sandy soil will put your plants under pressure and weekly watering will be beneficial.

Feeding Plants

All plants benefit from regular feeding during the growing season, encouraging them to grow healthier and produce more blooms, better crops and even more decorative foliage or fruits.

When to feed

Plants can only absorb food during their growing season, so feeding a plant when it is dormant is pointless.

If you are creating new areas in the garden, it is sensible to dig in the nutrients before planting. The normal regime for plants in beds and borders is to apply a base dressing of general-purpose granular fertilizer a few days before planting. For permanent plants, additional fertilizer is supplied as an annual topdressing in spring. This should be sufficient for most border plants, although some vigorous kinds that

Canna indica enjoys a liquid feed

UNDERSTANDING FERTILIZER NUTRIENTS

Most over-the-counter plant foods contain some nitrogen, some potash, some phosphates and a small amount of trace elements. The exact ratio of each is printed on the packet and this will help you to decide what to buy.

Nitrogen – Leafy plants need nitrogen to stay lush and green. The more the plant is grown for its foliage, the higher the percentage of nitrogen required. Bamboos, palms and any large-leafed plants, for example, need lots of nitrogen.

Potash – This helps plants to flower and fruit. Plants that would benefit from a high percentage of potash include cannas, agapanthus and hedychiums.

Phosphates – This helps the root system to grow and is most beneficial to trees and shrubs. Phosphates are best applied in the form of bonemeal sprinkled into the bottom of the planting hole before planting.

A well-fed and watered border will give handsome rewards

bloom prolifically may benefit from booster feeds of liquid fertilizer during the growing period, especially from the time they start flowering.

With hardy bulbs, as soon as flowering is over liquid feed with a general-purpose fertilizer once a week for two or three weeks to build up the bulbs, thus ensuring optimum flowering the following year.

Frequent feeding is needed by plants in containers such as patio tubs and hanging baskets, as plant foods are quickly leached out of containers due to frequent watering. Foods are supplied for the first six weeks or so by the new compost but once plants are established they will need to be fed weekly or fortnightly during the growing season with liquid fertilizer. Alternatively insert fertilizer tablets when plants are established.

What to use

Whatever fertilizer is chosen, provided the instructions are followed, more or less any feed is better than none. Understanding how various minerals benefit a certain area of the plant will determine your choice of fertilizer (see opposite, p78). As there are many organic gardeners these days, so there is a greater choice of both organic or chemical fertilizers.

Granular fertilizers

As the name suggests, these fertilizers are supplied as granules, which are easily sprinkled over the soil surface. Always lightly fork them into the soil, whether you are applying a base dressing or a topdressing. For flowers, widely available general-purpose fertilizers are suitable (some of these are available in organic forms) or a special flower-garden fertilizer can be used.

Slow-release tablets

These are ideal for hanging baskets, container plants or window boxes as they save so much time. Once buried in the compost surface they release plant foods steadily over the entire growing season. After about six weeks, when the supply of plant foods is diminishing from the new compost, insert tablets as directed on the carton. For permanent plants in containers, insert tablets in spring, at the start of the growing season.

Measure and dilute liquid feeds with water

TIP

One of the most useful types of plant food is a general-purpose fertilizer, which contains a good balance of the important plant nutrients, particularly for flowers. However, an alternative is to use a flower-garden fertilizer, which contains more potassium and less nitrogen, and therefore stimulates flower production.

Liquid feeds

There are numerous liquid fertilizers available, some of the most popular are based on seaweed. There are general-purpose types as well as fertilizers for specific plants or groups of plants. They are first diluted with water, according to the instructions, then watered around the plants with a watering can.

Applying feed

Fertilizers come in liquid, powder, tablet or granular form. All fertilizers contain at least one of the three major elements required by plants for healthy growth: nitrogen for leaf and stem growth, potash to help fruit and flower formation, and phosphate to encourage a strong, healthy root system (see p78–9).

'Straight' fertilizers contain one element only and the purpose of these is either to encourage one particular function of plant growth or to correct a particular deficiency.

'Compound' fertilizers, on the other hand, contain all three elements and are generally sufficient for most plants' needs. When buying general purpose compound fertilizers, look on the bag for the three numbers that will tell you the content: for example, 7.5.7 means that it contains 7 parts of nitrogen, 5 of phosphate and 7 of potash.

Liquid fertilizers are instantly available to the plants. The main disadvantage is that they don't stay in the soil very long and so have to be used regularly. The easiest way to apply it is to use a watering can. Measure the correct amount into the cap of the fertilizer bottle. Do not exceed the dosage as you may scorch the plant. Pour the liquid into the watering can and dilute with water. Water in thoroughly around the roots of the plant.

ALTERNATIVE COMPOUND FERTILIZERS

There are numerous organic and artificial fertilizers on the market, all suited to a particular purpose. The following are a small selection of the most popular.

Organic – Blood, fish and bone meal: a popular organic compound fertilizer that contains all three major nutrients. Simply sprinkle around the roots of the plant and then mix into the soil using a trowel or fork. Regular applications will help to maintain nutrient levels.

Chicken manure concentrate: an organic compound fertilizer available in either powder or pellet form, the latter providing a useful slow-release action.

Artificial – Growmore: one of the most popular artificial compound fertilizers. Its effects are rapid and it is particularly suitable for use on vegetables and as a lawn feed.

Rose fertilizer: one of several specialized compound fertilizers which can be used to feed all flowering plants, as well as fruit trees and bushes during the spring and summer.

Mulching

The main purpose of a mulch is to protect the soil surface by preventing weeds from germinating, providing moisture retention and helping to regulate soil temperature, making soil cooler in the summer and warmer in the winter.

When you apply organic mulches, these are eventually broken down and incorporated into the soil, benefiting the soil texture by improving water retention of lighter soils and helping heavy soils to drain more easily. Those with high nutrient content will also help feed the soil and boost fertility.

Organic mulches

Bark is an excellent organic mulch, as it is long-lasting and also looks attractive. Cocoa shells are an effective alternative to bark. Wood chippings have their uses but mainly for making paths through shrub areas rather than as mulches for beds. All of these wood- or husk-based mulches should not be used where fruit or vegetables are grown, as they have little or no nutritional value and will use up nitrogen from the soil as they rot down.

A peat mulch, on the other hand, provides plenty of nutrients but is only suitable for acid-loving plants, such as rhododendrons and heathers. A more environmentally friendly form, however, would be to choose a peat-substitute instead, as the mass demand for peat over the years has lead to the large-scale destruction of areas of wetland.

Leafmould is formed from composted leaves and will greatly improve the quality of

Cocoa shells provide an effective mulch but offer few nutrients

the soil, as will manure, but mulching with these two can turn into feeding, and with manure especially you can be encouraging weeds to grow.

The mulch should be layered roughly 5–10cm (2–4in) thick. Any thinner, and the mulch will not do its work; any deeper, and the plants will be swamped and the mulch could overheat.

Inert mulches

There are two main types of inert mulch: pea gravel and synthetic sheeting (woven polypropylene or polythene). They do not provide any nutritional benefits but are highly effective at controlling weeds. Pea gravel has an open nature, which prevents weed growth at the same time as providing a surface that can be walked on. Dwarf conifers in particular look good surrounded by pea gravel. In much the same way as organic mulches, make sure the depth of the pea gravel is roughly 5–10cm (2–4in) thick.

Sheet mulches, synthetic or otherwise, work by allowing rain and water to percolate through the sheet while at the same time reducing evaporation from the surface. They are great at controlling weeds, as established weeds and those which germinate under the mulch have no light and eventually die, while those which germinate above the mulch are unable to root through the sheet. Woven polypropylene is best, but black polythene sheeting or old polythene bags, such as compost bags, can also be used. Although these do not allow water to get through, provided they are no larger than 1m (3ft) sq, the water will run in to the soil from the sides.

TIP

Soft fruits particularly like a mulch of well-rotted farmyard manure, and all fruit requires a feed in winter in the form of top dressing. This operation simply involves replacing the top layer of compost (roughly 2.5cm/1in) with fresh compost. Your local riding stables will have an abundance of fresh manure!

Laying sheet mulches

To cover an entire shrub bed, use a full sheet. After you have prepared the soil, position the sheet mulch over the ground before you undertake any planting. On the sheet, mark out the positions of the plants where you want them to be in the bed and cut a cross for each one [A]. The size of the cuts is obviously dependent upon the size of the particular plant and its root system. You will now have four flaps. Fold them back and ease the plant through the centre [B], putting the flaps back around the stem after planting. To finish the effect, mulch around the plant with bark or cocoa shells [C].

For plants that are scattered around the garden, or for specimen shrubs, individual

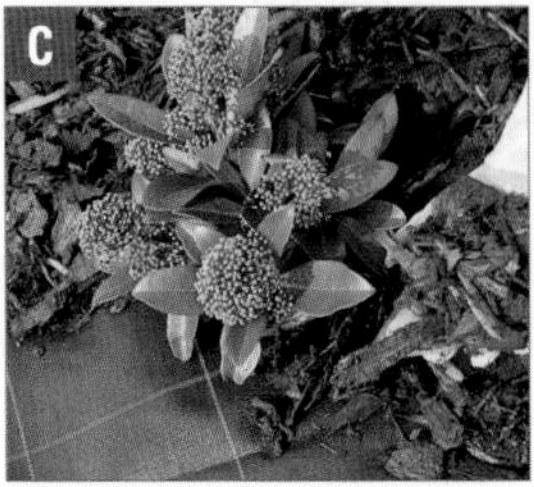

squares of sheeting are best. If the plant is small, cut a cross-shaped notch and plant through the hole. For larger plants, cut a slit from one side into the middle, then place it around the plant and overlap the sheeting to close the slit. Squares should be about 1m (3ft 3in) sq. Hold the squares in place by either using a spade to make slits in the turf or edge of the bed just in from each edge and then forcing the sides into the slit, or hold down the corners with turf or large stones.

TIP

The main drawback to synthetic sheet mulches is that once they are in place, organic matter cannot – very easily – be incorporated into the soil. If extra nutrients are required after the sheet mulch has been laid, this can be added by punching holes through the sheet with a dibber and then watered in to disperse into the soil.

Compost

Compost is the result of decayed organic household and garden waste and can make a great contribution to the productivity of the garden. In its best form, compost is a wonderfully dark, sweet-smelling, crumbly substance that can be dug into the soil or spread as a mulch.

Traditional compost heaps

Compost heaps are invaluable in large gardens which produce a lot of waste. You often find gardens that have completely open heaps, which, as well as looking untidy, are not very efficient in breaking down the material. The organic matter at the edges does not compost at the same rate as the material in the middle, and so the the heap needs to be turned regularly. It must not be allowed to dry out in the summer, but equally it should be covered with a sheet of polythene or old carpet to keep off heavy rain.

Ready-made compost bins

Ready-made plastic and metal bins on the market are becoming ever more popular. They are normally fully enclosed to allow the composted material to heat up evenly and rot down quickly. The composted material is also easy to get at from the bottom. The main disadvantage is that the bins are usually not big enough for the amount of material a large garden produces.

Making compost

For the material to heat up sufficiently, the heap or bin must be at least 1 cubic m (1 cubic yd) in size. To start off the compost, put a thick base layer down of rough material, such as straw or shredded

Digging in compost will greatly improve soil fertility

prunings, then sprinkle with either sulphate of ammonia (a dessertspoon per sq m/yd), any compost activator or animal manure to speed up the breakdown process. Continue in 15cm (6in) layers, adding a layer of lime now and then to neutralize the acidity of the compost.

Household organic material suitable for composting includes teabags, potato peelings, eggshells, shredded newspaper and even old rags. Ideal garden material includes dead flowers and leaves, bolted vegetables and old bedding plants, grass clippings, soft prunings, hedge trimmings and weeds (before they have set seed). If you fill the compost heap or bin with too much of any one material, such as grass clippings, the result will be a smelly, black slime.

Avoid adding cooked food, as this will attract vermin. Also, destroy and do not use diseased plants, seed bearing annual weeds or the roots of perennial weeds, such as ground elder and couch grass. These survive the composting process and you

COMPOST BINS

A compost bin should measure approximately 1.2m (4ft) in height by 1m (3ft) square.

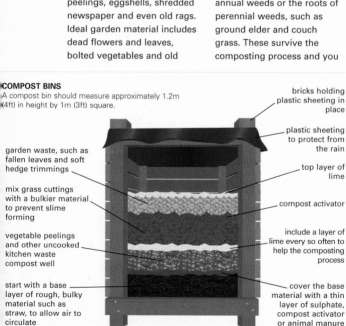

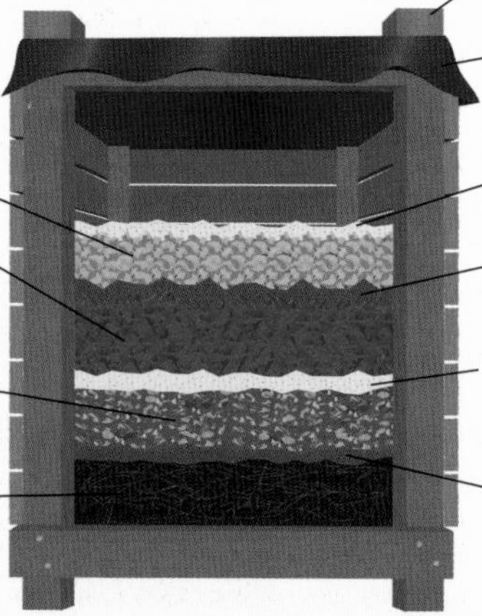

bricks holding plastic sheeting in place
plastic sheeting to protect from the rain

mix grass cuttings with a bulkier material to prevent slime forming

vegetable peelings and other uncooked kitchen waste compost well

start with a base layer of rough, bulky material such as straw, to allow air to circulate

> **TIP**
>
> If you have the space, try keeping two compost heaps or bins on the go at the same time. This will ensure a constant supply of compost, as material can be rotting down in one bin while you are still filling up the other. It is highly likely, once you start composting, that you'll find you need two bins anyway!

end up with more problems. Shred anything too woody or it will not compost.

Wormeries

These compost bins rely on a colony of worms reproducing on a large scale what they naturally do in the soil – that is, breaking down organic matter and improving the soil structure. In a specially-designed worm bin, worms are given fresh supplies of finely chopped household scraps every few days. A tray underneath collects liquid which can be drained off, watered down and used for plant food; the resulting compost is wonderfully rich.

Leaf mould

Leaf mould is made from rotted down leaves. The texture is crumbly and has a high nutritional value, making it ideal as a soil conditioner or even as a seed and potting compost.

Leaves rot down by means of cool fungal decay (a slower process), as opposed to compost heating up and then being broken down by bacteria.

You can make leaf mould simply by raking moist leaves into a pile as they will eventually rot down. Alternatively, make a wire cage with a roll of chicken wire nailed onto four wooden posts and fill with leaves. Smaller amounts of leaves can be put in sealed, black sacks with holes in them. Leaves may take up to a year to rot down, but to speed things up, shred the leaves and apply a leaf compost activator, and ensure the leaves do not dry out.

Well-rotted leaf mould is ideal as a soil conditioner

Weeding

Even the best prepared planting areas, where you have removed all traces of weed and dug the ground over, will be prone to wind-carried weed seeds after planting.

If the ground was cleared of perennial weeds before planting there should be little subsequent weeding required, apart from dealing with annual weeds – and not even these where the ground is mulched.

In beds and borders without mulch, control annual weeds by hoeing when they are in the seedling stage. Choose a warm, sunny day when the soil is dry on the surface so that they quickly die.

If the occasional perennial weed appears among the plants, treat it with glyphosate. This is available in gel form as a spot weeder, as a ready mixed solution in a spray bottle or as concentrated liquid for mixing in a watering can. Take care to avoid cultivated plants. Alternatively dig out the weeds, complete with roots.

Any annual weeds that appear in containers can be pulled out by hand.

Control annual weeds with regular hoeing

Weeds

As already mentioned in the section 'Preparing the Site' on pages 16–17, it is far better to achieve weed control before anything is planted. This ensures that new plants are not fighting with weeds for nutrients in the soil – and also because weeding is a lot more difficult with the plant in place.

If large weeds spring up, these can easily be removed by hand or by forking over the soil. Perennial weeds, such as couch grass, bindweed and nettles, are the biggest problem – even if you kill off their upper foliage, they can survive by retaining underground food stores in their roots and return each year.

The most effective way of removing perennial weeds is to kill them off at the roots. For this it is best to use translocated chemical weedkillers, such as those containing glyphosate. These are sprayed or painted on to the leaves and the chemical is then taken down to the roots by the plant. However, translocated weedkillers are not selective in what they kill and will attack weeds and garden plants alike. Most weedkillers can often take as long as several weeks before you can do any planting, so always read the label.

Prevention is always better than cure. Mulching with organic material, planting ground cover or using a synthetic sheet mulch will suppress weed growth.

Use a glyphosate-based weed killer to kill perennial weeds

TIP

If you do not like using weedkillers, try laying sheet mulches for several weeks or even months before planting in an effort to kill off the weeds. Do your planting through holes in the sheets and this will help prevent weeds coming through after planting. Alternatively, lay an organic mulch, at least 5cm (2in) thick. This also has the added benefit of enriching the soil.

Lawn Care

Keeping your lawn green and healthy is the aim of most gardeners. This can be achieved relatively successfully by applying a few simple techniques.

Mowing and edging

Mowing is one of the best ways to keep a lawn looking good. Regular mowing not only creates an attractive garden, it can also promote new growth and help keep the lawn healthy.

The lawnmower that is right for you depends on the size and condition of your lawn, and your preference for petrol, electric, battery or manual.

Before mowing, clear the lawn of any stones or branches, then set the mower slightly higher for the first cut, reducing each time until it cuts at the right height (usually one-third or less of the length of the blades of grass). To achieve straight lines, cut two opposite edges first and mow in straight lines in between.

A strimmer is best for edging

Petrol lawnmowers need the most maintenance

If you have lawn edging, such as pre-formed wooden battens or stones, then trim around the edges using a power edger, strimmer or long-handled cutters for a neater finish, rather than trying to mow up close.

Watering

Topping up the rainfall with a sprinkler is the best way to ensure your lawn receives sufficient water for healthy growth. The best time to water is in the evening or first

Raking the lawn of thatch

Sprinklers water the lawn evenly

thing in the morning as there is less chance of evaporation and the lawn will better absorb the water before the heat of the day.

The amount will vary depending on soil and grass types, as well as local weather conditions, but during the summer, give your lawn a good watering twice a week in hot conditions. There is usually no need to water in the autumn.

General maintenance

Any lawn can develop bare patches and most can be repaired by buying a lawn patch kit, which contains a mix of grass seed, fertilizer and compost. Raking the lawn to remove thatch (dead grass and moss) allows the air and moisture to penetrate down to the roots, ensuring stronger and healthier grass.

Sowing seed in bare patches

A healthy, well-groomed lawn

Plant Protection

Protecting plants, especially during harsh winters, is extremely important. And it is not only young, tender plants which need to be offered protection.

Horticultural fleece and even a sheet of plastic film are invaluable, as they warm up and dry out the soil, protecting plants from extremes of cold, as well as from pests.

Horticultural fleece works better than plastic as it allows light, air and water to pass through, giving plants the chance to breathe. Because it is light, it can be left on top of most plants, keeping away many pests and preventing wind damage.

Horticultural fleece should be wrapped around vulnerable plants to protect them from frost

Hotbeds

Hotbeds are an ingenious method of keeping tender plants warm, without the need for any elaborate electric heating cables. Fresh horse manure is used to warm plant roots; as the manure rots down it gives off heat, which is then trapped by the overhead frame.

To make your own hotbed

Dig a shallow hole in the ground. Fill it with a large amount of fresh manure – four wheel-barrow loads is plenty to make a good-sized pile – and leave for about five days to build up heat. If the weather is hot, turn the pile and sprinkle with water because the decomposition will slow down if it is allowed to dry out.

After about five days, flatten as much as possible and cover with a layer of loam roughly 7.5cm (3in) deep. Place a frame with a lid over the top to retain the heat. The lid can be opened if the temperature gets too high. Grow plants in the loam, but sow seeds in trays and place on top of the loam within the frame.

Raised beds can act like a hotbed as they warm up faster in spring

Wintering plants

Many tender plants used for summer bedding or containers can be kept from year to year if you rescue them before the frosts start in autumn. Tender perennials such as pelargoniums, fuchsias and osteospermums, for example, are propagated from cuttings in late summer or early autumn, and the resultant young plants are wintered in a cool but frost-free greenhouse. The parent plants are lifted and discarded as they are often too big to store under glass and not as good as young plants. Tender winter-dormant tubers such as dahlias, cannas and tuberous begonias are lifted, cut down and stored in boxes of peat substitute in a cool, frost-free place over winter.

Annuals, whether tender or hardy, are pulled up and discarded when frosts start, as they cannot be kept from year to year, although you may be able to save the seeds for sowing in spring.

TIP

Raised beds not only make it easier for the less able gardener, but they act in the same way as a hotbed, providing warmth and protection for plants. If you raise one side of the bed to be sloping towards the direction of the sun, this will warm the bed even more efficiently and promote early plant growth.

Protecting exotic plants

Choosing the right plants for the climate you live in will usually do away with the need to protect plants. However, if you really cannot live without a certain species or variety, to ensure their survival, the answer is to wrap them up for the winter.

When to wrap?

Wrapping up a plant for the autumn or winter all depends upon the local climate and the hardiness of the plant. Compare the average minimum temperature for your area during autumn and winter with the hardiness of your plants. One frosty night below the minimum will not kill them, but if a prolonged spell is forecast then they will need to be wrapped.

Artistic insulation

Protecting your plants need not mean staring out at ugly looking bubble-wrap for several months of the year. This method of wrapping will even create a talking point for your garden.

A hardy Japanese banana (*Musa basjoo*) is the exotic plant being artistically wrapped in this example.

TIP

Another method for wrapping up plants such as *Musa basjoo* is to use strips of hessian or a piece of carpet tied around the plant. These materials will help to trap any warm air and will act as an insulating layer through the colder months of autumn or winter. Use whichever method is more practical.

However, it is not strictly necessary to use wrapping, as this plant is root-hardy. You will ensure its survival by cutting it down to ground level, and it will grow back each year to a reasonable height. But to have the plant in full fruit and flower, however, you must keep and protect several years' growth, hence wrapping it up for the winter.

The best time to carry this out is usually during late autumn, when the leaves have been slightly damaged by the first hard frosts.

For this method you will need flue liners from your local plumber (about five for each plant), a ridge tile from a builders' merchant and a bale of straw. Remove all the leaves, cutting them back close to the stem, so that just the trunk of the banana tree remains [A].

Put the first flue liner round the stem [B] and stuff straw in between the liner and stem. Build up with more flue liners and straw [C] until you reach the top of the stem [D].

Finish off by placing a ridge tile on the top [E]. This will prevent rain from seeping through the 'flue' tower and rotting the main trunk.

A group of three or four plants growing in close proximity in the garden and all wrapped up similarly for the winter looks stunning.

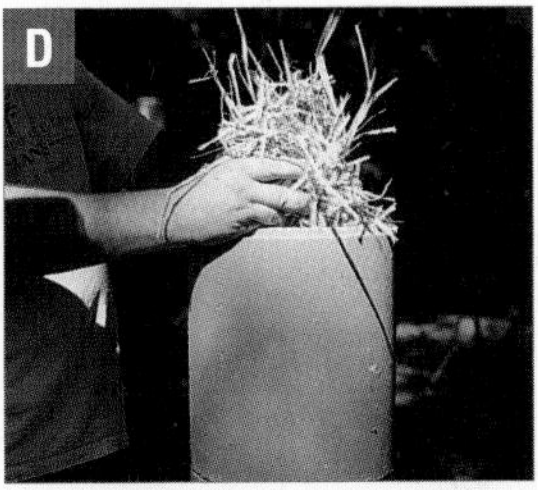

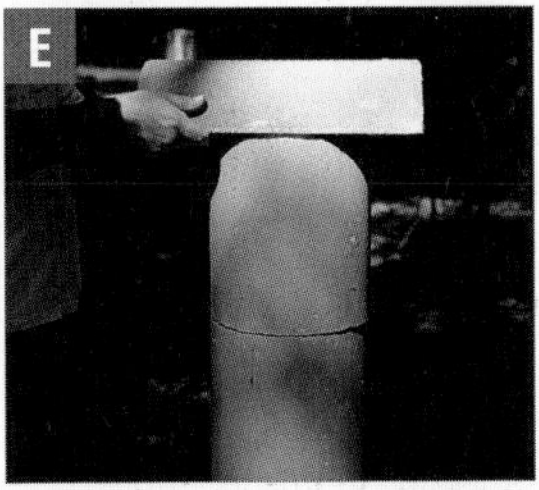

Inexpensive insulation

A cheaper method of winter wrapping can be employed where you have plants that are hidden from direct view. This is particularly useful if you are wrapping large numbers of plants, especially those which do not have the slender trunk of the *Musa basjoo*.

It is becoming common for another exotic plant, the cabbage palm (*Cordyline australis*), to be grown in gardens in less temperate climates. During really harsh frosts, however, these plants could be in trouble of surviving the winter. Although they nearly always re-shoot, if planted directly into the soil, they can take many years to grow back to their former glory. If a particularly cold spell is forecast, usually in deepest mid-winter, then you must insulate your *Cordyline australis*.

First of all, you will need a ball of string and a roll of agricultural (horticultural) fleece – available from most garden centres – and possibly a stepladder if you have seriously tall plants.

Gather up the foliage [A] and tie it together with string to secure it [B]. This will protect all the younger growth inside from the cold weather.

With the aid of a stepladder, if necessary, wrap several layers of the fleece around the plant [C]. Secure it with

D

string and cut off the fleece from the roll.

Tie the fleece securely in several places to prevent strong winds from blowing it away [D].

Protecting tree ferns

Among the most common exotic subjects that gardeners wish to grow in areas often far too cold to be suitable for them are tree ferns, such as *Dicksonia antarctica*. Away from urban centres in warm areas and mild coastal regions, they rarely survive unprotected during an average winter.

If you have tree ferns growing in pots, then they can simply be moved to somewhere frost-free for the winter, such as a conservatory, greenhouse or even a utility room.

For specimens growing in the ground, there are two methods of protection to consider.

The first method is to wait until the fronds have been hit by frost and gone brown, then cut them off as near to the trunk as you can. You will then be left with the most vulnerable part of the plant at the tip of the trunk, just inside the hollow bit at the top, where the new fronds will

TIP

Straw is great insulation and heat can start to build up inside very quickly, so as soon as temperatures rise, make sure you remove the straw straight away. Otherwise the heat could start to cook the foliage, leaving a soggy mess that will have to be cut off and will put paid to all your hard winter protection work.

Straw is a great insulation method, particularly for tree ferns

emerge. To prevent any winter damage, gently push straw or hessian into the hollow (see picture above), and fasten the remaining fronds together with string.

With the other method, you will need to have a good number of straw bales to hand (unless you have need of the straw afterwards, this could be quite an expensive means of protection!) Gather up the fronds vertically and hold them securely with string. Then stack the bales as tightly as possible around the trunk, gradually building them up to hide the entire plant. The result will look like a miniature haystack.

Other insulation

Total winter protection is not really feasible for larger shrubs and trees. Layers of straw is ideal for wrapping plants or covering up vulnerable areas of the plant. Straw or mulch can be used to cover around the base of semi-hardy trees and shrubs protecting new shoots from being damaged by frost. Newly planted trees and

TIP

To protect against late spring frosts, you can either insulate plants with a lighter material, such as fleece or net curtains, or spray susceptible foliage with water. This protects plants because heat is given off when water changes from liquid into ice. Always keep an eye on the weather if air frosts are forecast.

shrubs can be wrapped in straw and held together with a sheet of polythene or hessian material.

Smaller plants can be given temporary protection from light frosts by covering them with plastic bags or even cardboard boxes.

Evergreen boughs can be layered around plants or over perennials as a form of insulation. Placing the boughs in alternate directions for each new layer will provide the best insulation.

Pile dry leaves in a thick layer over perennials and cover with chicken wire or netting to keep the leaves from blowing away. As the weather warms, remove the top layers, eventually removing the mulch once new growth starts to emerge.

Protection from animals

Sometimes trees and shrubs need protecting from animals that like to strip bark or eat the foliage. The most effective method is to fence off vulnerable plants using a barrier of chicken wire or wire netting, secured in place and bent outwards and covered by soil to prevent burrowing animals breaking through. More practical on a small scale is to use a proprietary rigid or wrap-around stem or tree guard made from plastic or rubber.

Fruit trees and vegetables are the most vulnerable to attack from animals and especially birds. Plastic or mesh netting is the best solution to prevent your crop being eaten away.

Wire or plastic netting will keep hungry animals at bay when a young plant is becoming established

Training Climbers

Climbing plants look dramatic and are great for disguising ugly walls and corners, but they need help to get started. Training them properly will ensure that they flourish.

Vine eyes and wire lattice

Vine eyes are the most practical means for securing a climber's support on walls. They are long lasting (as long as you choose the galvanized variety), and they can support a lot of weight. They will also help thwart the effects of wind and storm damage to any plant attached to them. Remember that many climbers are extremely vigorous and will ride roughshod over any short-term measures to tie them up – leading instead to damage to both plants and masonry.

When planning the spread of climbers it is best to anticipate the area to be covered and put in enough vine eyes accordingly. Vine eyes can be driven or screwed directly into brickwork, mortar and masonry. Hold the vine eye steady and hammer, or screw it, into the wall. (If you have a traditional-shaped vine eye – that is, a long, round-headed shape – leave about 5cm (2in) of the vine eye showing on the outside.) Thread wire through the eye and twist it until it is fully taut, taking the wire across and linking up with the other vine eyes. This lattice of wire attached to vine eyes will provide a supporting framework strong enough for most climbers. The next step is to tie in the stems of the plant to the wire.

Train climbing roses and other heavy plants up a wire network attached to vine eyes

Tying in

There are many different products available for tying climbing stems to wire or trellis structures. Always check that the plant has not outgrown its ties each year or that the product used has not rotted and come away from its support.

String is the most useful method for tying up leading shoots of climbers, and for tying in pruned wands of climbers after fruiting. Other materials may be appropriate, depending on the nature of the climber, the amount of wind damage expected and the desired look for display plants. For example, you can buy different coloured string to camouflage the ties and hide their obtrusiveness.

Raffia and twines are useful for soft stems, and wire loops can be put on woody stems, so long as the stems are not permitted to grow into the wood. Paper-covered twist ties are ideal when planting up a clematis in a pot, for example, as the delicate stems are gently held in place by these ties and can be easily removed once the plant has taken hold and established itself.

Tie the tendrils of climbing plants to supports to help them become established

Netting and wire netting

For self-attaching climbers, an open net can be fixed to a wall and the plant encouraged to climb up it. There are many different types of netting available, often made of plastic, and in various colours. The problem with nets is that they can look awful until they are obscured with plants – and also, if you have a climber that needs to be cut down at the end of the season, untangling it can be tiresome. But they are great as a quick and easy means of providing support.

TIP

If you are using a wire framework to support your newly planted climbers, ensure that the wire does not start embedding itself in the stems and constricting growth. Plastic coated wire is the best type to use, which will also have the advantage of not rusting and adversely affecting the plant later on.

Plastic netting is generally quite floppy and therefore needs to be well secured to a wall or fence to prevent it falling down or blowing over in the wind, taking your climber with it. To make the actual netting seem less obvious to the eye before the plant covers it, try buying a plastic netting in a colour that blends in with the background surface. For example, if your wall is painted white, don't fix up black netting! Work with the material that you have to make the most of your support system.

Natural supports

Natural products look so much better as supports for climbers. Young shoots of a variety of plants can be used, ranging from hazel and willow to bamboo canes. These can be used singly or in a woven fashion to support climbers on their way up. They might be used as temporary support to get the climber into a hedgerow or tree branch, for instance, which will then take over the support role.

The more divided foliage of broom and hazel, cut in winter to avoid leaves forming, can be used to make small wigwams for shorter climbers on which to scramble. Larger supporting structures made of natural materials set the scene for a grand display of climbers in the garden.

Supports can be made out of rustic wood fashioned in any shape or structure, such as a trellis, an arbour or a gazebo. Even before the plant grows and scrambles up it, the structure can look

TIP

Be adventurous with your choice of support for your climbing plants. As well as trellis, climbers can be trained up through different coloured netting, an intricate wire arrangement, a free-standing pyramid in wood or raffia, a tripod of natural wood canes and, of course, a variety of brick or stone walls and wooden fences. Almost any kind of structure will do!

attractive and dynamic in its own right, introducing an interesting focal point for the garden.

An old stone wall that has seen better days can be attractively disguised by climbing plants. If the climber needs help to cling on to the surface before scrambling up and covering the whole area, unobtrusive wall attachments such as vine eyes will hide the fact that any support has been given.

Self-clinging climbers

Those types of plants most likely to need support are climbers. There are two main types: self-clinging climbers and those that require trellis or wire support, as mentioned on the previous pages.

Self-clinging climbers produce aerial roots along their stems to enable them to cling onto rough surfaces like brickwork or a pebble-dashed wall. There is no need to tie in this type of climber – simply direct them towards the surface you want them to climb up by planting them at an angle to the surface and let them get on with it.

Climbers that wind themselves around trellis include *Clematis armandii* and *Holboellia latifolia*. However, these must be tied in when first planted. New shoots naturally grow in one direction, upwards to the sun. As new lead shoots spring up and follow the sun – rotating slowly, unseen with the naked eye – wind them round its support in a *clockwise* direction or in a few days they will have unwound themselves.

Wind *Clematis armandii* clockwise around its support

Pruning

The mere thought of pruning a climber, shrub or tree can instill fear into the heart of many a gardener. The basic rule is to give it a go and not to panic.

Equipment and technique

A pair of secateurs is the best tool for most pruning tasks. Secateurs are either by-pass (with a sharp blade and a blunt blade cutting by a scissor action) or anvil (with a sharp blade chopping against the middle of a blunt anvil). By-pass secateurs do not bruise the shoot and so are better for finer pruning.

Shrub pruners are larger versions of secateurs and cut into branches up to 3cm (1¼in) thick. Use a pruning saw for larger branches or stems. Shears are useful for trimming hedges and other similar bushes.

A selection of tools of the pruning trade

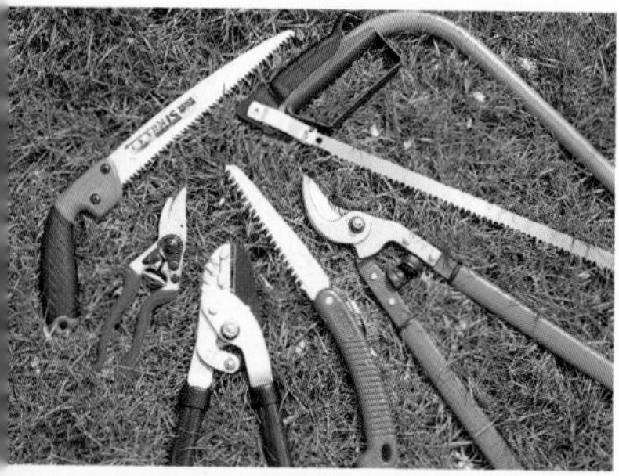

Training pruning

Training is the easiest type of pruning and involves maintaining the plant by removing dead branches or crossing limbs, or where limbs which grow in the 'wrong' direction. Most newly planted shrubs need initial training to encourage healthy growth and a balanced, open shape. After planting, prune back any dead or damaged stems and any stems that are crossing.

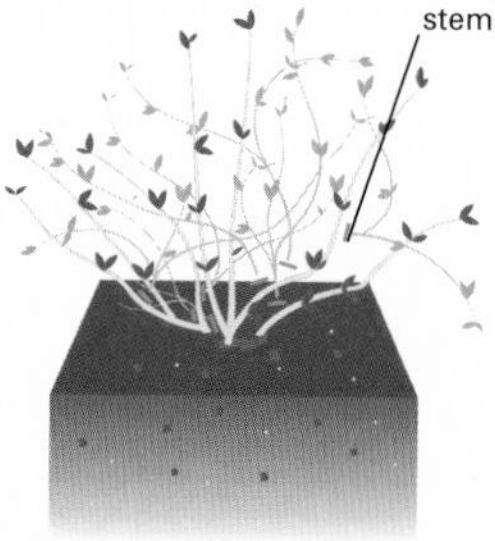
use secateurs to cut out any dead or damaged wood and weak, crossing stems

TRAINING PRUNING
With a young shrub, prune it carefully to create a balanced form and encourage vigorous growth

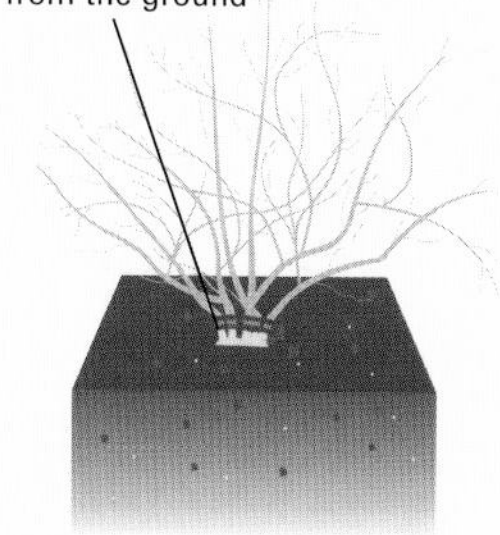
cut back hard all the plant's stems to about 7cm (2¾in) from the ground

COPPICING A SHRUB
To promote vigorous, colourful new growth, cut the plant back hard before new growth begins in spring

Coppicing

Shrubs that have outgrown their setting need to be reduced gradually or cut back hard ('coppiced'). Only shrubs that can regrow from dormant buds in the bark can be coppiced, however. Coppicing is not advisable for Cistus, Cytisus, Daphne and Hebe, and virtually all conifers.

To coppice a shrub, cut all growth back down to 7cm (2¾in) above ground level. Coppicing is best carried out in spring, but it can be done at any time of the year; yet it is best to avoid early autumn, as new growth is likely to be killed by winter cold.

Group 1 shrubs

These should be pruned immediately after flowering is finished. With Group 1 shrubs generally, restrict your pruning to the older shoots, leaving the newer shoots intact, as these shrubs tend to flower better on the spur shoots which are formed in the second year of a stem's life. Some do react well to being hard pruned, such as *Berberis stenophylla*, which makes a floriferous hedge if hard trimmed annually after flowering in mid-spring.

Group 1 shrubs include Abelia, Berberis, Camellia, Chaenomeles, Clethra, Cornus, Deutzia, Exochorda, Forsythia, many Hydrangea and Spiraea.

hard prune older stems immediately after flowering to encourage new growth

PRUNING GROUP 1 SHRUBS
Group 1 shrubs vary in how much regular pruning they require, but avoid pruning new and one year old stems

Group 2 shrubs

As these flower on this year's shoots, they can be hard pruned as growth begins in the spring. This encourages them to make vigorous new growths, which will either bear large trusses of flowers (*Buddleja davidii*) or simply more flowers, as with Hypericum and Lavatera.

Group 2 shrubs can either be cut down to 7cm (2¾in) above ground level, or to the bases of branches. Shrubs pruned in this manner will tend to flower later in the summer than if left unpruned.

Group 2 shrubs include *Buddleja davidii*, Caryopteris, some Ceanothus, Ceratostigma, *Hydrangea paniculata*, Hypericum, Lavatera, *Lupinis arboreus*, Perovskia and *Spiraea japonica*.

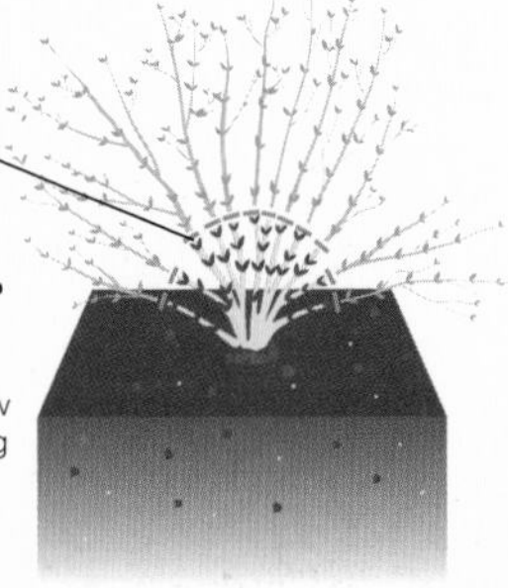
cut the shrub back hard to an even shape, 7cm (2¾in) above the ground or to the bases of branches

PRUNING GROUP 2 SHRUBS
These need to be hard pruned as new growth is beginning in the spring to encourage an immediate growth response

Small-leafed shrubs can be cut back with shears

Pruning Clematis

Whatever the species or cultivar, clematis are pruned in three different ways.

Group 1 clematis flower in the spring on last year's stems, so do not cut any old stems out. These include the alpinas and macropetalas, which are generally easy to contain and do not tend to spread all over the place. Occasionally, some will flower twice in one season if lightly pruned after the first flowering. For their early years, many Group 1 clematis often do not need any pruning.

Group 2 clematis – such as *Clematis* 'Marie Boisselot' – flower in early summer, also on last year's growth, so only cut these plants back in early spring before new growth begins, in this way leaving next year's crop of flowers unaffected. Remove all dead wood and leaves, and cut down to ground level if the main stem looks unsightly.

Group 3 clematis flower in late summer or early autumn on the current year's growth, so beware of taking away new growth once they have begun sprouting new stems. Some are vigorous growers, however, such as the 'Jackmanii' clematis, and these can be pruned back to a pair of good buds on old stems, about 30cm (12in) above ground level.

Watch out for the apparently 'dead' stems of clematis, particularly in Groups 1 and 2. These should not be pruned as they are usually alive and will break readily, losing at least one year's growth. Wait until the plant sprouts and tie the clematis up to avoid accidents and wind damage.

General pruning tips

Pruning is rarely done hard or frequently enough as most of us are too worried about causing harm to our plants. Here are a few basic points:

- Deciduous plants should be pruned when they are dormant.
- Evergreen plants need to be pruned according to when they flower, so as not to cut all the flower buds off.
- Prune foliage plants any time during the growing season.
- Cut herbaceous (non-woody) plants right back to the ground after the first frosts have scorched their leaves.
- Container plants can be clipped little and often throughout the growing season.

Large-leafed trees and shrubs should be pruned with secateurs

Brown-Bitting

Brown-bitting a plant – 'manicuring' the foliage by removing all the brown bits – will turn a healthy specimen into an even more stunning addition to the garden. This should be an integral part of general care for architectural plants in particular.

Removing tatty branches from trees or cutting off old, dead growth from herbaceous perennials is logical to most gardeners. However, old and scruffy foliage is often left on cordylines or yuccas, often due to a fear of harming them in some way. But the difference can be astonishing.

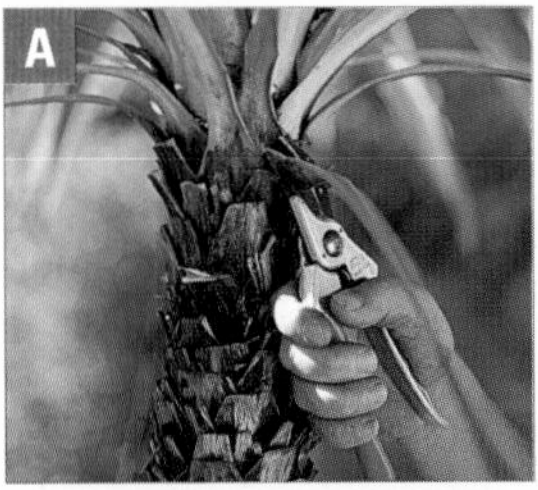

Basic technique

Cordyline australis is a good candidate for brown-bitting. The best time of year to do this is late spring or early summer, as any accidental damage will heal over more easily while the plants are still growing. If older leaves are not removed, they turn brown and droop, building up on themselves to form a bushy thatch.

Begin by taking the older, lower leaves first. Use a very sharp knife or a pair of secateurs, and pull the leaf taut, cutting as near as possible to the stem [A]. Remove the leaves one by one, gradually moving up the trunk [B]. When every brown leaf has been trimmed away [C], if there are any old flower stems, remove these, too.

Sculpting

A messy cordyline can be transformed into an exotic-looking tree with several beautiful corky tree trunks after brown-bitting. Yet you can take this further and give it a sculpted appearance.

The yucca, shown here, looks tatty [A]. Trim all the leaves to within a few centimetres (1–2in) of the trunk [B] to create a 'pineapple' effect [C].

Tree ferns often have highly sculptural trunk 'bark'. *Dicksonia antarctica*, for example, has a very wide trunk with a fibrous, dark chocolate-coloured bark, while *Dicksonia squarrosa* has a delicate, slender trunk with bark that is almost black. By cutting back all the old, brown fronds of a tree fern to the base, the plant will look so much more lush and cared for, and the beauty of its trunk will be able to be seen more clearly in all its glory.

Removing a branch

The main consideration when taking off a branch is to avoid making a tear that runs down the stem and rips off the bark, leaving a wound prone to infection. This is avoided by making the cut in three stages for branches over 15cm (6in).

Cut upwards underneath the branch about 30cm (1ft) from where you wish to remove the branch, only cutting to about a quarter of the thickness of the branch.

Then make a cut from the top of the branch 2 or 3cm (1in) beyond the first cut. When you are about half-way through, the branch should snap without tearing. This leaves a short stump which, as it weighs a lot less than the whole branch, is easier to remove with a final single cut. On smaller branches less than 15cm (6in), make two cuts below [A] and above [B] to give a neat cut [C].

Most trees and large shrubs have special defences for healing the wounds left after a branch has been removed, but the final cut must leave the collar intact around the base of the branch. This collar is thicker on the trunk-side than on the branch side and is normally at an angle across the branch; you must thus make the final cut with the saw angled so that the cut slopes away from the trunk.

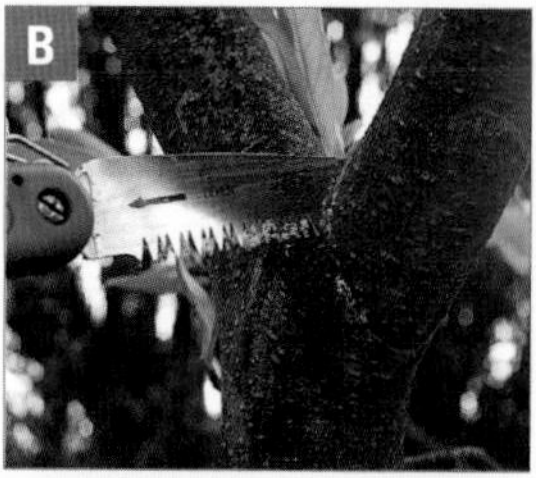

Coppicing and pollarding

As with smaller shrubs (see p105), trees and larger shrubs that have outgrown their setting can be cut back hard to just above ground level ('coppiced'). Pollarding is a form of coppicing; the main difference is that a pollard has a stem, often 2.5–5m (8–16ft) in height, and was often used to keep the new foliage out of the reach of cattle.

To coppice a tree or shrub, cut it down between 5–15cm (2–6in) above ground level, or leave the plant on a short stem or leg. Coppicing (pollarding) is best carried out in spring, but it can be done at any time; however, avoid early autumn as regrowth is likely to be killed by winter cold.

Only trees and shrubs that respond by regrowing from dormant buds in the bark can be coppiced or pollarded. Many broadleaved trees and shrubs respond, but old Fagus trees may be sensitive and liable to die. Almost all conifers apart from Taxus will die if cut back hard, as they must have green foliage from which to make new growth.

Pruning a mature tree

To keep a larger tree within bounds, this can be done by pruning. Do not just hack off branches at random, though, as this can promote disease from wounding. Reduce the density of branches as unobtrusively as possible. To reduce the density, remove any surplus branches, cutting them off where they join the trunk so as not to leave a 'snag'. Pruning can be carried out at any season on most trees, but if cutting back hard it's best to prune in early spring.

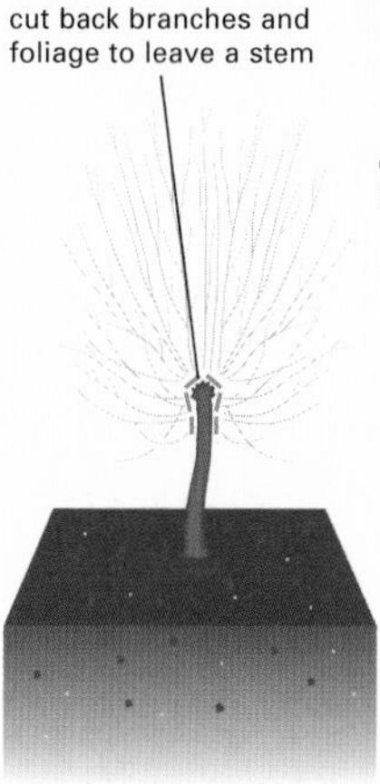
cut back branches and foliage to leave a stem

POLLARDING
In pollarding, the overgrown branches of a tree or shrub are cut right back

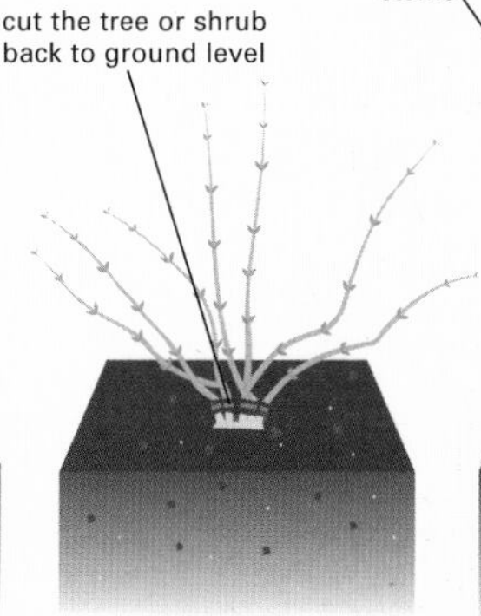
cut the tree or shrub back to ground level

COPPICING
This is a method used both to reduce and rejuvenate a tree or shrub

cut branches off where they join the trunk or main stems

PRUNING A MATURE TREE
Do not hack off branches at random. Gradually reduce the density of branches

Propagation

Increasing your stock (propagation) is both a rewarding and economical exercise. Whether raising seeds indoors or taking cuttings, you will be able to add new stock to your garden year after year.

Raising seeds indoors

In frost-prone climates, seeds of plants – such as tender perennials and annuals to be used for summer bedding and container display – are raised indoors. Ideally this will be in a frost-free greenhouse, although plants can also be raised on a warm windowsill in the house, provided there is good light to prevent them becoming weak and spindly. Seeds of various hardy perennials can also be raised indoors early in the year if desired. Other kinds, however, germinate better indoors rather than in the open ground (read the instructions on the seed packets before sowing).

Use a dibber to press large seeds into trays of compost

Containers and composts

Standard or half-size seed trays are suitable for large quantities of seed. However, most gardeners will be sowing small amounts of seeds, in which case 9–13cm (3½–5in) pots or half pots (less compost needed in the latter) are more suitable.

To save time pricking out or transplanting seedlings, seeds that are easily handled can be sown individually in 60-cell module trays. Very small seeds are best sown in a pot or half pot and the resultant seedlings pricked out.

Most gardeners use soilless composts for their sowings, traditionally made from peat but often consisting of peat substitutes, as peat is being phased out. Use either seed or multi-purpose compost. Traditionalists may prefer soil-based seed compost.

Sowing

Sowing techniques differ according to the type of container you are sowing in, but filling containers with compost is much the same whether you are using pots or trays. Simply fill the container to overflowing with compost, tapping it on the bench to get rid of any air pockets, then scrape off the surplus with a straight piece of wood to give you a smooth, level surface.

To sow seeds in seed trays or pots, take a pinch of seeds, hold it above the compost surface at an angle, and move your hand gently over the container so the seeds scatter evenly across the surface [A]. Sow as evenly and as thinly as possible.

To sow in 60-cell module trays make a shallow hole in the compost surface of each cell using a dibber and drop in a seed.

Most seeds need to be covered with a layer of compost, the depth equalling twice the diameter of the seed. Fine-grade vermiculite can be used instead of compost for covering seeds and is ideal for rapidly germinating subjects. Cover seeds with a 5mm (¼in) layer of vermiculite [B].

After sowing, containers with covered seeds should be watered [C], preferably with a watering can fitted with a fine rose. Otherwise, trickle the water over the containers very gently, as above.

Transplanting
Seedlings raised in ordinary seed trays or pots will need pricking out or transplanting as soon as they are large enough to handle, to give them more room to grow. Always hold seedlings by the seed leaves, never by the stems as these are easily damaged [A]. Separate them and make a hole for each seedling with a dibber, then gently push compost to cover the roots and lightly firm [B]. Ensure that the seedlings are evenly spaced [C]. Finally, water in the seedlings [D].

A

B

C

D

Raising shrubs by seed

Raising plants from seeds is often the quickest and best method for many shrubs. To do this, you must first obtain viable seeds, which need to be treated so that they will germinate. The resultant seedlings must be nurtured to produce a healthy plant that can then be hardened off and planted out where you want it to grow.

Collecting and storing seeds
Seeds can be collected from your own garden or bought from garden centres, nurseries or by mail order.

Collect seeds from shrubs as soon as they are ready

Collect seed as soon as the fruit is ripe – any later and you risk losing them to birds. Fruits in capsules will need drying to release the seeds. Lay these out in small trays but avoid using heat except for a few items such as pine cones. With fleshy fruits, remove the flesh to prevent it rotting. Store seeds in polythene bags or in small envelopes. Make sure seeds are dry. Store them in the fridge to keep them viable for longer.

Cuttings

Many hardy and tender perennials are grown from cuttings. Some are propagated on an annual basis, particularly chrysanthemums and dahlias, and tender perennials used for summer bedding such as zonal pelargoniums.

Basal stem cuttings These are taken in spring from shoots that grow from the crown of the plant. Shoots are removed close to the crown, so that each retains a piece of parent tissue or 'heel' at the base, when 5–8cm (2–3in) high. Remove lower leaves, insert in pots of cuttings compost and root in a temperature of 15–19°C (59–66°F). Pot off individually when rooted.

Semi-ripe cuttings Tender perennials used for summer bedding are propagated annually from semi-ripe cuttings in late summer. Use a non-flowering side shoot, remove lower leaves, dip the

A semi-ripe cutting from a fuchsia, with the base and lower leaves removed

base in hormone rooting powder, insert in pots of compost and root in a cold frame. Pot up when rooted.

Root cuttings Propagating from pieces of root is good for certain hardy perennials, including those that do not lend themselves to division. Lift a plant and remove a few thick roots (replant the parent straight away). Cut roots into sections 5–10cm (2–4in) in length. For thick root cuttings, cut the tops flat and the bases slanting [A] and insert into compost until the tops are just below the surface [B].

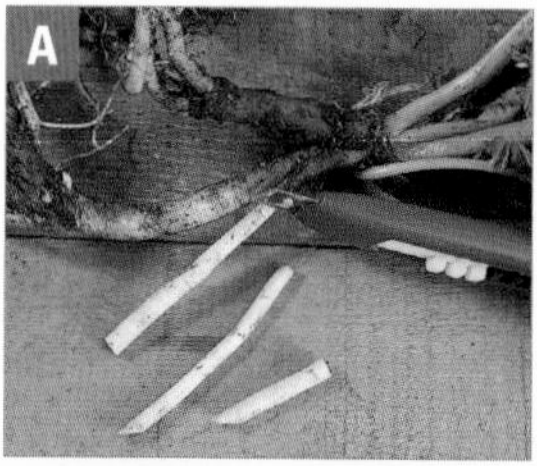

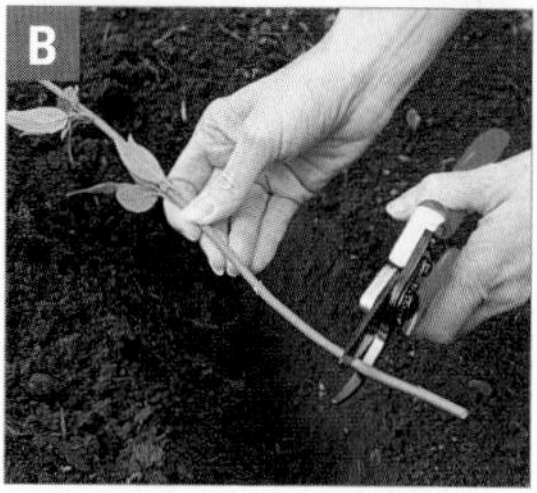

Hardwood cuttings

You do not get successful cuttings from deciduous trees or shrubs in late autumn, but they do propagate easily from hardwood cuttings taken in late winter when they are leafless or almost leafless. Ligustrum, Metasequoia and Salix are good examples of this.

Select a shaded bed in the garden and dig a trench about 17cm (7in) deep to hold the cuttings [A]. Put a few handfuls of sand in the bottom of the trench to help with drainage. Take healthy, mature sideshoots and cut them off just above the junction with the older wood of the main stem. Remove any remaining leaves and trim to about 25cm (10in) [B]. Put hormone rooting powder on the base, making a cut if necessary. Place in the trench and push soil over the cuttings [C], burying them to two thirds their length roughly 20cm (8in) apart [D].

Dig up the cuttings the following autumn and either plant out or grow them on in a nursery bed for a year.

Offsets

Offsets are new young plants sent up from the base of the parent plant.

Agave americana is one plant that produces offsets from its base. In mid-spring, take the plant out of its pot [A], select an offset at least 5cm (2in) long and remove it with a sharp and clean knife as close to the main plant as you can [B]. As the cut end will be moist, lay out the offset on a sunny windowsill until the cut end has dried out to prevent it from rotting. Push the base into a pot of

root system [B], into pots of loamy soil or straight back into the garden. Cut the canes back, removing all foliage except at the growing tip, and plant each individual section so that each cane can just be seen poking out of the ground [C].

gritty soil [C] (equal quantities of compost and fine gravel). Water in gently and leave until it has taken root – a few months. Do not be tempted to water. To test if the offset has rooted, give it a tug and if there is any resistance then roots must have formed. Once it has fully rooted, repot in a small pot filled with soil-based compost and a handful of grit.

Division

This is separating a single plant clump into several sections, each of which produces a new plant.

Dig up a mature clump of *Arundo donax* in early spring and divide it into new sections. Make sure you dig down far enough beneath the plant to lift under the roots. Chop the plant into sections, with one or two canes in each section [A]. Plant up the individual chunks, each with their own smaller

TIP

If you are taking leafy cuttings, pay attention to the time of day you take them. It is better to take cuttings early in the day rather than late afternoon, as plants tend to be more perky in the morning and slightly wilted looking by early evening.

Side-veneer grafting

This method of grafting is the most common technique. The aim is to match the 'cambium' of the scion (graft) with that of the rootstock. The cambium is the soft layer between bark and wood made up of cells which divide to make wood on the inside and bark on the outside. The thickness of the scion and rootstock should be equal, so that the cambiums can be matched on both sides of the cuts.

With a sharp knife, make a downwards slanting cut about 3cm (just over 1in) into the bark and surface wood of the rootstock around 5–10cm (2–4in) from the top of the rootstock. Remove the slither of wood with a nick at the base of the cut [A]. Take an equivalent slither from the bottom of the scion to fit into the cut on the rootstock [B]. Hold the scion in place by binding with a tie [C].

Keep the graft in a moist environment to unite the scion and rootstock, which will take up to six weeks. Then slowly allow more air into the environment; cut off bits of the rootstock down to the callus (the wound) to encourage the scion to make growth.

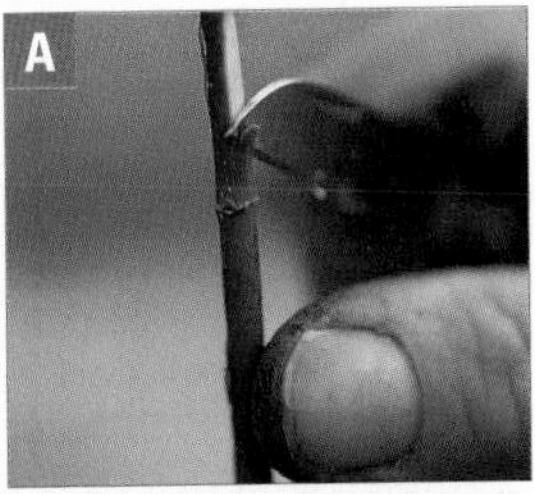

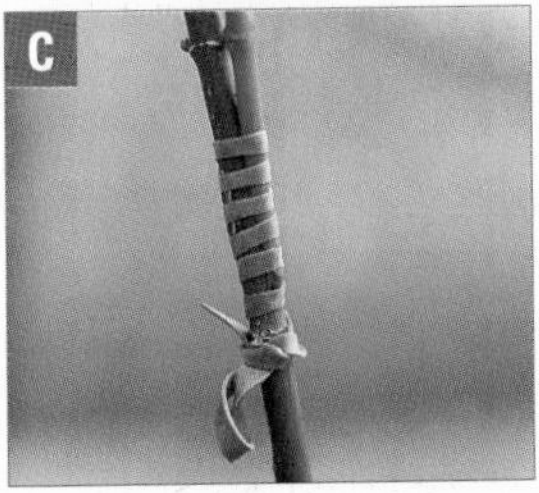

Storing Fruit and Vegetables

While freshly picked fruit, vegetables and herbs have an unequalled flavour, with careful preparation and storage there is no reason why you shouldn't be able to enjoy the results of your labours out of season.

Freezing

While previous generations relied mainly on bottling to preserve their produce, we have the advantage of the deep freezer, which means that now we only have to collect, bag and freeze.

The success of your freezing will depend on the varieties you grow. Certain cultivars have been specially bred for this purpose, so bear this in mind when you are buying seed. Pick your crop at a young age when the crops are still tender and bursting with flavour. There is absolutely no point in putting effort into preserving crops that are past their best and have become tasteless and tough as a result.

Vegetables can be tray dried – that is, cut out and spread on a tray so that they do not touch, then frozen – before being packed in bags for longer term freezing. However, most vegetables need to be blanched before freezing, as they are low in acid and contain high numbers of enzymes, which the blanching kills off and would otherwise cause them to deteriorate.

For delicate vegetables, blanching involves being lightly steamed. For tougher vegetables, place them in cold, unsalted water, bring to the boil, then skim the top, leave to simmer for a few minutes and drain. Plunge the

Many fruits can be frozen successfully for out of season usage

vegetables into cold water before drying off, and they will seem even fresher when defrosted.

Vegetables also freeze well when boiled and puréed. Those with a high water content, such as courgette and marrow, benefit from being lightly sautéed before freezing.

Root vegetables can be frozen, although they will store for a while left in the ground or in a cool, dry, dark place. While some, such as young, small carrots, can be frozen whole, most benefit from being puréed before freezing.

Soft fruits freeze whole particularly well and hold their flavour, while tree fruits are better puréed before freezing.

Certain herbs, such as mint and basil, will freeze well. Simply pick the leaves and freeze in the quantities you will require in small polythene bags, sealed with ties.

Drying

This is one of the most traditional methods of preserving food, possibly practised by our distant ancestors with nuts and roots. Drying fruit and vegetables correctly is something of a balancing act – if you dry them too fast at too high a temperature the fruit will lose nutrients and flavour as well as becoming tough and chewy. But if you dry them too slowly at too low a temperature, you run the risk of allowing micro-organisms to start to breed.

There are three basic methods of drying fruit and vegetables: sun-drying, which requires bright sunshine and a really hot, dry day and so is not suitable for the climate in some countries; oven-drying, which simply requires a reliable oven, preferably a convection oven; and air drying, which requires an airy, insect-free area.

DEFROST OR NOT?

When cooking frozen vegetables, do not defrost them completely (the exception to this is corn on the cob). Instead, place them in a small amount of water and allow the vegetables to defrost as they cook. This way you will get a better flavour from the vegetables and will not lose as much goodness from your precious crop.

Oven-drying

Some fruit and vegetables make better candidates for

oven drying than others. For example, any fruit with a high water content, such as melon and citrus, will lose much of their flavour. Similarly, small soft fruits containing lots of pips end up as all hard pips and no fruit when dried.

The time you need depends on what you are drying and how thick the slices or chunks are. As a rough guide, allow two hours for slices of 6mm (¼in), and four times that for 12.5mm (½in) slices. If you are planning to do this on a regular basis then it would be worth buying a commercial dehydrator. If it is only likely to be an occasional event, then a regular convection oven is sufficient.

Arrange the fruit and vegetables on trays, making sure that there is enough space on either side of the tray for air to circulate. There must be at least 7.5cm (3in) between the trays. These trays should be rotated and moved around the oven occasionally, so that the fruit and vegetables are evenly exposed to the heat. As soon as the juices have dried up, turn over the fruit and vegetables every now and again to ensure they dry at an even rate.

Air drying

This method is most suited to herbs. Harvest the herbs in the early morning, then discard all but the best and arrange these in bundles tied with string. Hang the bundles upside down in a dark, dry place – an airing cupboard is ideal – until dry. Once dry, strip the leaves from the stalks and store in airtight glass containers. Herbs will retain their taste for longer if kept out of the light.

Preserving in oil

Infused oils can add a totally unique element to dressings and marinades, and are so simple to make that anyone growing herbs could throw one together.

Use a lightly flavoured oil as the base for the more delicate herbs, such as basil and thyme. Stronger oils, like olive oil, will fight against the subtle flavours. Olive oil does, however, make a good base for the more robust flavours of garlic, mint and rosemary.

Fill half a bottle with oil then add whatever ingredients you wish to infuse, adding herbs as sprigs rather than leaves. Cover and leave for at least a couple of weeks. After this time if you want a clear oil then strain it, otherwise leave the flavourings in the oil – they will not decay and look very attractive.

Preserving in alcohol

Alcohol is a wonderful agent for preservation, being especially suited to fruit. As the fruit absorbs the alcohol it produces sugar, which gradually causes the surrounding alcohol to turn into a rich, strong, sweet syrup that can be spooned over the fruit when it is served.

As with infused oils, the method could not be easier. Pack a wide-necked jar with layers of different fruit, or just one type, then pour in the alcohol. Sherry, brandy and rum are ideal. Seal and leave for at least three weeks, turning the jar upside down occasionally to ensure the fruit receives equal coverage.

Olive oil infused with the flavours of garlic, chillies and bay

Planting Combinations

Ultimately, it is the gardener's individual taste which will influence the planting of any garden. However, some combinations of plants work better than others. The following pages aim to give you a few tips and ideas.

Gardens come in all shapes and sizes, and different areas can be used for different types of plants. Borders can be filled with a mixture of permanent shrubs, intermingled with flowers which change colour season by season. There can also be permanent areas of evergreen shrubs or architectural plants which remain a constant colour throughout the year, or areas of spectacular interest, where a specimen tree is surrounded by colourful blooms or interesting foliage from smaller trees or shrubs.

Experimentation

Play around with different planting arrangements before permanently positioning them. For instance, you could try choosing a range of upright, spiky subjects, such as Yucca, Forsythia or Crocosmia, to contrast with the more rounded Kolkwitzia or the tiered foliage of Viburnum.

Colour, height and varied form all combine to produce a classic mixed border

Evergreen shrubs surrounded by colourful annuals is an ideal scheme

Once you have selected a few plants of varying forms, bear in mind the obvious structural premise of putting the taller plants to the rear of any planting, so smaller or ground-cover plants are not hidden from view.

Seasonal considerations

Timing can be a factor in deciding what goes where. Because different plants flower at different seasons, they can be grown next to each other without fear of clashing. It also

Combine dwarf or low-growing plants in a rock garden

means that you can plant a variety to give colour over a prolonged season.

In flower beds and borders, plants should be combined in pleasing ways, taking colour, shape and size into account. For example, you may want to create dramatic or exciting contrasts in flower shape or colour, opt for more relaxing harmonious combinations, or even try single colour themes, such as an all-blue or all-red border, or even a combination green and white scheme.

Bedding schemes and annuals last for only one season, so even if you are not happy with certain choices, you can always try something different next year. Even hardy perennials and bulbs can be moved at the end of the season or the following year if you are not satisfied with their arrangement.

Feature planting

One idea for borders is to choose a major feature plant, such as a berberis, then decide on one or two other plants, for example, asters or ceratostigmas. These could be used as an edging to the bed

A wall is not only decorated with climbers but the eye is led to it by the planting beneath

Shrubs of different shapes, size and colour will mix well together

or as dot plants scattered randomly over the bed. Or they could be mixed more liberally with the main feature plant, across the bed as a whole.

The features in your garden play a large part in deciding on planting combinations. Borders add a certain height and interest to a completely flat garden. Fixed man-made features can be improved with the addition of plants. For example, climbers such as clematis or rambling roses will naturally decorate the vertical surface of a wall, but below there may also be a mixed border where you can combine colourful shrubs, such as Hypericum, with taller flowers like lupins, kniphofias or crocosmias, and low-growing plants such as Euphorbia and Cotoneaster. Not only is a rather dull, ugly surface covered up and made

Roses can be used as hedging to separate areas in the garden

attractive, but the whole effect is linked from the ground up to the top of the wall.

Larger shrubs combined with dwarf conifers grown next to a wall or shed add colour and interest, particularly if the green of the conifer is in contrast to the flowers of the shrub. *Juniperus pfitzeriana* looks especially good planted behind Euphorbia. A low juniper, such as *Juniperus horizontalis*, makes excellent ground cover on flat or sloping ground, and looks particularly attractive planted under *Acer palmatum*, or surrounded by a mix of columnar, shrub and ground cover conifers in various shades of green, for example *Chamaecyparis lawsonia*

Agaves can be used as a special feature plant within a mixed border

Buxus can be used to define a border filled with flowering plants

'Minima Glauca', *Cupressus glabra* 'Blue Ice' or *Picea abies* 'Reflexa'.

Slopes can also be covered with colourful heathers, such as the magenta coloured *Erica darleyensis* 'Kramer's Rote', the pink or red tipped foliage of *Calluna vulgaris* 'Flamingo' or the cream coloured *Calluna vulgaris* 'Spring Cream'.

If you have a large pond in your garden, then position larger shrubs or trees such as the willow (*Salix alba*) on the far side, where the water will not be hidden and they can be seen reflected in it.

Soil and climate

The soil type in your garden can make a big difference to the choice of plants. Dry, arid, free-draining soils can be a great idea for a desert combination planting. Desert plants have some of the best architectural shapes of all the plants. For example, plant *Agave americana* and *Agave salmiana* 'Ferox' together with *Chamaerops humilis*. Or maybe *Kniphofia* 'Royal Standard' and *Agapanthus* Headbourne Hybrids in a border.

Coastal gardens can present a bit of a challenge. However, with careful planning they can be made to look interesting all year round. Plants with lots of

Foliage plants among flowers of every colour look especially attractive

dense foliage are perfect for seaside combinations. Agaves are excellent for this location, along with *Chamaerops humilis*, *Cistus dansereaui* 'Decumbens' and the olive tree, *Olea europea*.

Container plants can also be placed alongside beds and borders

Tall kniphofias add height to a shrub bed full of low-growing plants

Planting effects

Bold statements can be made by bordering various plants with a low edging consisting of *Buxus sempervirens*. Buxus can be trained in a variety of topiary shapes, from straight hedging to rounded shapes, giving the border a more interesting and striking shape.

Hedging plants can be used to break up the vista of a flat garden, divide the garden into different areas, like rooms in a house, and even protect your house and garden against intruders.

The daisy bush (*Olearia macrodonta*) is very effective used as a hedging plant to section off areas of garden, even though its role is normally in the shrub bed.

Pyracantha is effective as a deterrent for unwanted visitors, with its needle-sharp thorns. Try combining groups of pyracanthas, such as the golden berries of *Pyracantha* 'Teton' with the amber fruit of 'Mohave', or planting masses of marigolds (Tagetes) around the base of *Pyracantha* 'Teton'.

The final piece of advice is to go with repetition and not get carried away planting every species and variety just because you can. Simplicity is a good word to keep in mind when planting – and is often the tactic which works the best.

Evergreen conifers look good surrounded by colourful, low-growing shrubs

A–Z of Plants

The following plant directory comprises more than 350 top garden plants arranged alphabetically by their Latin names. Follow the colour coding to move easily from one letter of the alphabet to another.

Whether you are seeking the ideal flowering shrub for an awkward shady corner, or vibrant summer flowers to brighten a patio or windowbox, this directory offers a plethora of choices across the entire spectrum of garden plants. Use the alphabetical organisation and colour coding to find your perfect plant and then follow the detailed margin cross-references to find good companion plants or those of a similar nature.

Abelia ABELIA

Abelias are grown for their delicate flowers and glossy looking foliage, and range in colour from white through to red. They are suitable for a sunny site in the garden but may not survive an especially cold winter.

There are around thirty species of Abelia and they can be either deciduous or semi-evergreen. The flowers tend to be on the small side, but are generally profuse and make an attractive display. The two to five sepals at the base of the flower give the shrub its colour, which remain when the petals eventually drop off. These sepals then develop as a crown to the dry, single-seeded fruit. The leaves are arranged in two or three clusters on the shoot, each no larger than 6cm (2½in).

Abelia schumannii

Abelia grandiflora

Abelias can be propagated by semi-hardwood cuttings taken in mid to late summer.

Abelias grow best up against a sunny wall for protection in colder areas, as they are not reliably hardy. Remove weaker growth only for pruning purposes. The early flowering Abelias should be pruned once flowering has finished (Group 1) but the post mid-summer flowering forms may be pruned hard in spring, according to Group 2 shrubs (see p104–6). This can be beneficial if a severe winter has cut them down to ground level.

MOISTURE	Thrives in any well-drained soil
SITE/LIGHT	Prefers the full sun, sheltered from cold, dry winds
GENERAL CARE	Mulch and fertilize with plenty of organic matter
PESTS & DISEASES	Generally trouble free from pests and diseases

SHRUBS see also 323

COMPANION PLANTS see pages 257 265

Abies SILVER FIR

Abies has around 50 species of evergreen conifers with regular whorled branches and generally soft foliage. The common name comes from the silvery-white bands on the underside of the needles. Silver firs make stunning specimen trees, as well as providing good screening.

Silver firs can be used in a number of different ways in the garden, as species can be chosen not only for their colour, but also for their size. *A. koreana* is a fairly small tree with attractive coloured cones and silvery foliage – ideal for a small lawn with not much space. On the other hand, *A. grandis* is a fast growing silver fir which will make a good specimen tree for a large garden. *A. concolor*, with its bluish-grey foliage, and the bright blue foliage of *A. procera*, are slower growing but will eventually make reasonably large trees.

Seed cones range from violet purple to green or brown. Female cones, which grow erect, ripen in autumn and break up, releasing the seed. The male cones hang below the lower branches to catch the wind and disperse pollen to trees nearby. Try propagating from seed in a cold frame as soon as they are ripe.

In general, Abies like fertile, fairly moist but well-drained neutral to slightly acidic soil. *A. procera*, however, must be grown in acidic soil.

Abies koreana

MOISTURE	Needs moisture but the soil must be well drained
SITE/LIGHT	Prefers full sun, but with shelter from cold winds
GENERAL CARE	Most species are shade tolerant, especially when young
PESTS & DISEASES	Aphids and honey fungus, especially young trees

TREES see also 373

COMPANION PLANTS see pages 172 296

Abutilon INDIAN MALLOW

Also known as the Flowering or Parlour maple, Abutilons are grown for their showy, largely bell- or cup-shaped solitary-hanging flowers.

Abutilon is a large genus from tropical and subtropical regions. The flowers usually have five petals which join together in a tube at the base. The foliage can also be variegated and attractive.

In cooler climes they tend not to be long lived, needing protection against a wall. In frost-prone gardens, grow Abutilons in a conservatory to be on the safe side. Keep well watered when growing, as this will hasten growth and ensure it flowers for a longer period.

Abutilon suntense is a deciduous, fast-growing variety with attractive mauve and white bowl-shaped flowers.

Abutilon suntense

Propagate by taking soft or semi-hardwood cuttings in summer.

They prefer well-drained, fertile soil in as hot and sunny a site as possible. Prune only to remove any wayward stems and branches.

MOISTURE	Grow in moderately fertile, well-drained soil
SITE/LIGHT	A sun-loving shrub, particularly good against a warm wall
GENERAL CARE	Keep well watered during growing period
PESTS & DISEASES	Pay attention to white fly and red spider mites

SHRUBS
see also
307

COMPANION PLANTS
see pages
262–3
362
390–1

Acacia WATTLE

As acacias originate from tropical to warm-temperate regions, they tend to prefer open sites in the garden in the full sun. The more sheltered situation, the better, preferably up against a warm, sunny wall.

Although wattles are members of the legume family, they do not produce the typical pea-like flowers in petals of five. Rather, the appeal of the flowers comes from its massed stamens. The flowers, which are mainly yellow, are produced in winter or spring. Some species have globular flowers but others are more cylindrical.

Acacia pravissima

Acacia retinodes

Propagate either from seed or by semi-hardwood cuttings in summer. Some species are able to sucker. Carefully lift these and grown on.

Wattles prefer open sites in the full sun. In fact, the shadier the position, the fewer flowers that will be produced. They like most well-drained soils but will not do well on shallow, chalky soils.

MOISTURE	Water freely in the growing season
SITE/LIGHT	A sun-lover which prefers a sheltered site
GENERAL CARE	Most wattles resent hard pruning
PESTS & DISEASES	Relatively trouble free from pests and diseases

TREES
see also
397

COMPANION PLANTS
see pages
201–4
440

Acanthus BEAR'S BREECHES

These vigorous, hardy herbaceous perennials have a distinctive form, earning them the description 'architectural plants'. They originate from dry, rocky sites, mostly in the Mediterranean and produce striking foliage and flowers.

The long, deeply lobed leaves, spiny in some species, are particularly attractive. The flowers, carried in bold spikes, appear beneath hood-shaped bracts.

Propagate by division in spring or from root cuttings in winter.

Bear's breeches are ideal as specimen plants in a garden to create focal points, but give them plenty of space to show off their form. A good choice for a gravel area or alongside paving or architecture and are excellent as cut flowers. *Acanthus spinosus* has tall racemes 1m (3ft) long, with pure white flowers and purple bracts from late spring to midsummer.

Acanthus spinosus

MOISTURE	Water moderately during the growing season
SITE/LIGHT	Plant in most soil types in sun or partial shade
GENERAL CARE	Thrives in deep fertile, well-drained loam
PESTS & DISEASES	Powdery mildew can cause problems

***FLOWERS* see also 232**

***COMPANION PLANTS* see pages 186 222**

Acer MAPLE

The maples are a large genus of over 100 species of evergreen and deciduous trees and shrubs. They are excellent for structural planting in the garden, offering a wide range of attractive features, including foliage, shelter or even the bark colour.

Maples are not only chosen for the colour of their foliage, but also the shape, which varies from boldly lobed leaves to the delicate, dissected leaves of some forms of Japanese maple. The colour is golden green in maples such as *Acer shirasawanum* 'Aureum', purple in many forms of *A. palmatum* and various shades of green in others. The colours can be especially spectacular

Acer griseum

Acer palmatum

TREES see also 249

COMPANION PLANTS see pages 296

in autumn, from a butter yellow in *A. cappadocicum* to brilliant red in *A. rubrum*.

A small tree maple, the paperbark, *A. griseum*, has a stunning autumn colour of red and scarlet, as well as an attractive cinnamon coloured flakey bark. *A. pseudoplatanus* 'Brilliantissimum' is a slow-growing, dome-shaped maple with brilliant shrimp pink foliage.

Propagate maples from seed, by cuttings and also grafting. Sow seed as soon as it is ripe and keep in a cool greenhouse or frame. Cuttings can be tricky, but are a good way of propagation if you can get them to make growth before they become dormant. Grafting takes place in mid to late summer.

Acer pseudoplatanus 'Brilliantissimum'

Acer shirasawanum 'Aureum'

Under-storey growing maples will tolerate some shade, whereas the forest types – the large tree maples – will only tolerate shade while young. However, all maples grow happily in full sun. They generally like all soil types but not waterlogged soils. Japanese maples especially do not like much chalk or lime in the soil, especially if the soil is thin. Smaller maples grow well in containers, as long as they are well watered.

MOISTURE	Do not over water or allow to get too dry
SITE/LIGHT	Plant in full sun or dappled shade in well-drained soil
GENERAL CARE	Protect from cold dry winds
PESTS & DISEASES	Prone to verticillium wilt, coral spot, tar spot and aphids

TREES
see also
137

COMPANION PLANTS
see pages
418
426

Achillea YARROW

The yarrows are hardy, mainly herbaceous perennials, although a few, especially the mat-forming rock garden species, are evergreen.

The tall border kinds are the most popular, especially those with flat, plate-like heads of flowers. Other species produce clusters of small, button-like flowers. The grey ferny foliage of some species is attractive, contrasting well with flowers. Yarrows are ideal for mixing with other hardy perennials of contrasting habit, especially spiky plants, and with ornamental grasses.

Achillea 'Coronation Gold' is a clump forming species producing tiny, golden yellow flowerheads in corymbs (clusters) 10cm (4in) across from mid-summer to early autumn. It can reach heights of up to 1m (3ft), so when planting, position at the back of a summer border.

Achillea 'Coronation Gold'

Propagate by division or from basal stem cuttings in spring.

Plant in full sun, as in shade yarrow becomes straggly and develops weak and floppy stems. Well-drained soil is best, but avoid overfeeding, especially with nitrogen-rich fertilizers. Yarrow tolerates poor soil that is low in nutrients, although it needs good drainage to prevent the plants from rotting.

Watch out for powdery mildew and aphids.

MOISTURE	Keep moist but not waterlogged
SITE/LIGHT	Prefers a well-drained site in the full sun
GENERAL CARE	Excellent grown in a wildflower or rock garden
PESTS & DISEASES	Prone to powdery mildew and aphids

FLOWERS see also 405 410

COMPANION PLANTS see pages 293 312 222

Aesculus HORSE CHESTNUT

Known as the horse chestnut or buckeye, Aesculus is a genus of around fifteen deciduous trees and shrubs from woodland areas in southeast Europe, the Himalayas and North America. Most horse chestnuts are suitable only as specimen trees for the larger garden.

Horse chestnut (*Aesculus hippocastanum*) is often known as the 'conker tree' from many people's childhood. It is also grown for its conical white blooms with pink, red or yellow spots in mid to late-spring. It grows at around 0.3–0.4m (12–16in) a year until 20m (70ft) in height. It is then a large tree with a high domed crown.

Aesculus indica

Another good species is the medium-sized Indian horse chestnut, *Aesculus indica.* It flowers roughly six weeks later than the horse chestnut with equally attractive cylindrical panicles.

Propagate horse chestnuts by seed, except for the variety 'Baumannii', which must be grafted, and *Aesculus parviflora* which grows from root cuttings in late winter.

Aesculus tolerates a wide range of soil types, from chalk to damp, heavy clays. Full sun is best but they will grow in shade. Be careful if children are around, as most parts can cause mild stomach upset if ingested.

MOISTURE	Keep moist and do not allow to dry out
SITE/LIGHT	Well-drained soil in sun or partial shade
GENERAL CARE	Enjoys fertile soil, with added mulch to retain moisture
PESTS & DISEASES	Prone to canker, leaf blotch, coral spot and scale insects

TREES
see also
172
256

COMPANION PLANTS
see pages
196
372
435

Agapanthus AFRICAN LILY

Herbaceous or evergreen clump-forming perennials, some are hardy while others are half hardy. African lilies have long, strap-shaped leaves and heads of tubular, lily-like flowers, mainly in shades of blue but also white. Many hybrids have been bred, especially for hardiness.

Plants need plenty of space so that their habit of growth shows to advantage. Grow them in a border with plants of contrasting form, such as spiky kniphofias. They are excellent plants for patio containers. The flowers are good for cutting.

Propagate by division in the spring and keep seedlings in a cold frame for the first winter in frost-prone climates.

In cold areas, mulch hardy hybrids, such as *Agapanthus* Headbourne Hybrids, during the winter months. Slugs and snails are keen on this plant!

Agapanthus Headbourne Hybrids

MOISTURE	Water freely in growing periods but sparingly in winter
SITE/LIGHT	Prefers full sun in fertile, well-drained soil
GENERAL CARE	Apply liquid fertilizer monthly from spring until flowering
PESTS & DISEASES	Prone to slugs and snails, and some viruses

FLOWERS
see also
315

COMPANION PLANTS
see pages
299
416

Agave

The Agave is a genus of more than 200 species of succulents from desert and mountainous regions of North, Central and South America, and the West Indies.

The leaves of these architectural plants are often rigid and fleshy, with sharp spines or toothed margins. *Agave americana*, or the Century Plant, is a beautifully shaped plant that looks stunning in the garden. The large, weighty leaves are blue-grey and are edged with rather sharp spines. Each leaf ends in a long sharp needle. Over thirty years, *A. americana* could reach 1.5m x 1.5m (5ft x 5ft) if grown in a suitable site.

Agave salmiana var. 'Ferox'

Agave americana

Agave salmiana var. 'Ferox' has large, vicious leaves that are wide and flat, olive green in colour, edged with sharp hooks and ending with a dangerous tip. A fully grown plant can reach 1.2m x 1.2m (4ft x 4ft).

Propagation is either from seed at 21°C (70°F) or by removing offsets in spring or autumn.

Agaves are great for growing in pots or containers but good drainage is important. Planting on a slope helps with drainage, as does gritty soil.

MOISTURE	Water in summer, reduce in autumn, keep dry in winter
SITE/LIGHT	Prefers full sun in a slightly acidic, moderately fertile site
GENERAL CARE	In frost-prone areas, grow under glass in full light
PESTS & DISEASES	Prone to scale insects, particularly on new growth

SHRUBS see also 441

COMPANION PLANTS see pages 249 358 423

Ageratum FLOSS FLOWER

These half-hardy annuals are dwarf, bushy plants with fluffy flowerheads mainly in shades of blue, but also hues of pink and white.

This genus comes from diverse habitats in tropical and warm temperate regions of North and South America. They can be erect, spreading or mound-forming in habit.

Floss flowers are the staples of summer bedding schemes, mixing well with many other plants. They are also extensively used in containers, including hanging baskets, and are good for edging beds and borders. *Ageratum* 'Blue Danube' produces many small, weather-resistant, lavender blue flowerheads.

For propagation, raise from seed in the spring under cover.

To ensure that Ageratum continually flowers throughout the summer, remove the dead flowerheads regularly. Watch out for black root rot.

Ageratum 'Blue Danube'

MOISTURE	Enjoys moist conditions; water freely in mid-summer
SITE/LIGHT	Prefers a sheltered but sunny site in well-drained soil
GENERAL CARE	Can also be grown in containers
PESTS & DISEASES	Prone to black root rot

***FLOWERS* see also 322 405**

***COMPANION PLANTS* see pages 235 321 396**

Alcea HOLLYHOCK

These short-lived hardy herbaceous perennials are generally tall, sometimes up to 2.4m (8ft), although dwarf cultivars have been bred. All produce sturdy, upright stems bearing fully double or single flowers in various colours, and pale green, hairy, lobed leaves.

Hollyhocks are popular for cottage garden borders, where they associate well with old-fashioned plants, including old roses, honeysuckles and peonies. Tall varieties may need staking. *Alcea rosea* cultivars are vigorous growers with long, terminal racemes of single purple, pink, white, yellow and even black flowers (*A. rosea* 'Nigra') in early to mid-summer.

Raise from seed in spring or early summer either under cover or outdoors in situ. If needed, transplant in the early autumn when two or three true leaves have developed.

Hollyhocks are best grown as annuals or biennials and look extremely attractive when grown up against a wall. Another advantage is that they attract butterflies and bees.

Alcea rosea cultivar

MOISTURE	Do not allow to become waterlogged
SITE/LIGHT	A sun-lover which is happy in well-drained soil
GENERAL CARE	May require staking in exposed sites
PESTS & DISEASES	Prone to hollyhock rust, aphids, capsid bugs and slugs

FLOWERS see also 232 238

COMPANION PLANTS see pages 323 358 390–1

Allium ORNAMENTAL ONION

Alliums are hardy bulbs valued for their rounded heads of tubular flowers in shades of blue, purple, pink or white. They have long leaves, either thin or strap shaped, which may die down before the flowers appear.

Allium cristophii

Most species have a single bulb which produces clusters of offset bulbs around it that gradually form clumps. *Allium caeruleum* has dense umbels of small, star-shaped bright blue flowers. *Allium cristophii* has large umbels, 20cm (8in) across of around fifty star-shaped, pink-purple flowers.

Propagate by removing offsets of bulbous species in the autumn or sow seed in trays in a cold frame when ripe or in the spring. Divide clump-forming species in spring.

Allium caeruleum

Onions are generally grown in a mixed border where they associate well with many perennials, including plants with spikes of flowers like lupins and plate-like heads such as achilleas. Try them also with ornamental grasses. Tall kinds are effective companions for shrub roses.

MOISTURE	Keep dry when dormant in summer
SITE/LIGHT	Grow in fertile, well-drained soil in full sun
GENERAL CARE	Contact with the bulbs may irritate the skin
PESTS & DISEASES	Prone to white rot, downy mildew and onion fly

FLOWERS see also 169 228–9

COMPANION PLANTS see pages 141 214 326

Alnus ALDER

Alders are usually found on poor or waterlogged soils. This is especially true of the common alder, *Alnus glutinosa*. Any type of garden soil will do, however, except shallow chalky ones. Some species look particularly effective planted right next to water.

Alnus incana

As well as being at home in the water garden, alders are suitable for many other sites. The male catkins can be attractive, expanding in late winter or early spring to give a purple (*Alnus glutinosa*), red (*Alnus incana*) or yellow (*Alnus cordata*) appearance to the tree. Woody, persistent, cone-like green fruits follow, which can be used as decorations or in flower arrangements. The forms of grey alder, *Alnus incana*, include the 'Aurea' with yellow green foliage, and also the weeping 'Pendula'.

Propagate alders by seed; small seeds can be sown on damp compost and covered with a thin layer of sand or grit. Root hardwood cuttings in winter or semi-hardwood shoots in summer. *Alnus incana* will throw suckers which can be cut and rooted.

The genus Alnus has a number of shrubby species which are useful in the wild garden. Use alders for shelter plantings in orchards. When they come into leaf and flower, which they do earlier than apples and other fruit trees, they can offer some protection for these trees against late spring frosts.

MOISTURE	Enjoys moist but well-drained conditions
SITE/LIGHT	Thrives in the full sun in moderately fertile soil
GENERAL CARE	Prune between leaf fall and mid-winter
PESTS & DISEASES	Prone to phytophthora root rot

TREES see also 395

COMPANION PLANTS see pages 170 332

Alstroemeria PERUVIAN LILY

Peruvian lilies are tuberous, herbaceous perennials and most are frost hardy. This plant's flowers are trumpet shaped, somewhat lily like, in bright or pastel colours. The leaves are generally lance shaped and in some species are greyish-green.

These plants are used in mixed borders, where they combine well with shrubs, including shrub roses. The flowers are suitable for cutting, often lasting for several weeks in water. The various coloured *Alstroemeria* Ligtu Hybrids are crosses between *A. ligtu* and *A. haemantha.*

Propagate by division in autumn or sow seed as soon as ripe. Plants benefit from a mulch of organic matter to protect roots from frost, and are best left undisturbed for as long as possible.

Alstroemeria Ligtu Hybrids

MOISTURE	Keep moist but water sparingly in winter
SITE/LIGHT	Well-drained, fertile soil in sun or partial shade
GENERAL CARE	Apply mulch for the first two years
PESTS & DISEASES	Prone to slugs, viruses and red spider mite under glass

FLOWERS *see also* 143 315

COMPANION PLANTS *see pages* 144 252 427–8

Amaranthus LOVE-LIES-BLEEDING

Amaranthus are half-hardy annuals that vary considerably in habit. Some, like *A. caudatus* (Love-lies-bleeding), have dangling, tassel-like flowers, while others, such as *A. cruentus* 'Plentitude', bear more upright plumes. Flowers can be red or green.

A. tricolor (Chinese spinach) is grown for its multicoloured foliage. Use Amaranthus as dot plants in summer bedding schemes, as container plants, hanging baskets or in subtropical plantings.

Raise from seed in spring under cover at around 20°C (68°F). *A. caudatus* can be sown in situ in mid-spring.

Amaranthus cruentus 'Plenitude'

Amaranthus 'Trompe d'Elephant'

A. 'Trompe d'Elephant' has interesting, gnarled foliage.

The flowers of Amaranthus are ideal for cutting and drying. Provide shelter and ensure that they are kept well watered during dry periods in the summer.

MOISTURE	Keep the soil moist, particularly during hot spells
SITE/LIGHT	Enjoys full sun in a sheltered site
GENERAL CARE	Mulching will help retain moisture
PESTS & DISEASES	Prone to aphids and viruses

FLOWERS
see also
215

COMPANION PLANTS
see pages
270
350

Amelanchier SNOWY MESPILUS

Also known as the Juneberry or Shadbush, Amelanchier is often grown for its snowy white flowers. Birds are also attracted to the spherical or pear-shaped purple-coloured fruits which appear from early summer.

Amelanchier is a genus of around 25 species of deciduous trees and shrubs, mainly originating from moist woodland areas or close to the banks of streams in Europe, Asia and North America. Its flowers emerge in late spring, along with, or just before, the foliage. The new foliage stays a coppery red for just a few days, especially in *Amelanchier lamarckii*, where it contrasts superbly with the flowers.

Snowy mespilus grows well on sandy heaths, as well as in fertile garden soils, although chalky soils should be avoided. They are excellent large shrubs to position in a border, as a boundary planting or as a specimen in the lawn.

They can be propagated by sowing seed as soon as it is ripe or by layers. Cuttings can be rather difficult to take root.

The fruits are black or purplish red, similar to miniature apples, and ripen in early to mid-summer before being eaten by birds. Autumn colours of red and orange are a stunning sight.

Amelanchier lamarckii

MOISTURE	Moist but well-drained conditions
SITE/LIGHT	Position in a sunny site or partial shade
GENERAL CARE	Little general maintenance is required
PESTS & DISEASES	Susceptible to fireblight

TREES
see also
329–30

COMPANION PLANTS
see pages
140
265

Anemone WINDFLOWER

A large and variable group of hardy herbaceous perennials. The dwarf *Anemone blanda* grows from tubers and produces blue, pink or white daisy-like flowers in spring. It is excellent for naturalizing in a woodland garden or among shrubs in a border.

A. coronaria also grows from tubers, and has large single or double flowers in blue, red or white, ideal for cutting. Grow this windflower in a cutting garden or mixed border and in hard-winter areas provide a permanent mulch of organic matter for frost protection. *A. hupehensis* and *A. x hybrida* (Japanese anemone) are taller, clump forming, fibrous-rooted perennials, valued for their late summer and autumn flowers in shades of pink and also white. Grow these in a mixed border with other late-flowering perennials such as Michaelmas daisies (asters), golden rod (Solidago) and sedums. *A. nemorosa* (wood anemone) is a dwarf rhizomatous perennial with blue or white spring flowers.

Anemone coronaria De Caen Group

Anemone blanda

Propagate by division in autumn or spring. It is possible to buy *A. blanda* in pots from garden centres in spring.

MOISTURE	Most like moist conditions
SITE/LIGHT	Sun or partial shade for most species of Anemone
GENERAL CARE	Mulch for protection in cold areas
PESTS & DISEASES	Prone to leaf spot, powdery mildew, slugs and snails

FLOWERS
see also
175

COMPANION PLANTS
see pages
163
405
410

Anthemis GOLDEN MARGUERITE

The species *Anthemis tinctoria* is a hardy, herbaceous perennial that freely produces yellow daisy-like flowers. However, it can be short lived.

The cultivars are indispensable border plants, mixing well with many other perennials, such as blue salvias and delphiniums. Try them also with blue cranesbills (geraniums).They are also a good choice for a gravel garden.

When flowering is over, cut plants back hard to encourage vegetative growth, as well as prolong their longevity. This is particularly useful for *Anthemis tinctoria*. The blooms of many species are suitable for cutting.

Propagate by division or from basal cuttings in spring, or sow seed in containers in a cold frame.

The main problems are aphids, powdery mildew, slugs and snails.

Anthemis tinctoria 'Wargrave Variety'

MOISTURE	Water during dry periods
SITE/LIGHT	Enjoys well-drained, sandy soil in full sun
GENERAL CARE	*A. marschalliana* prefers shelter and partial shade
PESTS & DISEASES	Prone to leaf spot, powdery mildew, slugs and snails

***FLOWERS* see also 394**

***COMPANION PLANTS* see pages 232 267 396**

Antirrhinum SNAPDRAGON

Antirrhinum is a genus of about forty species of annuals and perennials originating from mainly rocky sites in Europe, America and North Africa. They are often grown for the stunning variety of colour they give to gardens.

Antirrhinum majus cultivar

Cultivars of the common snapdragon, *Antirrhinum majus*, are grown as half-hardy annuals, although they are really short-lived perennials. They are bushy plants, producing spikes of two-lipped flowers in a huge range of colours over a long period.

Snapdragons are used for summer bedding and are also excellent for growing in patio containers. Very tall cultivars are better planted in a mixed border. Flowers are suitable for cutting, but choose tall varieties for this purpose. Dead-head regularly to ensure continuous flowering.

Raise plants from seed in late summer, early autumn or early spring under cover at 16–18°C (61–64°F).

The main problem is rust, so choose rust-resistant cultivars where possible, such as the *A. majus* Coronette Series.

MOISTURE	Do not allow to get waterlogged
SITE/LIGHT	Grow in sharply drained soil in the full sun
GENERAL CARE	Overwinter young plants under glass
PESTS & DISEASES	Prone to aphids, powdery mildew and rust

FLOWERS
see also
238

COMPANION PLANTS
see pages
321
394
416

Aquilegia COLUMBINE

This is a genus of about 70 species of clump-forming perennials from meadows, open woodland and mountain areas in the northern hemisphere.

Columbines are hardy herbaceous perennials that produce spurred flowers in many colours above attractive lobed, sometimes bluish-green foliage.

Grow them in a mixed border with other perennials such as lupins, delphiniums, peonies and irises. They are a good choice for cottage-garden borders, especially in combination with old roses. Dead-head regularly.

Aquilegia alpina

Aquilegia McKana Group

Propagate hybrids, such as *Aquilegia* McKana Group, by division in spring – divisions are slow to establish as columbines do not like to be disturbed.

The main problems are aphids, caterpillars of various kinds and powdery mildew.

MOISTURE	Keep moist but do not overwater
SITE/LIGHT	Full sun or partial shade in well- or sharply drained soil
GENERAL CARE	Most alpine species prefer cool conditions in summer
PESTS & DISEASES	Prone to aphids, caterpillars and powdery mildew

FLOWERS see also 280

COMPANION PLANTS see pages 293 326 358

Araucaria MONKEY PUZZLE

These coniferous, evergreen trees come originally from tropical rainforest areas which have a long dry season, such as New Guinea, Australia, New Hebrides, New Caledonia and South America.

Known as the monkey puzzle or Chilean pine, *Araucaria araucana* is a medium-sized evergreen tree with an open, whorled crown. The foliage can reach ground level, although it tends to lose lower branches the older it gets. *A. araucana* is perhaps the only Araucaria that thrives in cooler climates.

Monkey puzzles can be propagated by seed which comes from the fruits on large cones, 15–20cm (6–8in) across. Cuttings of vertical shoot tips can also be taken in midsummer.

Monkey puzzles make excellent specimen trees in the garden, but they do need space and would probably not thrive in tiny front gardens. They are, however, very tolerant of coastal exposure.

Araucaria araucana

MOISTURE	Keep moist and water freely in the growing season
SITE/LIGHT	Well-drained soil in the full sun, sheltered from cold winds
GENERAL CARE	Apply liquid fertilizer fortnightly in the growing season
PESTS & DISEASES	Prone to honey fungus

TREES see also 373

COMPANION PLANTS see pages 178 367

Arbutus STRAWBERRY TREE

Bell-shaped flowers categorise these evergreen trees and shrubs as being members of the heather family. Arbutus species, however, unlike most other family members, thrive on chalk and limey soils, as well as on acidic sands and other soils that are freely drained.

An attractive feature of the Arbutus genus can be its distinctive peeling, red-brown bark. The strawberry tree, *Arbutus unedo,* is the best example for flowers and fruits, as well as its shredding, red-brown bark. The white flowers open in the autumn, at the same time that the fruits from last year are ripening, producing a stunning display. *A. unedo* looks good in a shrub bed for its evergreen foliage and display season, but can grow up to 8m (25ft).

Arbutus unedo

Arbutus menziesii

Arbutus menziesii, or the madroñe, can eventually make a large tree, up to 15m (50ft) high – but over 100 years.

Propagate by taking basal cuttings in late winter, by layering or else by seed.

A. menziesii can be tender when young and will need some initial winter protection. When it is established it can be used to good effect as a specimen tree or as a focal point in the garden.

MOISTURE	Does not require much watering once established
SITE/LIGHT	Prefers well-drained soil in full sun to light shade
GENERAL CARE	*A. menziesii* needs acid soil; *A. unedo* tolerates alkaline
PESTS & DISEASES	Prone to leaf spot and aphids

TREES
see also
411

COMPANION PLANTS
see pages
220
251
435

Arctotis AFRICAN DAISY

In frost-prone climates the African daisy is grown as a half-hardy annual, although in warm climates it is a perennial. They tend to be short lived.

Daisy-like flowers in various bright colours including orange and red shades are freely produced. The lobed leaves are silvery green. They are ideal for summer bedding or for planting in bold groups at the front of a mixed border or in a gravel area. Excellent used as displays in patio containers. Blooms can be cut but do not last for long.

Propagate from seed in spring under cover, or from cuttings in late summer.

The flowerheads of modern cultivars, such as *A. x hybrida* 'Flame', tend to stay open longer, as they are bred for bedding display.

Arctotis x hybrida 'Flame'

MOISTURE	Water regularly and do not allow to dry out
SITE/LIGHT	Sharply drained, light soil in the full sun
GENERAL CARE	Root stem cuttings at any time
PESTS & DISEASES	Prone to aphids and leaf miners

FLOWERS
see also
394

COMPANION
PLANTS
see pages
163
321

Argyranthemum

These half-hardy evergreen sub-shrubs have a bushy or spreading habit and produce single or double daisy-like flowers in shades of pink (*Argyranthemum* 'Petite Pink'), yellow (*A.* 'Butterfly') or orange, as well as white.

Argyranthemum 'Butterfly'

The foliage is variable, from ferny to lobed, and green to grey-green. Argyranthemums are grown as annual summer bedding plants in frosty climates, and are good for mixed borders, patio tubs and window boxes. They mix well with other daisy-flowered plants such as brachyscome and gazanias.

Propagate from semi-ripe cuttings in late summer and overwinter young plants in a fairly temperate greenhouse.

They grow best in well-drained and moderately fertile soil in a hot, sunny site. They are excellent plants for coastal gardens as most species will tolerate salty sea winds.

Pinch out the tips of young plants to encourage a more compact shape.

Argyranthemum 'Petite Pink'

MOISTURE	Keep moist but not overwatered
SITE/LIGHT	Well-drained, moderately fertile soil in the full sun
GENERAL CARE	Apply a deep, dry winter mulch for protection
PESTS & DISEASES	Generally trouble free

***FLOWERS* see also 163 175**

***COMPANION PLANTS* see pages 264 394 420**

Aronia CHOKEBERRY

The chokeberry is a genus of deciduous, woodland, swamp and scrub margin shrubs originating from eastern North America. They are grown for their white or pink-tinged flowers and colourful autumn leaves.

The flowers of *Aronia arbutifolia*, the red chokeberry, come forth in mid to late spring in white clusters at the ends of the shoots. These are followed by persistent red berries, which ripen in early autumn.

One of the great features of aronias is the stunning autumn colours which the leaves adopt before falling to the ground, turning vivid reds and crimson.

Propagate in a cold frame in autumn or the early spring.

Aronias are excellent in shrub beds or for wild gardens. They particularly like damp sandy soils, and generally tolerate wet sites but are intolerant of shallow, chalky soils.

The berries of *Aronia prunifolia*

Aronia arbutifolia

MOISTURE	Enjoys lots of moisture
SITE/LIGHT	Sun or partial shade in damp, sandy soil
GENERAL CARE	Water moderately during growth
PESTS & DISEASES	New growth prone to slugs; birds attack the fruits

SHRUBS see also 370

COMPANION PLANTS see pages 167 171

Artemisia WORMWOOD

This is a large and varied genus ranging from annual herbs to woody plants, as well as hardy, clump-forming herbaceous perennials. They often have silky, hairy leaves, making them attractive as foliage plants.

The foliage of wormwood (also mugwort or sagebrush), is often aromatic, which is an attractive feature for the gardener.

Artemisia 'Powis Castle' is a woody-based perennial with dense, silver-grey leaves forming a clump.

Artemisia ludoviciana

Artemisia 'Powis Castle'

A. lactiflora is grown mainly for its flowers, although its deeply cut green leaves are attractive, while *A. ludoviciana* is more of a foliage plant with its striking silvery leaves.

Propagate by softwood or semi-hardwood cuttings in summer. They do not tolerate wet conditions.

MOISTURE	Extremely drought tolerant
SITE/LIGHT	Well-drained, fertile soil in the full sun
GENERAL CARE	Alpine species require sharp drainage
PESTS & DISEASES	Prone to powdery mildew, aphids and gall

SHRUBS see also 368

COMPANION PLANTS see pages 177 200

Arundinaria HIMALAYAN BAMBOO

Arundinaria anceps produces cascades of soft, evergreen foliage, making this bamboo highly attractive. Grow it as a single specimen or mass them together for screening.

This genus of one or two species of bamboo comes from the swampy areas in southeastern America. The canes are stout and rigid, up to 1.5–10m (5–30ft) high, with spreading rhizomes.

The most popular species, *Arundinaria anceps*, can even be used as hedging. This is a hardy, fast growing plant and can quickly fill a large space. Maximum height is usually no more than 4–5m (12–15ft).

Divide in spring for propagation, but when choosing a plant in the beginning, select a decent sized specimen, as small seedlings are often difficult to bring on.

Arundinaria anceps

Arundinaria anceps

A. anceps is best planted in a sheltered site out of strong winds. The more shelter you provide the bamboo, the greener and healthier the foliage will become. During the first couple of seasons, do not allow this particular bamboo to dry out. Feed every four weeks from mid-spring to early summer with a mixture of blood, fish and bone sprinkled around the base of each plant.

If it is to be grown as a hedge, clip regularly during the growing season.

MOISTURE	Keep moist and do not allow to dry out
SITE/LIGHT	Enjoys a sheltered position in full sun or partial shade
GENERAL CARE	Clip back with shears to keep under control
PESTS & DISEASES	Prone to aphids

SHRUBS see also 372

COMPANION PLANTS see pages 214 355 400

Aster

The plants included here are hardy herbaceous perennials. There are both tall and dwarf cultivars, producing single or double daisy-like flowerheads in shades of blue, violet, purple, red and also white.

Aster x frikartii 'Mönch'

Aster novae-angliae 'Harrington's Pink'

Some flower in late summer but many are of great value in the autumn garden, combining well with other late-flowering perennials such as rudbeckias, helianthus and anemones, as well as with shrubs noted for autumn leaf tints and berries, such as rhus and berberis.

Propagate by division in spring or sow seed in a cold frame in spring or autumn. Divide *Aster novae-angliae* cultivars every two or three years to keep them young, vigorous and free-flowering.

A. x frikartii 'Mönch' is an attractive variety with long-lasting lavender-blue flowerheads.

As asters dislike drying out, maintain a permanent mulch of organic matter. Be on the lookout for wilting caused by drought. Support tall plants with twiggy sticks as they start into growth.

MOISTURE	Keep moist and do not allow to dry out
SITE/LIGHT	Generally thrives in full sun to partial shade
GENERAL CARE	Mulch annually after cutting back in late autumn
PESTS & DISEASES	Prone to aphids, slugs, snails, grey mould and leaf spot

FLOWERS
see also
159

COMPANION PLANTS
see pages
152
386
394

Astrantia MASTERWORT

Masterworts are hardy, clump-forming herbaceous perennials. The flowers, on tall upright stems, are pink, red or green and surrounded with a collar of coloured bracts.

Deeply lobed or hand-shaped leaves make an attractive background for the summer blooms. Grow in mixed borders and woodland gardens, or around shrubs, combining them with foliage perennials such as hostas and the new heucheras or coral flowers with coloured foliage. The flowerheads can be cut and dried.

Dead-head if you do not want plants to self seed.

Astrantia major 'Ruby Wedding'

Astrantia major 'Sunningdale Variegated'

Propagate in spring by division or by transplanting self-sown seedlings. Most *Astrantia major* variants will tolerate drier conditions.

MOISTURE	Most enjoy moist conditions
SITE/LIGHT	Grow in humus-rich soil in sun or partial shade
GENERAL CARE	*A. major* 'Sunningdale Variegated' – full sun for leaf colour
PESTS & DISEASES	Prone to aphids, powdery mildew, slugs and snails

FLOWERS
see also
141

COMPANION PLANTS
see pages
282
285

Aubrieta

These hardy evergreen carpeting perennials produce masses of small, four-petalled flowers in blue, red-purple, mauve, pink or white. The small leaves are roughly oval and can add colour to drab walls.

Aubrieta x cultorum

Indispensable spring flowering plants for the rock or scree garden in combination with aurinia, arabis and helianthemums. When flowering is over, cut back plants to ensure a compact habit.

Propagate from semi-ripe cuttings taken in midsummer or from seed sown in containers in a cold frame in autumn or spring. Hybrid forms are usually grown in preference to the species, especially from seed.

Aubrieta enjoys moderately fertile, preferably neutral or alkaline soil, as long as it has good drainage. It produces blooms more abundantly if it is positioned in a warm, sunny site in the garden, cascading over brick walls or planted in masses on a sunny bank.

Aubrieta hybrid

MOISTURE	Does not need much watering
SITE/LIGHT	Prefers the sun in well-drained neutral/alkaline soil
GENERAL CARE	Cut back after flowering to maintain compactness
PESTS & DISEASES	Mainly prone to aphids, also eelworms and flea beetles

FLOWERS
see also
166
321

COMPANIOI PLANTS
see pages
166
277

Aurinia GOLD DUST

A hardy dwarf evergreen perennial, Aurinia produces masses of sunshine yellow flowers above mounds of grey-green foliage and are very robust plants.

Aurinia saxatilis

A favourite companion for aubrieta on rock and scree gardens, this plant is also suitable for covering a well-drained, sunny bank.

Aurinia saxatilis (Gold dust) bears its profuse flowers in late spring and early summer.

Propagate in early summer from softwood cuttings or sow seed in containers in a cold frame in the autumn.

Grow Aurinia in moderately fertile soil with good drainage in the full sun. Cut back after it has finished flowering to maintain a compact shape.

Aurinia saxatilis

MOISTURE	Do not allow to become too wet – prefers little water
SITE/LIGHT	Moderately fertile soil with good drainage in full sun
GENERAL CARE	Cut back after flowering to maintain compactness
PESTS & DISEASES	Prone to aphids

FLOWERS *see also* 321

COMPANION PLANTS *see pages* 165 277

Azara THE VANILLA TREE

Originating from South America, this is a genus of ten species of evergreen shrubs and small trees that are often found at the margins of woodland or beside lakes.

Azara microphylla is an attractive weeping tree with lots of tiny, glossy leaves hanging from delicate branches. Even after ten years, it is unlikely to be more than 4m (12–15ft). It originates from Chile and is tough and hardy in many colder climates. In severe winters, it can be cut back to the ground by frost, but nearly always recovers.

Azara microphylla

A. microphylla is vanilla-scented due to its tiny yellow flowers in the early spring – an added delightful feature for a small garden.

To propagate, root semi-ripe cuttings in the summer.

Grow in moist, fertile soil. Light shade is best, as too much sun will turn the leaves slightly yellow and too much shade will thin the crown too much. Shelter from strong winds, although slight coastal breezes will be fine. Although not a lime hater, avoid chalky soil unless constant watering and feeding can be given. If left to grow naturally, it develops into a large shrub.

MOISTURE	Prefers moist but not wet conditions
SITE/LIGHT	Grow in fertile, humus-rich soil in light shade with shelter
GENERAL CARE	Annual sprinkling of blood, fish and bone in spring
PESTS & DISEASES	Generally trouble free

SHRUBS see also 170

COMPANION PLANTS see pages 160 171

Begonia

This is a huge group of very tender perennials. In frost-prone climates tuberous and fibrous-rooted begonias are used for summer bedding and for containers such as patio tubs, window boxes and hanging baskets.

Begonia semperflorens 'Olympia Red'

They flower profusely, producing blooms in shades of red, pink, orange, yellow or white. The trailing Pendula tuberous begonias are especially suitable for hanging baskets, while the tuberous Multiflora and giant-flowered Tuberhybrida begonias are better in tubs and window boxes. The compact, bushy, fibrous-rooted *Begonia semperflorens* cultivars are generally used for massed summer bedding in combination with other bedding plants such as ageratum, impatiens and lobelia. The leaves are often flushed with bronze. Deadhead all plants regularly.

Begonia Multiflora Nonstop Series

Propagate from seed in late winter or early spring under cover.

The Multiflora and Pendula begonias are generally treated as annuals and raised from seed each year.

MOISTURE	Water moderately in growth, sparingly during winter
SITE/LIGHT	Humus-rich, well-drained slightly acid soil in partial shade
GENERAL CARE	When grown under glass, shade from direct sun
PESTS & DISEASES	Prone to vine weevils, aphids, grey mould and mildew

FLOWERS
see also
267

COMPANION PLANTS
see pages
145
291
321

Bellis DAISY

Hardy perennials grown as biennials, the cultivars of *Bellis perennis*, the common daisy, are dwarf, rosette-forming plants with large, double or semi-double flowers in shades of pink, red or white.

The leaves are somewhat spoon shaped in appearance. Daisies are often used in spring bedding schemes, in combination with other spring bedding plants and bulbs such as tulips, hyacinths, forget-me-nots (Myosotis) or wallflowers (Erysimum). They are also good for tubs and window boxes.

Propagate from seed outdoors in early summer in shallow drills, or divide in spring or else after flowering.

Remove dead flowerheads regularly. For winter-flowering container specimens, grow in loam-based potting compost.

Grow in moderately fertile, well-drained soil in a warm, sunny site or partial shade.

Bellis perennis 'Tasso Red'

MOISTURE	Moderate watering
SITE/LIGHT	Moderately fertile soil in full sun to partial shade
GENERAL CARE	For winter-flowerers, water moderately
PESTS & DISEASES	Generally trouble free

FLOWERS
see also
147
228–9

COMPANION PLANTS
see pages
245
286
341

Berberis BARBERRY

This is a large genus, with species across all continents except Australia and Antarctica. Berberis adds a stunning orange-yellow colour to the garden, which the majority of other flowering shrubs generally lack.

Barberries are usually grown for their foliage and flowers. Flowers are carried on last year's shoots in spring and early summer, but some develop in the autumn in the more floriferous varieties such as *Berberis darwinii*. The flowers are followed by berries, which are either red or blackish-blue.

Berberis thunbergii 'Rose Glow'

The spiny stems of barberries can be useful for planting as a hedge to stop unwanted visitors to your house or garden!

Propagate by semi-hardwood cuttings in summer or hardwood cuttings in a cold frame in autumn.

B. thunbergii comes in a wide variety of colour forms, both purple-reds and golden greens.

Berberis darwinii

MOISTURE	Moderate watering needed
SITE/LIGHT	Any well-drained garden soil in sun or partial shade
GENERAL CARE	Prune to remove weak or broken branched
PESTS & DISEASES	Prone to rust, leaf spot, powdery mildew and aphids

SHRUBS see also 167

COMPANION PLANTS see pages 170 290 331

Bergenia ELEPHANT'S EARS

Hardy dwarf evergreen perennials, bergenias have large, showy heads of bell-shaped flowers carried on thick stalks, in shades of pink (*Bergenia* 'Abendglut'), red and magenta, as well as white (*B.* 'Bressingham White').

The large leathery, shiny, rounded or oval leaves, which give these their common name, may become tinted with red or purple in winter. These are excellent plants for the front of mixed borders, perhaps surrounding shrubs and interplanted with winter and spring bulbs, and for woodland gardens.

Propagate from rhizome cuttings in autumn, or by division after flowering. Seed-raised plants usually produce hybrids.

Bergenias benefit from a permanent mulch of organic matter and most species dislike extremes of heat and drought. However, they do not mind poor soil conditions or even being positioned in an exposed site.

Check the plants regularly for leaf spot, slugs, snails and vine weevil grubs.

Bergenia 'Bressingham White'

Bergenia 'Abendglut'

MOISTURE	Keep moist but not overwatered
SITE/LIGHT	Happy in most soils either in the sun or partial shade
GENERAL CARE	Apply mulch in the autumn and beware of frosts
PESTS & DISEASES	Prone to slugs, snails, vine weevil grubs and leaf spot

FLOWERS see also 243

COMPANION PLANTS see pages 393 436

Betula BIRCH

With around 60 species to choose from, birches are grown for their stunning bark – in silver, copper or mahogany, their attractive male catkins and their autumn foliage. They are surface-rooting and so will compete for moisture with other plants.

Birches can be suitable for small gardens as specimen trees and over 30 years can grow up to 10–15m (33–48ft) in height. *Betula jacquemontii, B. ermanii* and *B. papyrifera* have vivid white or creamy white barks. However, for those who prefer copper and mahogany barks there is *B. nigra* 'Heritage', and some forms of *B. utilis* have peeling sheets of burnished copper.

Propagate from seed, root softwood cuttings in summer or graft some varieties in winter.

Birches like well-drained soils but not shallow chalk ones. Yellow-brown, pendent male catkins provide an attractive display in spring before the leaves emerge.

Betula nigra 'Heritage'

Betula jacquemontii

MOISTURE	Prefers moist conditions
SITE/LIGHT	Moderately fertile, well-drained soil in sun or light shade
GENERAL CARE	Do not allow the roots to dry out when transplanting
PESTS & DISEASES	Generally fine but watch out for birch rust and fungus

TREES see also 139–40 142

COMPANION PLANTS see pages 196 423

Bidens

This is a short lived, slender, somewhat spreading, half-hardy perennial. Suitable for containers or hanging baskets. It is grown as an annual in frost-prone climates.

The daisy-like, rich yellow flowers of this plant are produced over a long period, the bright green ferny foliage making a pleasing background.

Bidens ferulifolia is excellent for providing summer colour in patio tubs, window boxes and hanging baskets. *B. triplinervia* var. *macrantha* has bright golden yellow flowerheads which are carried above foliage on slender stalks in the autumn.

Bidens triplinervia var. *macrantha*

Propagate from seed in spring under cover.

Bidens is not usually troubled by pests or diseases but beware of sharp frosts.

Bidens ferulifolia

MOISTURE	Keep the soil moist
SITE/LIGHT	A sun-lover which is happy in any type of soil
GENERAL CARE	Can be grown under glass in cooler climates
PESTS & DISEASES	Generally trouble free

FLOWERS
see also
212

COMPANION PLANTS
see pages
262–3
291

Brachyglottis NEW ZEALAND SENECIO

Species of these evergreen shrubs are often listed under Senecio and originate from New Zealand and Tasmania. They are grown for their attractive foliage and flowers.

Brachyglottis have silvery or buff coloured hairy foliage which give the leaves a felt-like, velvety feel. The felt stays on the shoots and undersides of the leaves, but soon comes away from the leathery upper surface of the leaf, which then turns mid- to dark green or grey.

Propagate by semi-hardwood cuttings in the summer, or by seed.

New Zealand Senecio look good placed in mixed and shrub borders as long as they are given full exposure to the sun, as well as a hot part of the garden. Do not position in the shade, nor on poorly drained soils.

Hard pruning in the spring will help them produce more foliage, however this will be at the expense of flowers.

The other option is to lightly trim the plant once it has flowered to retain a neat shape. This applies particularly to the variety *Brachyglottis senecio* 'Sunshine', which tends to be rather sprawling in its habit.

Brachyglottis senecio 'Sunshine'

Brachyglottis senecio 'Sunshine'

MOISTURE	Moderate watering only
SITE/LIGHT	Most are suitable in well-drained soil in full sun
GENERAL CARE	Grow *B. hectoris* in fertile soil in partial shade
PESTS & DISEASES	Generally trouble free

SHRUBS see also 396

COMPANION PLANTS see pages 275 396

Brachyscome SWAN RIVER DAISY

Cultivars of the half-hardy annual *Brachyscome iberidifolia* have daisy-like, blue, purple, pink or white flowers on bushy plants, and finely divided, grey-green leaves.

Brachyscomes are excellent plants for summer colour in patio tubs and window boxes, and for mixed borders. Grow with other daisy-flowered plants, such as osteospermums. Young plants should have growing tips pinched out, as this encourages the plants to become well branched or bushy and therefore to produce many more daisy-like flowerheads.

B. iberidifolia 'Bravo'

Propagate from seed in spring under cover.

During the growing season, ensure the plants are well watered (but not waterlogged) and a balanced liquid fertilizer is applied twice in the season.

Check regularly for signs of slugs and snails near the plants.

MOISTURE	Water in the growing season and keep moist in winter
SITE/LIGHT	Enjoys a sheltered site in the full sun
GENERAL CARE	Grow in a loam-based potting compost under glass
PESTS & DISEASES	Prone to slugs and snails

FLOWERS see also 152

COMPANION PLANTS see pages 309 357

Bracteantha STRAWFLOWER

The strawflower *Bracteantha bracteata* is a half-hardy annual with papery, daisy-like flowerheads on strong, upright stems.

Bracteantha bracteata 'Sundaze Golden Yellow'

Cultivars of Bracteantha, mainly with double flowers, come in shades of yellow, orange, pink, red and also white. Grow in a mixed border or cutting garden. Low-growing cultivars can be used as edging or for a window box and tall cultivars should be supported.

Propagate from seed in spring under cover.

The flowers of *Bracteantha bracteata* are suitable for cutting and drying.

Bracteantha bracteata

MOISTURE	Keep the soil moist
SITE/LIGHT	Enjoys moderately fertile, well-drained soil in full sun
GENERAL CARE	Stake up tall-growing cultivars
PESTS & DISEASES	Generally trouble free but prone to downy mildew

FLOWERS see also 394

COMPANION PLANTS see pages 351 405

Buddleja BUTTERFLY BUSH

Buddlejas are some of the most popular garden plants, primarily grown for their large, honey-scented flowers which attract butterflies mid-summer, as well as for their use as fast-growing hedge plants.

Flowers are usually borne in dense, conical panicles in various colours including white (*Buddleja davidii* 'White Profusion'), lilac-blue (*B. davidii* 'Nanho Blue'), red-purple, lilac-pink and lavender.

Propagate by semi-hardwood cuttings in summer.

Buddleja davidii 'White Profusion'

Buddleja davidii 'Nanho Blue'

To produce the largest flowers, Buddleja requires a fertile soil, but it will grow on any well-drained soil, self-seeding into piles of gravel and chalk cliffs. Most are suitable for a mixed border and climbers grow well against a warm, sunny wall.

MOISTURE	Water freely in growing season
SITE/LIGHT	Fertile, well-drained soil in full sun
GENERAL CARE	Grow tender species in a cool greenhouse
PESTS & DISEASES	Prone to capsid bugs, caterpillars and red spider mites

SHRUBS see also 287

COMPANION PLANTS see pages 333 354

Buxus BOX

With its small evergreen leaves and its tolerance of clipping, box is one of the best shrubs for topiaries and living sculptures, as well as hedging. Dwarf boxes can be grown for edging, ground cover or in a rock garden.

Buxus is found in habitats throughout Europe, Asia, Africa and Central America. In the garden its architectural uses are many, depending on the skill of the gardener. The common box (*Buxus sempervirens*) can be left as a wild species to make a narrow crowned tree over time.

Box can be propagated from cuttings, taken either in the spring or autumn.

Buxus is happy on a wide range of soil pH, from about 5.5 to 7.4. In the wild it is found on soils derived from chalk and limestone. Whatever the soil type, the most important factor is good drainage.

Buxus sempervirens

MOISTURE	Do not allow to dry out or become waterlogged
SITE/LIGHT	Tolerates the sun but prefers partial shade
GENERAL CARE	Drought will produce poor, dull foliage
PESTS & DISEASES	Generally trouble free but watch out for red spider mite

SHRUBS see also 196

COMPANION PLANTS see pages 306 384 427–8

Calceolaria POUCH FLOWER

The species *C. integrifolia* is a shrubby, evergreen, half-hardy perennial but is generally grown as an annual in frost-prone climates. Cultivars are usually grown and these have yellow, orange or red pouched flowers over a long period, and grey-green leaves.

Pouch flowers or slipper flowers are good for summer colour in containers, including hanging baskets. They can also be used in summer bedding schemes, and look good with *Salvia farinacea* cultivars.

The ancient and very brittle stemmed *Calceolaria* 'Kentish Hero' and its deep orange pouch-like flowers are an interesting feature for the garden. *C.* 'Sunset Red' bears larger, vivid red flowers.

Propagate from seed in spring under cover, or from semi-ripe cuttings in late summer.

Most species require cool, moist conditions to flower abundantly, with not too much bright sunlight. Water freely and apply a balanced liquid fertilizer once a month during the growing season.

Calceolaria 'Sunset Red'

Calceolaria 'Kentish Hero'

MOISTURE	Keep moist but do not allow to become waterlogged
SITE/LIGHT	Prefers sun or partial shade on fertile acid soil
GENERAL CARE	Alpine species grow well in well-drained, gritty soil
PESTS & DISEASES	Prone to aphids, slugs and snails

FLOWERS see also 154

COMPANION PLANTS see pages 396

Calendula ENGLISH or POT MARIGOLD

The hardy annual English marigold produces double or single daisy-like flowers over a long period. Colours include shades of orange, apricot, yellow and cream. Flowers have conspicuous darker centres, usually brown or purplish.

The strongly aromatic leaves are generally spoon shaped. Dwarf and tall cultivars are available. Calendulas are a good choice for cottage-garden borders, plus ordinary mixed borders, and the flowers are suitable for cutting. Blue cornflowers make good companions.

Propagate from seed sown in flowering position in spring or autumn.

Calendula officinalis 'Fiesta Gitana' is a dwarf variety, usually with double-flowerheads in orange and yellow. All varieties should be dead-headed regularly to ensure continuous flowering.

Most varieties thrive even in poor soil, as long as it is well drained in the sun or partial shade.

These plants are prone to aphids and powdery mildew.

Calendula officinalis 'Fiesta Gitana'

MOISTURE	Water moderately
SITE/LIGHT	Grow in full sun or partial shade in well-drained soil
GENERAL CARE	Dead-head regularly
PESTS & DISEASES	Prone to aphids and powdery mildew

FLOWERS see also 416

COMPANION PLANTS see pages 193

Callicarpa BEAUTIFUL FRUIT

Grown mainly for their profusion of bead-like fruit, Callicarpa make an ideal shrub border. The berries in the variety 'Profusion' are a remarkable violet purple and grow prolifically during hot summers.

Callicarpa bodinieri var. *giraldii* 'Profusion'

The fruits are produced in dense, rounded clusters, ripening in late autumn. The flowers are carried in mid-summer and are lilac in colour.

Callicarpa bodinieri var. *giraldii* 'Profusion'

Callicarpa can be propagated by seed or by cuttings with a heel in spring.

Callicarpa grows on a wide range of sites, preferring damp fertile soils with a sunny aspect as they do not fruit well in shade. They can be used as specimens, as well as in shrub or mixed borders. The leaves turn yellow to purple in autumn.

MOISTURE	Keep damp during growing season
SITE/LIGHT	Thrives in full sun or dappled shade
GENERAL CARE	Water sparingly during winter
PESTS & DISEASES	Generally trouble free

SHRUBS see also 160

COMPANION PLANTS see pages 220 251 408

Callistemon BOTTLE BRUSH

Bottle brushes get their common epithet from the way in which the colourful flowers are carried, resembling a bottle brush. They look great grown up a house wall or in a shrub border.

The leaves of the bottle brush are willow-like, lasting for two years and the shoots tend to be pendulous. The flowers are produced in summer in cylindrical spikes which eventually change to become the next length of foliage.

Callistemon prefer hot sunny sites with freely drained but moisture retentive soil. They are often killed, or reduced to ground level, by hard winters.

Propagate either from semi-hardwood or fully ripe cuttings with a heel in summer, or by seed. Sow seed into a damp compost. Plant out in the spring once frosts are over.

Try planting beside a sun-facing wall in cooler climates. *Callistemon citrinus*, the crimson bottle brush, produces brilliant crimson-red flowers in 10–15cm (4–6in) long spikes from early summer to autumn.

Callistemon citrinus

Callistemon citrinus

MOISTURE	Keep moist and water during dry periods
SITE/LIGHT	Moderately fertile, well-drained soil in full sun
GENERAL CARE	Remove crowded stems; tolerant of pruning
PESTS & DISEASES	Trouble free but susceptible to winter cold

***SHRUBS* see also 374**

***COMPANION PLANTS* see pages 260 292 440**

Calluna LING or HEATHER

The genus is made up of the single species, *Calluna vulgaris.* The species is widespread and is found in moorland and lowland heaths from Europe, as far east as Siberia, and down to Morocco and the Azores.

Although Calluna grows vigorously on fertile soils, it prefers dry acidic conditions, and has been found growing on soil with an extremely low pH of 1.9. It can also be found growing on the top of chalk downland, surviving there in pockets of acidic clay above the chalk.

In the garden it is very useful as ground cover and for planting in clumps. Many selections have gold, red or other coloured foliage, adding colour all seasons of the year.

Calluna vulgaris 'Silver Knight'

Calluna vulgaris 'Spring Torch'

To propagate, root semi-ripe cuttings in midsummer.

Calluna vulgaris 'Silver Knight' has a grey foliage, deepening to purple-grey with mauve flowers. *C. vulgaris* 'Spring Torch' produces green leaves with cream, orange and red tips in the spring. All callunas prefer the full sun.

MOISTURE	Do not allow to become waterlogged
SITE/LIGHT	Like full sun in an open site
GENERAL CARE	Trim in spring before new growth begins
PESTS & DISEASES	Prone to phytophthora root rot and grey mould

SHRUBS see also 244

COMPANION PLANTS see pages 285 369 437

Camellia

Camellia is a large genus of shrubs with showy flowers that are prolonged during the winter/spring season. It is also prized for its bright or glossy evergreen foliage.

Camellia williamsii 'J.C. Williams'

Plant camellias as specimen shrubs in woodland garden settings and shrub borders, where their early flowering season can be enjoyed in comfort. The flowers look stunning, but do need regular dead-heading.

The flowering season starts in late autumn and early winter with *Camellia sasanqua* varieties, whose flowering can last into early spring. *C. japonica* and *C. williamsii* forms follow in mid-winter, usually producing a succession of blooms from late winter to late spring.

Camellia can be propagated at almost any time of the year. Generally, take semi-hardwood cuttings in late summer.

Camellias like deep moisture-retentive but well-drained soils and dislike lime.

Glossy, evergreen *Camellia* leaves

Camellia japonica 'Lavinia Maggi'

MOISTURE	Keep the soil moist
SITE/LIGHT	Site must be well drained, preferably partially shaded
GENERAL CARE	Maintain a mulch of leaf mould or bark
PESTS & DISEASES	Prone to phytophthora root rot, scale insects and aphids

SHRUBS see also 384–5

COMPANION PLANTS see pages 329–30 380

Campanula BELLFLOWER

This is a huge group of plants, those listed being hardy herbaceous perennials, although *Campanula medium* is a hardy biennial and *C. portenschlagiana* is evergreen. Habit is variable, although most have bell-shaped flowers produced over a very long period.

Some species have star-shaped or saucer-shaped blooms. Flower colours are mainly shades of blue, plus pink, purple and white. The taller kinds such as *C. glomerata* (clustered bellflower), *C. lactiflora* (milky bellflower) and *C. persicifolia* (peach-leaved bellflower) are ideal for mixed borders and combine effectively with many other summer-flowering perennials and shrubs, including shrub roses.

Propagate by division or basal cuttings in spring.

Dwarf campanulas such as *C. carpatica, C. portenschlagiana* (Dalmation bellflower) and *C. poscharskyana* are suitable for rock or scree gardens. Support tall bellflowers as these can be battered by strong winds. Insert twiggy sticks around clumps before growth.

Campanula lactiflora 'Loddon Anna'

Campanula glomerata 'Superba'

MOISTURE	Keep moist but not wet, especially in winter
SITE/LIGHT	Generally well-drained soil in sun or partial shade
GENERAL CARE	Grow less hardy species under glass
PESTS & DISEASES	Prone to slugs, snails, powdery mildew and rust

FLOWERS see also 369

COMPANION PLANTS see pages 267 390–1 432

Canna INDIAN SHOT PLANT

These half-hardy herbaceous perennials grow from thick rhizomes. They have long, broad leaves, purple, bronze, variegated or blue-green in some cultivars, and lily-like flowers, often in brilliant colours.

Cannas, with its brilliant red, yellow or orange colours, give a tropical touch to gardens in frost-prone climates where they are used as dot plants in summer bedding schemes and patio containers. Cut down in autumn and store the dormant rhizomes in slightly moist peat substitute in a frost-free place for the winter.

Canna indica

Canna 'President'

Propagate by dividing rhizomes in spring, each with a growth bud, and start into growth under glass.

Canna indica is a hardy, fast-growing variety and *C.* 'President' has gladioli-like scarlet-red blooms.

MOISTURE	Keep moist and do not allow to dry out
SITE/LIGHT	Enjoys the full sun in a sheltered, humus-rich site
GENERAL CARE	Water freely in dry spells
PESTS & DISEASES	Prone to slugs and snails

FLOWERS see also 146

COMPANION PLANTS see pages 138 291 292

Carpenteria TREE ANEMONE

This is a genus of one species native to hot, dry, sunny situations in California and so is best sited in sun-facing borders or against sun-drenched walls. The leaves are evergreen and leathery in appearance.

Carpenteria californica is ideal as a shrub in a border, as well as situated against a wall. The flowers are carried in a terminal cluster of three to five blooms on the new growths in early to mid-summer, and some varieties also produce them singly from the leaf axils. The fragrant flowers are white, 5–8cm across (2–3in), with a boss of yellow stamens. C. 'Bodnant' and *C. californica* 'Ladham's Variety' are particularly good forms.

Propagate Carpenteria by hardwood cuttings in spring or by semi-ripe cuttings in summer.

Provide shelter from cold, dry winds and remove old shoots occasionally once they have flowered.

Carpenteria californica

MOISTURE	Keep moist and do not allow to dry out
SITE/LIGHT	A sunny, well-drained site with shelter
GENERAL CARE	Mulch in the autumn to protect the base
PESTS & DISEASES	Generally trouble free

SHRUBS see also 367

COMPANION PLANTS see pages 201–4 323 438

Cassiope

This genus of dwarf, evergreen shrubs originates from diverse habitats in arctic and alpine regions of North Europe, North Asia and North America. They are low growing, rarely reaching more than 15cm (6in) high.

Cassiopes produce large, white, bell- or urn-shaped flowers in late spring to early summer. They prefer a moist humus-rich site, such as in a rock garden. They are attractive when established, but they do need plenty of moisture, particularly during the growing season, and will generally not tolerate any chalk or lime in the soil.

Cassiope can be propagated by taking softwood or semi-hardwood cuttings in summer, or else by layering.

They will grow in either full sun, especially if kept moist, or in partial shade, and are best situated in a sheltered spot. Try planting Cassiope on a peat bank or in open areas in a woodland garden.

Cassiope 'Muirhead'

Cassiope 'Muirhead' has white flowers with yellowy centres and has a low, mound-forming habit. The species *C. tetragona* does tolerate some lime in the soil.

MOISTURE	Keep moist during summer but not waterlogged
SITE/LIGHT	Prefers humus-rich soil in full sun to partial shade
GENERAL CARE	Provide shelter if there are strong winds
PESTS & DISEASES	Generally trouble free

SHRUBS *see also* 244

COMPANION PLANTS *see pages* 139–40, 297, 408

Catalpa BEAN TREE

Catalpa is often grown for its large erect panicles, carried in mid- to late summer like candles or lanterns above the green foliage. The bean-like fruits hang down in strands, lasting long into the winter and open up to release the small, two-winged seeds.

Bean trees have large, heart-shaped thin leaves which are susceptible to damage by strong winds. Therefore site in a sheltered spot during the growing season. Catalpa are ideal trees for parkland settings and large gardens.

Propagate by seed, graft in late winter, or take softwood cuttings in summer and root them in late winter.

C. erubescens 'Purpurea' can be coppiced and will make a good foliage plant for a shrubbery, with the new foliage (particularly in spring) very deep purple, almost black.

Generally bean trees like a wide range of well-drained, moisture retentive soils, but *C. bignonioides* will tolerate heavy clays.

Catalpa bignonioides

Catalpa erubescens 'Purpurea'

MOISTURE	Keep moist but not waterlogged
SITE/LIGHT	Well-drained soil in the full sun, but a sheltered site
GENERAL CARE	Protect young plants from frost during the winter
PESTS & DISEASES	Generally trouble free

TREES see also 361

COMPANION PLANTS see pages 381 435

Ceanothus CALIFORNIA LILAC

This genus, originating mainly from America, is found in scrubs and woodland on dry slopes. They all produce an abundant display of small flowers in large clusters, with the majority of the species having flowers which are mainly blue or varying shades of blues.

California lilacs have two main seasons of flowering: in the spring and in late summer or early autumn. Evergreen forms mainly flower in the spring, while the deciduous ones bloom in late summer/autumn. *Ceanothus* 'Cascade', an evergreen shrub, flowers from spring to early summer. The plants range from prostrate or mound forming shrubs to tall upright ones.

The different flowering forms each have separate pruning regimens. The evergreen forms (Group 1) need minimal trimming after flowering, whereas the deciduous forms (Group 2) should be pruned back close to the previous year's shoots in early spring (see pages 104–6).

Propagation is by softwood to semi-hardwood cuttings taken in summer.

The mound forms can be used for ground cover whereas the taller ones fit well into a shrub bed or mixed border. In colder districts they may need the shelter of a wall and prefer full sun. All species tolerate acid sands to chalky soils, but demand good drainage.

Ceanothus 'Cascade'

MOISTURE	Keep moist but not waterlogged
SITE/LIGHT	Good drainage in full sun or no more than light shade
GENERAL CARE	Mulch and fertilize after pruning
PESTS & DISEASES	Prone to root rot on wet soils

SHRUBS
see also
177

COMPANION PLANTS
see pages
137
260
387

Cedrus CEDAR

Originally found in the western Himalayas and the Mediterranean, cedars are majestic looking trees and require an ample sized garden due to the potential size of some species when established.

Cedars need lots of light. They like hot, dry sunny sites, and are not fussy whether the soil is acidic or alkaline, as long as it is well drained. In the shade they look ragged and lose the lower foliage.

Cedars can be raised from seed in spring or by grafting onto seedling rootstocks. Male cones emerge above the branches in autumn and the female cones expand the next summer and ripen late summer, breaking up some time over winter or spring.

The Deodar cedar (*Cedrus deodara*) is one of the best choices for a small garden, whereas the Atlas cedar (*Cedrus atlantica*) is ideal for slightly larger spaces, showing off its silvery blue foliage.

Cedrus deodara

Cedrus atlantica (male cones)

MOISTURE	Water moderately
SITE/LIGHT	Tolerates most soils, but likes plenty of sun
GENERAL CARE	Prune for shape or to keep in check
PESTS & DISEASES	Prone to honey fungus and aphids

TREES see also 373

COMPANION PLANTS see pages 161 174 275

Celosia COCKSCOMB

Cockscombs are half-hardy perennials grown as annuals in frost-prone climates. The Plumosa Group of *Celosia argentea* is the most popular, with brightly coloured plume-like flowerheads.

Celosia spicata Flamingo Series

These plants give an exotic touch to summer bedding schemes, patio tubs and window boxes and the flowers are good for cutting. Coleus (solenostemon) are good companions. *Celosia spicata* Flamingo Series produces spikes of flowers on branching plants.

Propagate from seed in spring under cover.

Cockscombs are especially suitable for a mixed border, and the flowers are ideal for cutting and drying. In frost-prone areas grow under glass in containers. Outdoors, make sure there is no further risk from frost, then plant in moist, fertile soil with good drainage in a sheltered and sunny position.

Watch out for foot and root rot and leaf spot, as well as aphids, whiteflies and red spider mites under glass.

MOISTURE	Keep moist and water freely in dry periods
SITE/LIGHT	A situation with good drainage, shelter and lots of sun
GENERAL CARE	Under glass, ensure there is adequate ventilation
PESTS & DISEASES	Prone to foot and root rot, and fungal leaf spot

FLOWERS see also 312

COMPANION PLANTS see pages 168 402 434

Centaurea CORNFLOWER or KNAPWEED

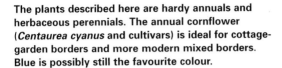

The plants described here are hardy annuals and herbaceous perennials. The annual cornflower (*Centaurea cyanus* and cultivars) is ideal for cottage-garden borders and more modern mixed borders. Blue is possibly still the favourite colour.

Cornflowers associate well with shrub roses and the perennials are excellent for prairie-style borders, planted alongside ornamental grasses. *Centaurea dealbata* 'Steenbergii' is a clump former and *C. montana* forms mats. As they can grow up to 90cm (36in) high, you need to provide supports for both. Flowers are good for cutting.

Propagate *C. cyanus* from seed sown in the flowering position and the perennials by division, both in spring.

C. cyanus can be grown in containers for winter flowering. Another feature of this genus is that they attract bees and butterflies, wonderful for any garden, especially a wild garden.

Keep an eye out for powdery mildew.

Centaurea cyanus 'Blue Diadem'

MOISTURE	Keep moist but not overwatered
SITE/LIGHT	Most prefer full sun or partial shade
GENERAL CARE	Can be naturalised easily in grass
PESTS & DISEASES	Prone to powdery mildew

FLOWERS see also 147

COMPANION PLANTS see pages 146 218 396

Ceratostigma

These hardy herbaceous perennials and shrubs are valued for their late-season blue flowers. *Ceratostigma plumbaginoides* is a perennial, woody at the base, while *C. willmottianum* is a true shrub.

The foliage of both these varieties takes on autumn tints. Ideal for mixed borders, combined with plants for late summer and autumn colour such as Michaelmas daisies (asters), nerines, rudbeckias, Schizostylis, sedums, Rhus and Berberis.

Propagate from semi-ripe cuttings in summer.

Ceratostigma griffithii

Ceratostigma willmottianum

C. griffithii is a rounded shrub with attractive red stems.

In spring, cut back flowered shoots of shrubs to just above older growth and cut down dead herbaceous growth in spring.

MOISTURE	Keep moist but not too wet
SITE/LIGHT	Prefers a sunny, sheltered spot with good drainage
GENERAL CARE	Great planted up a warm, sunny wall
PESTS & DISEASES	Prone to powdery mildew

FLOWERS
see also
235

COMPANION PLANTS
see pages
163
170
404

Chaenomeles JAPONICA

Also known as the flowering or Japanese quince, this genus has three species of deciduous, often spiny, shrubs from mountain woodland in China and Japan. The cup-shaped flowers open before the leaves.

An effective way of growing Chaenomeles, particularly the frequently flowering quinces, is to train them in a fan or espalier shape against a wall. They are just as attractive grown as free standing shrubs, either in a border or as an isolated specimen.

Propagate by semi-hardwood cuttings with a heel in summer or by layering.

Try growing *Chaenomeles speciosa* 'Nivalis' for its pure white flowers or *C. superba* varieties for their spreading habit and abundant flowers.

Chaenomeles superba

Chaenomeles speciosa 'Nivalis'

MOISTURE	Keep moist but not too damp
SITE/LIGHT	Position in a fertile site with sun and light shade
GENERAL CARE	Be careful of the spines which can be quite vicious
PESTS & DISEASES	Can be prone to fireblight and scale insects

SHRUBS see also 170

COMPANION PLANTS see pages 367 417

Chamaecyparis CYPRESS

Cypresses are evergreen, coniferous trees from the forests in Taiwan, Japan and North America. Species vary from rounded, dwarf bushes up to tall, conical shaped trees reaching up to 40m (130ft) high.

Dwarf or slow-growing forms are obviously ideal for the smaller garden and can be clipped to maintain their shape. Taller forms include some varieties of the *Chamaecyparis lawsoniana* such as 'Columnaris', which is a columnar tree reaching 10m (30ft) high. Another tall grower but with billowing foliage is *C. pisifera* 'Squarrosa Sulphurea'.

Chamaecyparis pisifera 'Squarrosa Sulphurea'

Chamaecyparis lawsoniana 'Columnaris'

Propagate semi-hardwood cuttings in late summer, or grow from seed in spring.

Treat small globe forms as plants for mulched beds, in tubs or the rock garden; in mixed or shrub beds they may be swamped by faster growing plants. The upright taller forms need positioning in the garden to highlight their shape and height.

MOISTURE	Keep moist and water during dry spells
SITE/LIGHT	Any type of well-drained soil in the sun or light shade
GENERAL CARE	Avoid planting in hollows as this will waterlog the plant
PESTS & DISEASES	Prone to phytophthora root rot and honey fungus

TREES see also 420

COMPANION PLANTS see pages 142 172 178

Chamaerops DWARF FAN PALM

Only one species makes up this genus – *Chamaerops humilis,* which comes from rocky or sandy slopes in regions of the western Mediterranean.

Chamaerops humilis

This shapely plant is a low-growing bushy palm that sends up numerous suckers around the base throughout its life, rather than forming a single trunk. In frost-prone areas, *C. humilis* is best grown in a cool greenhouse or even inside as a houseplant.

Foliage is plentiful and the whole clump can become very dense, enabling it to withstand strong winds, making it a suitable palm for coastal areas.

To propagate, it is best to separate suckers from established plants during late spring.

Chamaerops humilis

C. humilis prefers full sun, although the fronds are a more attractive green if grown in light shade. Larger specimens are much hardier than small plants. It is a good choice for a pot on a balcony or terrace. Do not confuse young plants with *Trachycarpus fortunei* (see p423).

MOISTURE	Drought tolerant but water regularly during growth
SITE/LIGHT	Sun or light shade in fertile, well-drained loam
GENERAL CARE	Remove brown leaves as soon as they appear
PESTS & DISEASES	Prone to brown leaf spot; red spider mite under glass

SHRUBS see also 423

COMPANIO PLANTS see page 162 237

Chionodoxa GLORY OF THE SNOW

These hardy dwarf bulbs produce starry, blue, white-centred flowers. Of extremely easy culture, they are ideal for naturalising in mixed borders, planted around deciduous spring-flowering shrubs.

Glory of the snow combines well with bergenias and dwarf yellow daffodils (narcissus). Plant the bulbs among the bergenias. Chionodoxas are also among the best small bulbs for rock gardens.

Propagate from offsets while dormant in summer or early autumn. Plants may self-seed freely.

C. forbesii varieties have star-shaped blue or pink flowers.

Chionodoxa forbesii 'Pink Giant'

Chionodoxa forbesii

MOISTURE	Keep moist but do not allow to become saturated
SITE/LIGHT	Any well-drained soil in the full sun
GENERAL CARE	Plant bulbs 8cm (3in) deep in the autumn
PESTS & DISEASES	Generally trouble free

FLOWERS see also 304

COMPANION PLANTS see pages 195 257 387

Chrysanthemum

Annual chrysanthemums provide summer colour with their single, daisy-like flowers on branching stems. There are also half-hardy to hardy perennial forms.

The hardy Rubellum hybrids, such as *C.* 'Clara Curtis', are especially good for mixed borders. The early-flowering florists' chrysanthemums, such as the Sprays, are grown in borders, too, but generally are not so hardy. The hardy dwarf kinds, especially the Pompons, such as *C.* 'Brown Eyes', are ideal for patio tubs as well as mixed borders. The flowers of all chrysanthemums are excellent for cutting.

Chrysanthemum 'Clara Curtis'

Propagate from basal cuttings in spring; Rubellum hybrids can also be propagated by division in spring. Sow seed of annuals during spring in flowering positions.

Pinch out tips of young plants to encourage branching. Side shoots can also be pinched out. The taller chrysanthemums will need stakes for support.

Chrysanthemum 'Brown Eyes'

MOISTURE	Keep moist and water freely during dry periods
SITE/LIGHT	Full sun in well-drained, neutral to slightly acid soil
GENERAL CARE	Apply well-rotted manure or a mulch
PESTS & DISEASES	Prone to aphids, earwigs, capsid bugs and fungal rot

FLOWERS see also 228–9

COMPANION PLANTS see pages 152 349 404

Cistus ROCK ROSE

Found on dry, rocky areas in the Canary Islands, North Africa and South Europe, the showy blooms of rock roses last for only a day once open. In the early summer, though, the shrubs are smothered with colour.

They require hot, dry and rather barren sites, faring badly on fertile sites as they grow too fast and are hit by even the mildest winters. They are great in rockeries and sun-facing banks, and look good in containers on patios.

White is the main colour, then pink, but most have petals marked with various blotches. The individual bloom has five wide spreading petals which resemble those of the wild roses.

The simplest method of propagation is from softwood or semi-ripe cuttings in the summer, but they can also be layered.

The foliage can look attractive, especially that of *Cistus dansereaui* 'Decumbens', which has oblong-shaped, sticky, dark green leaves, complementing its pretty white flowers with yellow and crimson at the base of each petal.

As rock roses are fast growing plants, fairly short-lived and not particularly hardy, it is often not worth continuing to prune back old, leggy plants; rather, they would be better replaced with annual backups kept over winter in a frost-free environment.

They tolerate coastal exposure, windy sites and thrive on a wide range of soils.

Cistus dansereaui 'Decumbens'

MOISTURE	Does not require much watering
SITE/LIGHT	Enjoys any well-drained soil in a sunny position
GENERAL CARE	Remove dead wood and winter damage
PESTS & DISEASES	Generally trouble free

SHRUBS
see also
187

COMPANION PLANTS
see pages
275
379
388

Clematis OLD MAN'S BEARD

With well over 1,500 species, hybrids and cultivars to choose from, clematis offers unparalleled variety to the gardener. It can be used to enhance any garden, as it is one of the most versatile of all climbing plants.

Gardening with clematis is a rewarding experience for any gardener because the variety in colour and form of the plant is remarkable – in some years over 100 new varieties have been added. There are red, purple, white, yellow and blue clematis, and flowers that are bell-shaped, tubular, starry, single, double, reflexed or the size of dinner plates. The breathtakingly colourful display of clematis can be simply stunning. Indeed, there

Clematis recta

Clematis texensis 'The First Lady'

SHRUBS
see also
292

COMPANION PLANTS
see pages
390–1

Clematis montana rubens

are only a few months in the year when there is not a species of clematis flowering in the garden. The different qualities and seasonal displays which characterize the various species shine through from their original roots in the wild – from the mountains of Europe or North America, to areas around the Mediterranean.

Clematis are versatile enough to grow in window boxes, pots, in tubs on patios, on trellises, on decks, or even in a classic herbaceous border. Many are hardy, while others – like the hybrids – often need sheltered, sunny aspects.

Generally, clematis are fast growers, but there is a tendency for newer cultivars to be less vigorous and more suitable for today's smaller gardens. In fact, 'selective breeding' is targeting the plants that produce the most flowers and which are grown exclusively in small pots. Growth rates may vary across Europe and North America, while gardeners in New

Clematis 'Mrs Cholmondeley'

SHRUBS
see also
_294_

COMPANION PLANTS
see pages
_315_

Clematis 'Prince Charles'

Zealand can expect up to 20 per cent extra growth than is recommended elsewhere.

Among the varieties pictured in these pages, *Clematis recta*, native to southern Europe, has several known cultivars and subspecies, including some with dark foliage. It is perfect for planting in the herbaceous border and, with the help of adjacent plants or support, can grow to around 1.5m

Clematis tangutica

(5ft). Late flowering, the scent of *C. recta* attracts colourful butterflies and useful hoverflies, whose larvae feed on those troublesome aphids which will try and attack the plant. As an herbaceous clematis, this species dies back to ground level during the winter.

C. 'Mrs Cholmondeley' is an ideal candidate for a container and will scramble to about 1.5m (5ft) along trellises. As long as it is well watered, this variety will produce quite a number of large blue-purple flowers, each up to 20cm (8in) across. It is in flower by the early summer and continues flowering sporadically until late summer.

SHRUBS* *see also* *323

COMPANION PLANTS* *see pages* *293

If taken out of the container after a few years, it will double its size and do very nicely trained up a tripod within an herbaceous border. After flowering, perhaps after an early autumn flush of flowers, prune it well back to a pair of fat buds, so that in the following spring these will become the lead shoots that will start the plant off for the new season.

Clematis integrifolia

C. 'Prince Charles' has a bluish-purple flower that is somewhat variable in colour, depending on how much sunlight the plant receives. It has characteristic yellow anthers, and the flowers are borne freely, giving the impression they are nodding. The flowers are up to 10cm (4in) across and the plant grows energetically up to 2.5m (8ft).

Clematis 'Natacha'

As a general rule, keep all clematis well watered before and during flowering.

Prune plants regularly according to their flowering season and specific requirements.

MOISTURE	Water regularly before and during flowering
SITE/LIGHT	A sun-lover which is happy in any well-drained soil
GENERAL CARE	Mulch all clematis in late winter with compost or manure
PESTS & DISEASES	Prone to clematis wilt, aphids and whiteflies

SHRUBS
see also
422

COMPANION PLANTS
see pages
299
367

Cleome SPIDER FLOWER

The spider flower is a tall, frost-tender annual with large heads of spidery flowers with long stamens, in shades of pink and red plus white, and large hand-shaped leaves.

Cleome originate in sandy plains and mountain valleys in tropical and sub-tropical zones worldwide.

Grow in a mixed or sub-tropical summer flower border, creating an exotic effect. The flowers are suitable for cutting in the summer. Dead-head regularly and ensure that there is plenty of water for the plants in dry conditions.

Propagate from seed in spring under cover. Once the danger of frost has gone, harden the young plants off before planting out.

Cleome speciosa

C. hassleriana 'Sparkler Lavender'

The purple-flowered *Cleome hassleriana* 'Sparkler Lavender' and pure white *C. speciosa* are particularly attractive varieties.

MOISTURE	Do not allow to dry out and water regularly when hot
SITE/LIGHT	Enjoys fertile, preferably sandy, well-drained soil in the sun
GENERAL CARE	Dead-head regularly to prolong flowering
PESTS & DISEASES	Prone to aphids

FLOWERS see also 145

COMPANION PLANTS see pages 262–3 363

Clerodendrum CHANCE TREE

A genus of around 400 species mainly found in woodland in tropical and sub-tropical regions in Africa and Asia. These shrubs are usually grown for their showy, often fragrant, flowers which are produced late in the summer.

Clerodendrum is suitable for warm borders in the garden and climbers can be trained over a trellis or other support.

Clerodendrum bungei

The glory flower, *Clerodendrum bungei,* is a sub-shrub, 2m (6ft) high, which is often cut back to ground level in all but the mildest winters, producing fragrant, purplish-red blooms with large heart-shaped leaves. *C. trichotomum* and its variety *fargesii* are taller growing, making 3–6m (10–20ft) in time. The fragrant flowers have white petals subtended by the reddish purple calyx with prominent stamens.

Propagate by softwood and semi-hardwood cuttings, by root cuttings, by division of suckers and by seed.

All Clerodendrum like a well drained fertile soil, in sunny positions.

Clerodendrum trichotomum

MOISTURE	Keep moist and do not allow to dry out
SITE/LIGHT	Prefers a sunny site in well-drained, fertile soil
GENERAL CARE	Feed or mulch to maintain soil fertility
PESTS & DISEASES	Relatively trouble free

SHRUBS see also 300

COMPANION PLANTS see pages 170 220 425

Clethra LILY-OF-THE-VALLEY TREE

Clethra are flowering shrubs that carry attractive, bell-shaped blooms that produce a wonderful spicy fragrance able to fill the garden with its perfume. They are very suitable sited in a woodland garden.

Also known as white alder or summer-sweet, another feature of Clethra is that they flower towards the end of summer, at a time when most shrubs have finished flowering. An added attraction for some species is their peeling bark.

Propagate from seed, the best method for *Clethra delavayi*, or by division of root suckers (*C. alnifolia*) or from semi-hardwood cuttings taken with a heel in mid- to late summer.

Some evergreen species are less hardy than the two deciduous ones mentioned. Evergreens require a more sheltered site, preferably in the shade.

Clethra are not suitable for dry sandy soils, nor for those containing even a hint of lime or chalk.

Clethra alnifolia 'Rosea'

MOISTURE	Enjoys relatively moist conditions
SITE/LIGHT	Prefers the semi-shade
GENERAL CARE	Mulch regularly to retain organic-rich soil
PESTS & DISEASES	Generally trouble free

SHRUBS
***see also* 287**

***COMPANION PLANTS* see pages 384–5**

Colchicum AUTUMN CROCUS

These hardy corms, also known as naked ladies, are grown for their large, crocus-like flowers in autumn, in shades of pink or purple, plus white. The large leaves appear in spring and need plenty of space to develop.

Colchicum speciosum

Colchicum are best grown around shrubs in a mixed border or around deciduous trees in a lawn. They can be easily naturalized in long grass. Smaller species are suitable for a rock garden or a scree bed. All parts of the plant are harmful if ingested and may cause mild skin irritation.

Propagate by separating corms during summer dormancy.

Colchicum speciosum is a vigorous grower producing attractive goblet-shaped, pale pink flowers with oblong-shaped leaves.

Colchicum speciosum

Half-hardy species, such as *C. boissieri*, are best kept in a bulb frame or alpine house. Be careful to avoid the foliage and flowers when watering, and keep completely dry when dormant.

MOISTURE	Water moderately during growth
SITE/LIGHT	Enjoys a sunny position in well-drained soil
GENERAL CARE	Apply low-nitrogen liquid fertilizer at start of growth
PESTS & DISEASES	Prone to grey mould, slugs and snails

FLOWERS
see also
223

COMPANION PLANTS
see pages
163
199

Convallaria LILY-OF-THE-VALLEY

A well-loved, hardy, carpeting herbaceous perennial spreading vigorously from rhizomes. The tiny bell-shaped flowers are highly scented and are produced through a mass of fresh green oval leaves.

Use as ground cover in moist, shady situations such as around and beneath shrubs or in a woodland garden. *Convallaria majalis* does well in full shade, producing waxy white flowers.

Propagate in autumn by teasing the rhizomes apart and replanting, keeping moist until established. Seeds can be sown in containers in a cold frame or greenhouse. Remove the flesh from the seeds before sowing.

Lily-of-the-valley benefits from a permanent mulch of organic matter such as composted chipped bark or leafmould applied in autumn. The flowers are ideal for cutting.

The seeds of *C. majalis* can cause mild stomach upsets if accidentally eaten.

Lily-of-the-valley is only really affected by grey mould.

Convallaria majalis

MOISTURE	Keep moist and do not allow to dry out
SITE/LIGHT	Position in humus-rich soil in full or partial shade
GENERAL CARE	Top-dress with leafmould in autumn
PESTS & DISEASES	Prone to grey mould (botrytis)

FLOWERS *see also* 310

COMPANION PLANTS *see pages* 285 380

Convolvulus BINDWEED

Not to be compared with the notorious weed, ornamental bindweeds are desirable plants. All produce characteristic flaring, trumpet-shaped flowers.

Convolvulus cneorum

Frost-hardy *Convolvulus sabatius,* a perennial with trailing stems, is a good rock-garden or container plant. The pots can be moved into an unheated greenhouse if winters are excessively wet and cold. The hardy annual *C. tricolor* has a somewhat spreading habit and is suitable for the front of mixed borders. they are good plants for infertile soils.

Propagate in spring, *C. sabatius* by division, *C. tricolor* from seed in flowering positions, and *C. cneorum* by semi-hardwood cuttings in summer or by seed in spring.

C. cneorum can be tender and is not particularly long lived. The evergreen foliage is covered with silky hairs, giving it a silvery appearance and its common name, silverbush. It needs a hot, dry and well-drained site for best effect.

Convolvulus sabatius

MOISTURE	Water freely during growth and keep moist in winter
SITE/LIGHT	Full sun in most well-drained soils
GENERAL CARE	Dead-head annuals to prolong flowering
PESTS & DISEASES	Relatively trouble free

SHRUBS see also 292

COMPANION PLANTS see pages 201–4 227

Cordyline CABBAGE PALM

Neither cabbage-like nor a palm, this fast-growing tree has become more popular over the years, even for more temperate regions, possibly due to milder winters.

A bushy head of long, narrow leaves tops a corky trunk. It is very tolerant of salty winds, making it an excellent choice for a coastal garden. Flowers blossom into large, white fragrant clusters. After flowering, the head of foliage will divide into two or three branches, which will grow into a huge mass.

Cordyline australis 'Red Star'

Trees can reach 5–6m (15–20ft). The variegated form *Cordyline australis* 'Albertii' is often available from garden centres or specialist nurseries, although the green variety is far superior and much hardier. *C. australis* 'Red Star' has very attractive leaves.

Propagation is best by rooting well-established suckers in spring, although seed can be sown in spring.

C. australis can be grown in pots and containers, in which they should remain for one season only and then be planted in the ground. Grow in fertile, well-drained soil in the full sun or partial shade.

Regular brown-bitting is necessary to keep it looking its best.

MOISTURE	Too much moisture will cause root rot
SITE/LIGHT	Prefers sun or light shade in good quality loam
GENERAL CARE	Consider winter wrapping for protection
PESTS & DISEASES	Trouble free outside but prone to red spider mite indoors

***SHRUBS* see also 441**

***COMPANION PLANTS* see pages 275 285 294**

Coreopsis TICKSEED

Hardy herbaceous perennials include *Coreopsis* 'Goldfink', *C. verticillata* and *C. grandiflora*, although gardeners usually grow the latter as an annual. *C. tinctoria* is a true hardy annual and is very useful for filling gaps in mixed borders.

All have colourful daisy flowers and are ideal for prairie-style borders, combined with ornamental grasses. *C. verticillata* 'Grandiflora' has extremely attractive dark yellow pointed flowerheads. Tickseeds are ideal for ordinary mixed borders where they associate well with spiky plants such as delphiniums. A good plant for cut flowers. Taller cultivars, such as *C. verticillata* 'Moonbeam', will need some support.

Coreopsis verticillata 'Grandiflora'

Coreopsis verticillata 'Moonbeam'

Raise annuals from seed in spring, in flowering positions; perennials under glass in winter. Propagate perennials by division in spring.

MOISTURE	Water moderately
SITE/LIGHT	Enjoys fertile soil with good drainage in sun or partial shade
GENERAL CARE	Good for cut flowers and attracts bees
PESTS & DISEASES	Prone to slugs and snails

FLOWERS see also 159

COMPANION PLANTS see pages 214 232 355

Cornus DOGWOOD

This large group of plants includes deciduous shrubs and small trees. Shrubby dogwoods are grown mainly for their twig colour, but are also attractive with their elegant habit, fruits, star-shaped flowers and foliage.

Dogwoods are useful wherever winter twig colour or summer foliage is required. They look good by the side of ponds where the winter stems can be reflected in the water, or as a specimen plant in the centre of a lawn. They thrive on heavy wet sites, but will grow on a wide range of soils, including shallow chalk or limy soils.

Cornus stolonifera 'Flaviramea'

They can be easily propagated from 20cm (8in) lengths of stem inserted as hardwood cuttings.

Cornus kousa var. *chinensis* 'Satomi'

Bracts change colour in autumn and make a vivid display towards the end of the winter, from bright crimson in *Cornus alba* 'Sibirica', to yellow to olive-green in *C. stolonifera* 'Flaviramea'. *C. kousa* var. *chinensis* 'Satomi' has dark pink bracts and red-purple autumn foliage.

MOISTURE	Prefers fairly wet, damp conditions
SITE/LIGHT	Relatively unfussy but grows best in moderate shade
GENERAL CARE	Mulch during summer to keep soil moist
PESTS & DISEASES	Trouble free

SHRUBS see also 307

COMPANION PLANTS see pages 244 323 395

Cortaderia PAMPAS GRASS

These hardy perennials are among the largest of the ornamental grasses, forming clumps of evergreen, arching leaves with very sharp edges.

The traditional use of pampas grass is as a lone specimen in a lawn, making an imposing addition to any garden. But modern uses include mixed borders, combined with daisy-flowered perennials and shrubs noted for autumn leaf colour, and gravel areas.

In early spring, cut out all dead leaves and stems – wear pruning gloves to avoid cuts from the leaf edges. Cutting back can be quite savage – even as low as ground level every other year – but will improve older clumps. New foliage will soon grow up again. Propagate by division in spring.

Cortaderia selloana is very forgiving of most sites, provided it is given shelter from strong winds. However, pampas grass will perform much better if grown in rich, moist loam with adequate irrigation.

Cortaderia selloana

MOISTURE	Ensure it is kept adequately moist
SITE/LIGHT	A sunny, sheltered site in rich, well-drained loam
GENERAL CARE	Cut off dead plumes after flowering has finished
PESTS & DISEASES	Relatively trouble free

***SHRUBS* see also 162**

***COMPANION PLANTS* see pages 212 278**

Corydalis

Dwarf hardy perennials of varied habit and needs. *Corydalis flexuosa* is best sited in partially shady conditions such as a woodland garden or beneath large deciduous shrubs, while *C. lutea* is ideal for a sunny rock garden or bank, or the front of a mixed border.

C. flexuosa, with its gorgeous brilliant blue flowers, becomes dormant in summer, while *C. lutea*, with its golden yellow blooms, is evergreen. Both have attractive ferny foliage.

C. solida, known as fumewort, is a perennial with beautiful pink to red flowers in spring. It blends well with *Dicentra spectabilis* (bleeding heart).

Corydalis can be propagated by division in autumn or from seed when ripe in a cold frame. Some species need a dry dormant period in summer and protection from excessive wet in the winter.

Corydalis solida

Corydalis flexuosa 'China Blue'

MOISTURE	Keep moist but not excessively wet
SITE/LIGHT	Relatively fertile, well-drained soil in sun to partial shade
GENERAL CARE	Grow shade lovers in a peat bank or woodland area
PESTS & DISEASES	Prone to slugs, snails and aphids

FLOWERS see also 150

COMPANION PLANTS see pages 236 258 329–30

Corylopsis FLOWERING HAZEL

This plant makes a beautiful shrub for any site with dappled shade. Flowering hazels have primrose yellow flowers, which are highly fragrant, flooding the garden with a wonderful aroma.

The shrubs are ideally suited to a woodland garden or in a shrub border, as they prefer

Corylopsis sinensis

some shade and also a degree of shelter from cold dry winds. *Corylopsis pauciflora* carries blooms in few flowered racemes but in such large numbers that they make a stronger and slightly earlier floral display than *C. sinensis*.

Corylopsis can be propagated from the shiny black seeds or from softwood or semi-hardwood cuttings in summer. They can also be layered.

Corylopsis prefer moisture retentive soils that are fertile and acidic to neutral. *C. pauciflora* tolerates a moderately deep chalk soil, although on shallow chalk soils the plant will become chlorotic. However, *C. sinensis* and the other species in the genus will not thrive in these conditions.

Corylopsis pauciflora

MOISTURE	Keep fairly moist
SITE/LIGHT	Prefers light to moderate shade and in a sheltered site
GENERAL CARE	Mulch to conserve water during dry spells
PESTS & DISEASES	Generally trouble free

SHRUBS see also 435

COMPANION PLANTS see pages 382 390–1

Corylus HAZEL

Hazels are most often grown for their attractive foliage, as well as their yellow male catkins. Larger species or cultivars make excellent specimen trees for a garden.

The male catkins open during the late winter, lasting into early spring. The female flowers are fairly small, comprising crimson stigmas which only just poke out from a green bud.

Corylus avellana 'Contorta' is an interesting form with twisted branches, which has lost the ability to grow shoots in a straight line.

Corylus avellana

Corylus avellana 'Contorta'

Hazels can be propagated by seed that is best sown fresh or by layering.

C. avellana and *C. maxima* are shrubs, reaching around 6–8m (20–27ft) and are usually multi-stemmed. On the other hand the Turkish hazel, *C. colurna*, is a tree with a single straight bole, making 15m (50ft).

Some hazels, such as cultivars of *C. avellana* and *C. maxima*, produce nuts that are edible.

MOISTURE	No particular watering requirements once established
SITE/LIGHT	Sun to partial shade in well-drained soil, even chalky soil
GENERAL CARE	Give coloured-leaf variants as much sun as possible
PESTS & DISEASES	Prone to caterpillars, mites, aphids and honey fungus

TREES see also 381

COMPANION PLANTS see pages 196 435

Cosmos

Cosmos can be either annual or perennial plants. *Cosmos atrosanguineus* is a tuberous, frost-hardy herbaceous perennial while *C. bipinnatus* and *C. sulphureus* cultivars are annuals – one half-hardy and the other tender, respectively.

All Cosmos plants have ferny foliage and daisy-like flowers. They are best grown in mixed borders with ornamental grasses and other daisy-flowered plants. *Cosmos atrosanguineus* looks particularly good grown in a container on the patio.

Cosmos sulphureus 'Sunny Gold'

Cosmos atrosanguineus

Propagate in spring; annuals from seed under glass and *C. atrosanguineus* from basal cuttings.

Winter tubers of *C. atrosanguineus* under glass when the weather is severe. These plants are prone to aphids, grey mould, slugs and snails.

MOISTURE	Keep plants moist at all times
SITE/LIGHT	Enjoys full sun in well-drained soil
GENERAL CARE	Dead-head regularly to prolong flowering
PESTS & DISEASES	Prone to aphids, grey mould, slugs and snails

FLOWERS
see also
278

COMPANION PLANTS
see pages
193
240

Cotinus SMOKE TREE

Smoke trees are deciduous shrubs that are often grown for their reddish-purple, slightly rounded leaves. The common name comes from the way in which the bushes are smothered by filament-like flowers from early summer onwards.

Most cultivated forms have purple foliage, with the flower stalks also having a purplish tinge. In their naturalised green form they start off a shade of fawn and end as smoky-grey. In the autumn, colour changes to a strong, vivid red and even orange-red in some forms. They look impressive in a shrub border or as a specimen plant.

Propagate by semi-hardwood cuttings with a heel of older wood in summer, by layering and by seed.

Cotinus coggygria 'Royal Purple' bears red-purple foliage and *C.* 'Grace' is a bushy shrub or small tree with leaves turning a delicious translucent red in autumn.

Do not overfeed or plant on very fertile sites as this will affect the autumn colour.

Cotinus coggygria 'Royal Purple'

Cotinus 'Grace'

MOISTURE	Keep shrubs moist
SITE/LIGHT	Tolerant of any well-drained soil in full sun
GENERAL CARE	Prune only to remove damaged stems
PESTS & DISEASES	Prone to powdery mildew and verticillium wilt

SHRUBS *see also* 170

COMPANION PLANTS *see pages* 253 275 424

Cotoneaster

Cotoneaster is a genus of mainly evergreen, with a few deciduous, shrubs which can even make small trees. Most forms have masses of white to light pink flowers, which, along with their berrying fruits, make them attractive to bees and birds.

Cotoneasters have lots of uses in the garden, including providing winter food for many birds. They are excellent in the shrub bed, especially *Cotoneaster salicifolius*, as an evergreen screen or trained against a wall or fence, such as *C. horizontalis*. The deciduous species can produce superb autumn colour, such as *C. dielsianus*.

Cotoneaster salicifolius

Cotoneaster horizontalis

Propagate by semi-hardwood cuttings taken in summer, or from seed. However, seed can take up to five years to germinate.

Cotoneaster grows in almost any well-drained soil, including chalky ones and acidic sands. Deciduous species prefer full sun, with larger evergreens thriving both in the full sun or partial shade. Give dwarf evergreens a sunny site to encourage fruiting. Evergreens need protection from cold, dry winds in areas with long periods below freezing.

MOISTURE	Fairly drought tolerant once established
SITE/LIGHT	A sun-lover which is happy in any well-drained soil
GENERAL CARE	Tolerates pruning and trimming back
PESTS & DISEASES	Prone to fireblight, honey fungus and silver leaf

SHRUBS see also 379

COMPANION PLANTS see pages 157 294 323

Crataegus MAY or HAWTHORN

Hawthorns are particularly attractive small flowering trees. *Crataegus monogyna*, especially the wild white form, makes a domed crown with hanging branches full with clusters of white flowers, which are then followed by maroon-red fruits in autumn.

Flowers can be scented, and some cultivars of *C. monogyna* (May), such as 'Biflora' (sometimes known as 'Glastonbury Thorn'), produces fragrant white flowers during mild winters, as well as a flush in late spring. The forms of *C. laevigata*, also known as the Midland hawthorn, produce pink or scarlet, single or double flowers and make attractive small trees.

Hawthorns can be propagated by seed, taking two or more years to germinate, or by grafting.

All have thorns to a greater or lesser extent and love the sun. They will grow just the same in moderate shade, but may not flower as well. They tolerate all soils except wet ones, and are happy on clays and chalky soils.

Crataegus laevigata 'Rosea Flore Pleno'

MOISTURE	Keep moist but avoid overwatering
SITE/LIGHT	Tolerates most well-drained soils in full sun to light shade
GENERAL CARE	Clip back to maintain shape – and beware of the thorns!
PESTS & DISEASES	Prone to various insect and fungal problems

TREES see also 332

COMPANION PLANTS see pages 265 329–30 382

Crocosmia MONTBRETIA

These hardy herbaceous perennials grow from corms and are valued for their brilliantly coloured, somewhat funnel-shaped flowers. They produce clumps of erect, sword-shaped or grassy leaves.

Originating from grassland in South Africa, montbretias are an excellent flower to brighten any garden border. Grow montbretias in mixed borders with other late-flowering perennials. Good in sub-tropical plantings, especially *Crocosmia* 'Lucifer'. They also look good planted among ornamental grasses. Flowers can be cut and arranged indoors.

Propagate by division in spring or sow seed in containers in a cold frame as soon as the seeds are ripe.

Provide a permanent organic mulch for montbretias in hard-winter areas. Some species will need twiggy sticks to support the foliage which can flop in wet weather, smothering nearby plants. Congested clumps should be divided in spring.

Crocosmia 'Lucifer'

MOISTURE	Keep the plants moist
SITE/LIGHT	Deep, humus-rich, well-drained soil in sun or partial shade
GENERAL CARE	Lift and divide congested clumps in spring to help vigour
PESTS & DISEASES	Red spider mites may be a problem

***FLOWERS* see also 186**

***COMPANION PLANTS* see pages 138 141 355**

Crocus

Crocuses are dwarf in habit, with most being hardy. Flowers are similar, irrespective of species, being wine-glass shaped and opening best in full sun. Some crocuses flower in autumn, others in winter or spring.

All are most effective when planted in bold, informal drifts. They can be grown at the front of mixed borders and around the base of deciduous trees, especially the large-flowered Dutch crocuses like *Crocus* 'Jeanne d'Arc' and *C.* 'Pickwick'. Small-flowered kinds, such as the *C.* Chrysanthus hybrids 'Blue Pearl' and 'E. A. Bowles', are good for rock gardens. Some are suitable for naturalizing in short grass, particularly *C. speciosus* and *C. tommasinianus*.

Crocus 'Jeanne d'Arc'

Crocus tommasinianus

Propagate by removing and replanting cormlets while parent corms are dormant. Some species, such as *C. tommasinianus*, self-seed prolifically.

MOISTURE	Water freely during the growing season
SITE/LIGHT	Most enjoy full to light shade in fertile, well-drained soil
GENERAL CARE	Some species need a dry summer dormancy
PESTS & DISEASES	Prone to mice, squirrels, birds and corm rot in storage

FLOWERS *see also* 208

COMPANION PLANTS *see pages* 139–40 251 213

Cuphea

These tender sub-shrubs are usually grown as annuals. They are neat, bushy plants, producing masses of brilliantly coloured tubular flowers throughout the summer.

Cuphea ignea

Used in summer bedding schemes, including sub-tropical displays, and in containers such as patio tubs and window boxes, Cupheas provide a pleasing display over many months, although some species may be shorter lived than others.

Cupheas mix effectively with purple verbenas, as well as with many other summer bedding plants. *Cuphea llavea* bears pretty vermilion flowers in the early summer. *C. ignea* has cigar-shaped flowers.

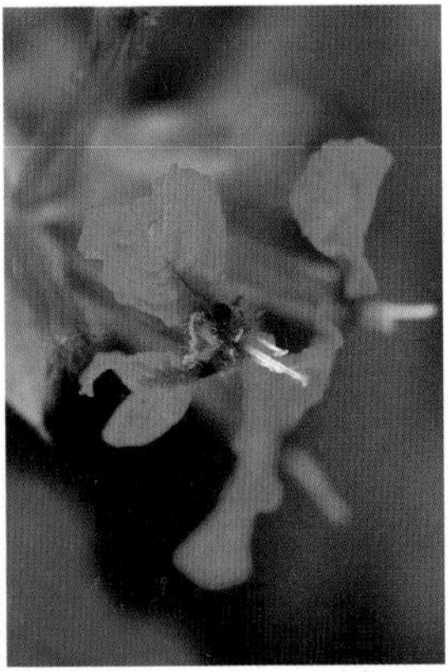
Cuphea llavea 'Tiny Mice'

Raise plants from seed sown under glass in early spring. Plants can also be propagated from cuttings of young shoots in spring.

In the growing season, make sure they are well watered and apply a liquid fertilizer every three or four weeks. Water sparingly during the winter.

MOISTURE	Water well in growing season, sparingly in winter
SITE/LIGHT	A sunny site in moderately fertile soil with good drainage
GENERAL CARE	Apply a liquid fertilizer regularly during growing season
PESTS & DISEASES	Prone to aphids and whiteflies

FLOWERS see also 262–3

COMPANION PLANTS see pages 201–4 350 433

Cupressus CYPRESS

Cypresses are evergreen, coniferous trees which are tolerant of drought and chalky soils. Mature bark often peels off into curling scales. The cones can take two years to ripen. As well as making excellent specimen trees, they can be used as a hedge or screen.

Cupressus sempervirens is mainly grown as the narrow crowned form typical of the Mediterranean landscape. *C. macrocarpa* is a conical, spiky-topped tree, eventually growing up to 30m (100ft) high over many years. It needs regular and careful trimming if it is to be used as a hedging plant. 'Goldcrest' and 'Golden Pillar' are two foliage forms.

Cupressus macrocarpa 'Goldcrest'

Cypresses can all be grown from cuttings taken in late summer. Plant them out as small trees and grow in pots, as the root systems are wide ranging and they do not transplant well.

The hardiest cypress is the Nootka cypress (*C. nootkatensis*). It occurs in areas with high winter snowfall and tolerates wet soils. The cones ripen in the second year but usually remain on the tree.

The Leyland cypress is a hybrid between *C. macrocarpa* and *C. nootkatensis* and is usually called *Cupressocyparis leylandii*.

MOISTURE	Once established does not require regular watering
SITE/LIGHT	Prefers a sunny site in well-drained, acidic to alkaline soil
GENERAL CARE	When pruning, do not clip into brown branches
PESTS & DISEASES	Prone to phytophthora root rot and corynium canker

TREES see also 191

COMPANION PLANTS see pages 178 375 420

Cyclamen SOWBREAD

Cyclamen are tuberous perennials, all the species described here being hardy. The flowers of these miniature plants have swept-back petals and the rounded or heart-shaped leaves, often patterned with silver, make attractive carpets.

These are ideal plants for rock gardens, woodland gardens and for planting in the partial shade of deciduous shrubs. Plant them in generous drifts to make the most of their attractive blooms. *Cyclamen coum* produce leaves that are often patterned with silver.

Propagate Cyclamen from seed sown as soon as ripe and germinated in a cold frame. The species *C. hederifolium* self-seeds prolifically.

Cyclamen can be permanently mulched with leafmould, applied when dormant.

The main problems are mice, squirrels and vine weevil larvae.

Cyclamen coum

MOISTURE	Keep moist but not too wet; do not allow to dry out
SITE/LIGHT	Enjoys partial shade in fertile soil
GENERAL CARE	Mulch regularly or apply a liquid fertilizer
PESTS & DISEASES	Prone to vine weevil larvae, mice and squirrels

FLOWERS see also 236

COMPANION PLANTS see pages 139–40 236 310

Cytisus BROOMS

Brooms are excellent shrubs for the mixed border, especially useful on hot dry banks. The lower growing forms with mound-shaped habits are very effective when trained to grow over a low wall.

Brooms produce abundant, pea-like flowers, followed by greenish pods. *Cytisus* 'Lena' produces impressive clusters of dark yellow flowers with stunning red backs. By contrast, *C. praecox* 'Warminster', also known as Warminster broom, has creamy yellow flowers.

Brooms can be raised from seed sown in spring, but taking cuttings is a much more reliable method for propagation.

They will grow on a wide range of soils but insist on good drainage if they are to thrive. As they are plants from hot, dry and sunny climates, they will not tolerate more than light shade and should ideally be sited in full sun.

Brooms are fast growing but short lived shrubs and do not respond to hard trimming.

Cytisus praecox 'Warminster'

Cytisus 'Lena'

MOISTURE	Water sparingly during winter
SITE/LIGHT	A sunny position in any soil with good drainage
GENERAL CARE	Trim, do not hard prune, only after flowering
PESTS & DISEASES	Relatively trouble free

SHRUBS see also 265

COMPANION PLANTS see pages 220 299 363

Dahlia

Dahlias are half-hardy herbaceous perennials with tuberous roots. Dahlias can be grouped into border or bedding cultivars that are propagated vegetatively, and those that are grown as annuals from seed.

Dahlia 'Bishop of Llandaff'

Dahlias are grown for their long and prolific display of flowers in summer and autumn. The border dahlias are tall and ideally suited to mixed borders, while the bedding cultivars are shorter and used for summer bedding or planting in patio tubs.

Flowers are classified according to form, such as Anemone-flowered, with crested blooms; Ball, with large ball-shaped flowers, such as *Dahlia* 'Stolze von Berlin; and Cactus, with double, spiky flowers, such as *D.* 'Yellow Happiness'. Others include Collerette, with an inner collar or ring of shorter petals;

Dahlia 'Dahlietta'

FLOWERS see also 199

COMPANION PLANTS see pages 186 365 396

Decorative, with wide-petalled, double flowers, such as *D.* 'Snowstorm'; Pompon, with small ball-shaped flowers; Semi-cactus, whose double flowers have pointed petals; Single, with one or two circles of petals; and Waterlily, with flattish flowers. The Miscellaneous group contains dahlias that do not fit into any

Dahlia 'Snowstorm'

Dahlia 'Stolze von Berlin'

Dahlia 'Yellow Happiness'

of the other groups, such as *D.* 'Bishop of Llandaff'. Dwarf dahlias grown as annuals from seed are ideal for summer bedding or patio containers.

All dahlias combine well with cannas, chrysanthemums, gladioli, petunias, salvias and verbenas. The flowers are ideal for cutting.

Propagate from basal stem cuttings in spring or plant out dormant tubers in mid-spring – large clumps can be divided. Raise annual types from seed under glass in early spring.

Pinch out tips of young plants to encourage branching. When flowering starts, liquid feed weekly with high-potash fertilizer. Dead-head all dahlias.

MOISTURE	Keep well watered in dry weather
SITE/LIGHT	Enjoys a sunny site with good drainage
GENERAL CARE	Support tall cultivars with canes or wooden stakes
PESTS & DISEASES	Prone to aphids, caterpillars, powdery mildew and slugs

***FLOWERS* see also 270**

***COMPANION PLANTS* see pages 262–3 433**

Danae ALEXANDRIAN LAUREL

Danae is a genus of clump-forming, shrub-like, evergreen perennials consisting of one species, *Danae racemosa*, originating in woodland in Turkey and Iran.

Danae racemosa

Danae racemosa, often classified as just an evergreen shrub, can be described as a mixture between a miniature bamboo and asparagus. The new shoots give the plant its asparagus look, sprouting up in mid- to late spring. Many shoots are sent out each spring which remain all year round. Larger clumps of these shoots start to form as the plant matures, giving the plants its bamboo appearance.

After a very warm summer, bright red berries will appear, usually during the early autumn. *D. racemosa* is a very slow grower, only reaching 1m (3ft) or so after about ten years.

It is easy to propagate either from fresh seed or by division in early spring.

D. racemosa is extremely useful for sites in the garden where little else will grow, as dark shade can be tolerated by this plant, as well as dry conditions. However, light shade in moist soil would be the preferred position. Old shoots should be cut back to ground level in the spring. Plants can also be grown in pots or containers, but vine weevil can be a problem.

MOISTURE	Although moist conditions are best, dry soil is acceptable
SITE/LIGHT	Light to deep shade in most soil types
GENERAL CARE	Generally maintenance free
PESTS & DISEASES	Trouble free in the ground, but vine weevil in pots

SHRUBS *see also* 381

COMPANION PLANTS *see pages* 155 185

Daphne

The flowers of most Daphne are fragrant and mainly white to mauvy-purple in colour, but yellow and yellow-green flowers also exist. They like slightly acidic to slightly alkaline soil, generally tolerating some lime.

The flowers are four-lobed and tubular. As well as being grown for their flowers, the foliage can also be a feature. Foliage is usually evergreen, but *Daphne mezereum* is deciduous, as are *D. bholua* and *D. burkwoodii.*

Daphne looks good in mixed borders, on rockeries and as specimen plants in tubs. Beware if children and pets use the garden as the berries and foliage are poisonous.

Propagate by seed sown as soon as it is ripe, but it may take longer than one year to germinate. Cuttings of semi-hardwood can be taken in summer and rooted in a closed frame. The suckering forms can be divided and grown on until well rooted. They can also be grafted in late winter.

In the garden, the more vigorous forms, such as *D. mezereum* and *D. laureola*, can be sited in light shade but Daphne mainly prefers a bright, sunny position. Mulch regularly to keep the roots cool and retain the moisture. Watch out for aphids, leaf spot and grey mould.

Daphne burkwoodii 'Astrid'

MOISTURE	Keep moist and do not allow to dry out
SITE/LIGHT	A sunny site with dappled shade and good drainage
GENERAL CARE	Mulch to keep the soil moist
PESTS & DISEASES	Prone to aphids, leaf spot, grey mould and viruses

SHRUBS see also 294

COMPANION PLANTS see pages 190 329–30 356

Delphinium

Delphiniums are mainly hardy herbaceous perennials but some are grown as annuals. Characterized by their spikes of flowers, they are split into several groups.

The Elatum Group (which includes 'Blue Nile') has fat spikes of flowers and is the most popular. The Belladonna Group (such as 'Casablanca') has loose, branching spikes. The Pacific Hybrids (including the Summer Skies Group) are rather like Elatum delphiniums but are grown as annuals. Delphiniums are ideal for mixed borders, including cottage-garden borders, and combine effectively with many other plants including roses (particularly shrub roses), and plants with flat heads of flowers such as achilleas.

Delphinium 'Blue Nile'

Delphinium 'Casablanca'

Raise annuals from seed under glass in early spring. Propagate Belladonna and Elatum cultivars from basal stem cuttings in spring.

The flowers are excellent for cutting. Tall delphiniums need canes for support, one cane per stem. Support shorter cultivars with twiggy sticks.

MOISTURE	Water well during dry periods
SITE/LIGHT	Enjoys a sunny site in fertile, well-drained soil
GENERAL CARE	Dead-head regularly and cut down all stems in autumn
PESTS & DISEASES	Prone to leaf spot, powdery mildew, slugs and snails

FLOWERS see also 270

COMPANION PLANTS see pages 141 155 390–1

Deutzia

This is a genus of mainly deciduous, flowering shrubs which have five-petalled, cup- to star-shaped flowers. Many mature species have attractive peeling bark.

The shrubs have particularly fragrant flowers which are borne in spring or early summer from buds on last summer's growth. The individual, showy flowers are around 1cm (½in) wide and carried in clusters, often sprouting above the arching shoots. Deutzia produces star-shaped hairs on all its parts, and in the ten stamens with winged stalks.

Propagation is by seed, sown in containers in a cold frame during the autumn, by softwood cuttings in summer or by hardwood cuttings rooted in the autumn.

Most forms are deciduous but some Chinese species are evergreen. They are suitable planted in a sheltered spot in the half shade or in an open sunny border.

Deutzia 'Strawberry Fields' is an early summer flowerer which produces pink blooms.

Deutzia 'Strawberry Fields'

MOISTURE	Keep well moist
SITE/LIGHT	Full sun to partial shade in well-drained soil
GENERAL CARE	Mulch regularly to keep soil moist
PESTS & DISEASES	Relatively trouble free

***SHRUBS* see also 177**

***COMPANION PLANTS* see pages 170 190 213**

Diánthus CARNATIONS or PINKS

A large group of perennials, annuals and biennials providing plants for various parts of the garden. The species mentioned here are all completely hardy. Sweet williams (*Dianthus barbatus*) are favourite biennials, much used in cottage-garden borders.

Carnations grown as annuals, such as *D. caryophyllus* and *D. chinensis* (Indian pink), make a good display in mixed borders or containers. With perennial Dianthus, some are alpines and suitable for rock gardens, including *D. alpinus* and 'La Bourboule'. Old-fashioned pinks, including 'Dad's Favourite' and 'Mrs Sinkins', are great for cottage-garden borders. Modern pinks including 'Doris', 'Joy' and 'Laced Monarch', and border carnations, such as 'Lavender Clove', are better for modern mixed borders.

Dianthus chinensis 'Strawberry Parfait'

All carnations are suitable for borders, and combine well with roses – particularly shrub roses – and with grey- or silver-leaved shrubs and perennials such as santolinas and artemisias respectively.

Raise annuals from seed in early spring under glass and sweet williams from seed in an outdoor seed bed in late spring to early summer. Propagate perennials from cuttings in summer.

Flowers are excellent for cutting and many are highly fragrant. All types are good for alkaline soils. Tall kinds may need the support of twiggy sticks. Dead-head regularly.

MOISTURE	Water moderately in the spring and summer
SITE/LIGHT	Full sun in mainly neutral to alkaline, well-drained soil
GENERAL CARE	Support taller forms with sticks
PESTS & DISEASES	Prone to aphids, leaf spot, slugs and snails

FLOWERS see also 199

COMPANION PLANTS see pages 272 390–1 398

Diascia

Diascia are frost-hardy, herbaceous perennials with a rather spreading habit. They produce masses of lobed, tubular flowers on upright stems over a long period.

Excellent for the front of mixed borders, banks and patio tubs or window boxes. Diascias combine well with alchemillas, cerinthes, eryngiums, lavenders and small bush or groundcover roses. *Diascia* 'Lilac Belle' is a free-flowering variety.

Propagate by division in spring or from semi-ripe cuttings in summer.

In colder areas, young plants need greenhouse protection in their first winter. Remove dead flowerheads regularly to ensure continuous flowering.

Diascia 'Lilac Belle'

MOISTURE	Keep moist and water during dry periods
SITE/LIGHT	A sun-lover which is happy in fertile, well-drained soil
GENERAL CARE	Put young plants under glass to protect in winter
PESTS & DISEASES	May be damaged by slugs and snails

FLOWERS *see also* **267**

COMPANION PLANTS *see pages* **306 390–1**

Dicentra

These are hardy, herbaceous perennials with attractive, divided, ferny foliage and dangling, heart-shaped flowers. Dicentras are among the best plants for the dappled shade of woodland gardens.

Dicentras associate well with spring or early summer flowering shrubs, as well as with woodland and shade-loving perennials such as ajugas, corydalis, epimediums and hostas, and also deciduous shrubs.

Dicentra spectabilis 'Alba'

Bleeding heart, *Dicentra spectabilis,* has an arching habit and has a more robust variety, 'Alba', producing white flowers.

Propagate by division, ideally as soon as plants become dormant in autumn.

Dicentras enjoy moist, preferably neutral or slightly alkaline soil. Keep mulched to ensure soil retains its moisture. Slugs and snails are the main problems.

Dicentra spectabilis

MOISTURE	Keep moist at all times
SITE/LIGHT	Generally prefer semi-shade in fertile, humus-rich soil
GENERAL CARE	Mulch regularly to maintain moisture and richness
PESTS & DISEASES	Prone to attacks from slugs

FLOWERS
see also
262–3

COMPANION PLANTS
see pages
215
243
285

Dicksonia TASMANIAN TREE FERN

Dicksonia is a genus of around 25 species of evergreen or semi-evergreen ferns. They make attractive specimen plants either outdoors or inside in a conservatory.

The tree fern is a stunning looking plant and is an excellent feature for any garden. *Dicksonia antarctica* starts to form a trunk only after five years. A thick, fibrous trunk is topped with large, deeply-cut fronds 2m (7ft) long. It is a slow grower, making only 30cm (1ft) every ten years, so patience is required to see it develop into a spectacular specimen tree.

For the really patient, these ferns can be propagated by sowing spores at 15–16°C (59–61°F) as soon as they are ripe.

This fern is extremely fussy about where it is situated. A sheltered, shady position away from the wind and also from anyone brushing past it is essential. Ideally, the trunk should be sprayed twice daily during the hot summer months.

Mild gardens are essential to keep it outside all-year-round. Otherwise, keep in a large pot and over-winter in a shady, cool conservatory.

Dicksonia antarctica

MOISTURE	Keep moist; spray twice a day during hot summers
SITE/LIGHT	Humid, sheltered and shady site in well-drained peat
GENERAL CARE	Irrigate regularly during the growing season
PESTS & DISEASES	Generally trouble free

SHRUBS see also 423

COMPANION PLANTS see pages 236 252 293

Digitalis FOXGLOVE

These plants are treated as hardy biennials, although some may live for a bit longer. Foxgloves are distinctive plants with spikes of longish, bell-like flowers. Being woodland plants, they look at home in the dappled shade of woodland gardens.

Alternatively, foxgloves can be grown in similar conditions in a shrub or mixed border, among large deciduous shrubs, where they will make a striking effect.

Digitalis purpurea

Digitalis purpurea Excelsior Hybrid

Propagate from seed sown in pots in a cold frame during late spring.

Digitalis purpurea Excelsior hybrids are particularly great for cut flowers. Remove dead flowerheads to prevent self-seeding.

MOISTURE	Does not like very wet or very dry conditions
SITE/LIGHT	Prefers humus-rich soil in partial shade
GENERAL CARE	Dead-head after flowering to prevent self-seeding
PESTS & DISEASES	Leaves are susceptible to leaf spot and powdery mildew

FLOWERS see also 232

COMPANION PLANTS see pages 243 252 280

Doronicum LEOPARD'S BANE

Hardy herbaceous perennials valued for their early colour, doronicums have cheerful, yellow daisy-like flowers carried above heart-shaped leaves.

Essentially mixed-border plants, doronicums also look at home in the dappled shade of a woodland garden and combine beautifully with blue-flowered perennials such as lungworts (pulmonaria) and corydalis, and with biennial forget-me-nots (myosotis). Other good companions are dicentras, as well as spring-flowering shrubs such as yellow kerrias and various white-flowered spiraeas.

The flowers are excellent for cutting.

Propagate by division in autumn, preferably early in the season.

Doronicum orientale 'Magnificum' produces golden yellow flowerheads 4–5cm (1½–2in) across in mid- to late spring.

Problems with Leopard's bane include leaf spot and powdery mildew. Overly wet soils, especially with *D. orientale* species, encourage the roots to rot.

Doronicum orientale 'Magnificum'

MOISTURE	Needs to be kept moist
SITE/LIGHT	Enjoys partial or dappled shade in humus-rich soil
GENERAL CARE	*D. orientale* prefers moist but well-drained soil
PESTS & DISEASES	Prone to leaf spot, powdery mildew and root rot

FLOWERS *see also* 267

COMPANION PLANTS *see pages* 215 298 341

Echinacea CONEFLOWER

A tall, upright, hardy herbaceous perennial, echinacea has large daisy-like flowers, each with a conspicuous, brownish, cone-shaped centre, carried on reddish stems.

An ideal plant for modern prairie-style borders. Mix it with ornamental grasses, asters (including Michaelmas daisies), late heleniums, helianthus, monardas, rudbeckias and golden rods (solidago). They are also good planted close to shrubs noted for autumn leaf colour, such as rhus (sumachs). When flowers are over, cut back the stems to encourage more blooms.

Propagate by division in spring or by root cuttings in winter.

Echinacea purpurea 'White Swan' produces large, white flowerheads with orange-brown centres, 11cm (4½in) across.

Coneflowers are not troubled by pests or diseases.

Echinacea purpurea 'White Swan'

MOISTURE	Keep moist but not overly wet
SITE/LIGHT	Deep, well-drained, humus-rich soil in the full sun
GENERAL CARE	Cut back stems after flowering
PESTS & DISEASES	Generally trouble free

FLOWERS *see also* 163

COMPANION PLANTS *see pages* 276 278 337

Echinops GLOBE THISTLE

Hardy herbaceous perennials, echinops are valued for their distinctive globe-shaped flowerheads. The grey-green spiny foliage is often deeply cut and is a further attraction.

Excellent subjects for mixed borders, they combine well with shrubs of all kinds, perennials such as flat-headed achilleas, and with ornamental grasses, including Miscanthus. Globe thistles, being reasonably unfussy plants, are also suited to more natural areas of the garden and will grow in infertile soils.

Echinops bannaticus 'Taplow Blue'

Echinops ritro

Propagate by division in spring or from root cuttings during winter.

The flowers can be dried for winter arrangements. Remove dead flowerheads to encourage further flowering.

Echinops ritro is a compact, perennial, producing metallic-blue flowerheads in late summer, which become a brighter blue when mature. *E. bannaticus* 'Taplow Blue' is one of the tallest varieties.

MOISTURE	Requires only little moisture in order to thrive
SITE/LIGHT	Best in fairly poor, well-drained soil in the full sun
GENERAL CARE	Dead-head to prevent self-seeding
PESTS & DISEASES	Prone to attack from aphids

FLOWERS see also 147

COMPANION PLANTS see pages 141 336 414

Echium VIPER'S BUGLOSS

This genus is a hardy biennial of branching habit, carrying spikes of bowl-shaped flowers, each surrounded with a conspicuous green calyx. Blue is probably the most popular colour, but there are cultivars available in other colours.

Viper's bugloss is suitable for filling gaps in mixed borders where it associates with many annual or perennial flowers, including poppies (papaver). It can also be used in patio tubs and window boxes.

Echium vulgare 'Blue Bedder' is an upright, bushy bristly biennial which has extremely attractive light blue flowers which become blueish pink towards the end of the season and is suitable for a wildflower garden.

Raise plants from seed sown under cover in early summer, winter young plants in a frost-free greenhouse and plant out in spring.

Slugs and snails are the main pests.

Echium vulgare 'Blue Bedder'

MOISTURE	Water freely in growth, but sparingly in winter
SITE/LIGHT	Loves a sunny site in fairly fertile soil with good drainage
GENERAL CARE	Winter young plants in a greenhouse for protection
PESTS & DISEASES	Prone to attack by slugs when young

FLOWERS see also 248

COMPANION PLANTS see pages 350 351 359

Epimedium BARRENWORT

Epimedium are hardy, herbaceous or evergreen perennials of dwarf habit, spreading vigorously by rhizomes. Heart-shaped leaves may take on autumn tints in some species, while spring foliage is often flushed with bronze.

Clusters of small bowl- or cup-shaped flowers appear through the leaves and come in various colours.

Epimedium x versicolor

Epimediums are excellent for ground cover in woodland gardens, under deciduous trees, or around large deciduous shrubs in a mixed border. A permanent organic mulch in hard-winter areas is beneficial. Cut down the old leaves of herbaceous species in late winter.

Propagate by separating the mats of rhizomes in autumn, or take rhizome cuttings in winter.

Epimedium grandiflorum 'Snow Queen' produces large, pure white flowers, whereas *E.* x *versicolor* has lovely pink and yellow flowers with red tints in mid- to late spring.

Epimedium grandiflorum 'Snow Queen'

MOISTURE	Keep plants moist
SITE/LIGHT	Provide shelter in partial shade in well-drained soil
GENERAL CARE	Provide a deep mulch for winter protection
PESTS & DISEASES	Prone to powdery mildew

FLOWERS *see also* 436

COMPANION PLANTS *see pages* 139–40 252 285

Erica HEATHER

Erica, with around 700 species of prostrate to tree-like shrubs, is similar to Calluna (p183) but differs in its flowers which have prominent, bell-shaped corollas.

Ericas are suitable for planting in drifts or with dwarf conifers, providing colour all year round. Most ericas like acidic conditions, on moist soil with good drainage. However, several species go against the family trend of disliking lime and will grow, even thrive, on chalky soil. These include *Erica carnea, E. darleyensis* and *E. erigena.* These species (which will also grow on acidic soils) are also useful in their flowering

Erica erigena 'Irish Dusk'

Erica vagans 'Mrs D.F. Maxwell'

period, from late autumn into mid-spring. *E. vagans* grows in any soil type.

Propagate ericas by semi-hardwood cuttings in summer.

They are sun-loving plants, disliking more than the lightest shade. They enjoy adequate soil moisture, but not boggy conditions.

Erica darleyensis 'Silberschmelze'

MOISTURE	Keep extremely moist but not saturated
SITE/LIGHT	A sun-lover, mainly preferring acidic, well-drained soil
GENERAL CARE	Grow more tender species under glass
PESTS & DISEASES	Prone to phytophthora root rot on wet sites

SHRUBS
see also
183

COMPANION PLANTS
see pages
135
191
196

Erysimum WALLFLOWER

Erysimums flower freely and come in many bright and pastel colours. They are traditionally used in spring bedding schemes along with tulips and forget-me-nots (myosotis).

Wallflowers are also useful gap fillers for mixed borders and are essential for cottage-garden borders. The dwarf compact kinds are suitable for patio containers and window boxes. Erysimums are ideal for alkaline soil, but avoid very wet conditions over winter which can lead to the roots rotting off.

Erysimum 'Apricot Twist'

Raise plants from seed sown in an outdoor seed bed in late spring or early summer. Transplant seedlings to a nursery bed. Plant young plants in flowering positions in autumn.

E. cheiri 'Harlequin'

The cultivars of *E.* x *allionii* (Siberian wallflower) and *E. cheiri* are hardy dwarf evergreen perennials grown as biennials. *E.* 'Apricot Twist', on the other hand, is a short-lived perennial. Wallflowers are prone to clubroot and affected plants should be discarded.

MOISTURE	Keep moist but not too wet
SITE/LIGHT	Lots of sun in fertile, well-drained, neutral or alkaline soil
GENERAL CARE	Clubroot is more likely to occur on acid soils
PESTS & DISEASES	Prone to leaf spot, powdery mildew, slugs and clubroot

FLOWERS see also 341

COMPANION PLANTS see pages 344–5 427–8 437

Erythronium DOG'S-TOOTH VIOLET

Erythroniums, also known as trout lily, are hardy dwarf bulbs producing nodding, lily-like flowers with swept-back petals. Long, wide leaves are also attractive and some species have dramatic bronze-marbled foliage.

As these bulbs like broken shade, grow them in a woodland garden, or below large deciduous shrubs or trees in a mixed border.

Propagate by division of clumps in summer or autumn while dormant.

Erythronium dens-canis

Erythronium californicum 'White Beauty'

Erythronium dens-canis (European dog's-tooth violet) is suitable for naturalizing in grass, provided it does not grow too long and dense. *E. californicum* 'White Beauty' is a vigorous grower, with a rusty red ring in the base of each flower.

Watch out for attack by slugs and snails.

MOISTURE	Do not allow to dry out
SITE/LIGHT	Humus-rich soil in dappled to light shade
GENERAL CARE	Keep bulbs slightly damp during storage
PESTS & DISEASES	Prone to damage from slugs and snails

FLOWERS see also 315

COMPANION PLANTS see pages 139–40 157 298

Escallonia

These evergreen shrubs flower over a long period, often lasting from summer well into autumn. Funnel-shaped flowers are carried at the ends of the current season's shoots, in colours ranging from white to deep pink.

Escallonia foliage is often aromatic when touched and is glossy green in all forms. They are ideal for coastal sites and milder areas, and can be used as specimen

Escallonia rubra var. *macrantha*

shrubs, in shrub beds or trained up against a wall. They also make excellent hedges and windbreaks.

Propagate by seed and by most forms of cuttings – softwood in early summer, semi-hardwood in later summer and hardwood cuttings in a frame in autumn.

Escallonia rubra var. *macrantha* is a vigorous grower that can reach up to 4m (13ft). Conversely, *E.* 'Pride of Donard' is a compact variety, only making 1.5m (5ft). Most plants tolerate shallow chalk soils and medium to heavy clay soils.

Escallonia 'Pride of Donard'

MOISTURE	Keep moist and do not allow to dry out
SITE/LIGHT	Sun or light shade in any well-drained soil
GENERAL CARE	Apply a good mulch to retain moisture
PESTS & DISEASES	Relatively trouble free

SHRUBS see also 417

COMPANION PLANTS see pages 262–3 287 354

Eschscholzia CALIFORNIA POPPY

These hardy annuals have brilliantly coloured bowl-shaped flowers and attractive pale or grey-green ferny foliage. These slim, dwarf plants can be used to fill gaps in a mixed border and for growing in gravel areas and on rock gardens.

Eschscholzia californica hybrids

These flowers combine well with small ornamental grasses, brachyscome, cerinthes and felicias. They are particularly good for infertile, dry soils. The flowers need direct sun to fully open.

Propagate from seed sown in flowering positions in spring or early autumn. Make successive sowings several weeks apart for a long display.

Eschscholzia californica varieties have attractive ferny foliage to complement the exquisite blooms.

Eschscholzia californica

MOISTURE	Do not require excess watering
SITE/LIGHT	A sun-lover which is happy in poor, well-drained soil
GENERAL CARE	Excellent for cut flowers
PESTS & DISEASES	Generally trouble free

FLOWERS
see also
359

COMPANION PLANTS
see pages
175
255
336

Eucalyptus GUM TREE

Originating from Australia, most species are not hardy but many can still be grown in cooler climates and make excellent, fast-growing specimen trees.

Most of the hardy species, such as *Eucalyptus glaucescens* and *E. niphophila,* known as 'gums', have evergreen, aromatic leaves and attractive barks that peel to reveal white, green and yellow at different stages.

Eucalyptus tolerates a wide range of soils, from acidic to chalky, but does not like being transplanted. Buy small, container grown plants. Propagate also by seed; pot on when large enough to handle and plant out as soon as the risk of frost is past.

Eucalyptus glaucescens

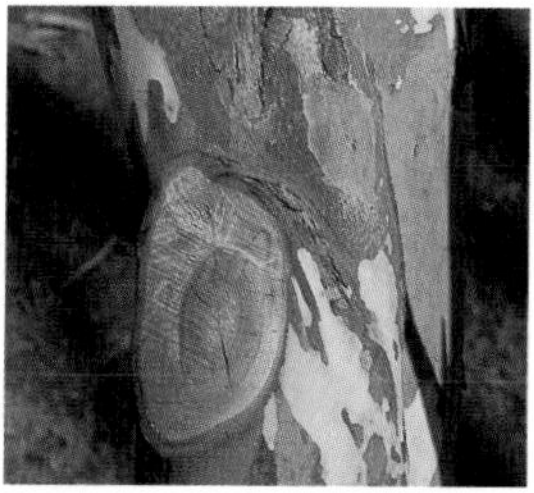
Eucalyptus niphophila

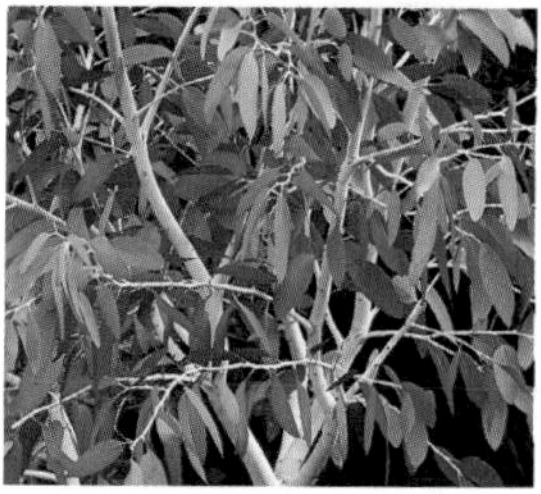
E. niphophila 'Debeuzevillei'

MOISTURE	Fairly drought resistant once established
SITE/LIGHT	A real sun-lover; most enjoy any poor, well-drained soil
GENERAL CARE	Stake new plants to support fast-growing foliage
PESTS & DISEASES	Prone to phytophthora root rot and silver leaf

TREES see also 172

COMPANION PLANTS see pages 252 436

Eucryphia

This genus of evergreen trees and shrubs is mostly grown for its upright habit, leathery leaves and showy, saucer-shaped, fragrant white flowers.

Eucryphia glutinosa is the hardiest species which can withstand more exposure than other eucryphias. It makes a bush 4–5m (12–18ft) in height and spread with two seasons of display – flowering in mid- to late summer and its foliage turning orange and red in the autumn.

Eucryphia glutinosa

Other forms make upright trees, especially *E. nymansensis*, which can reach 15m (50ft) in 30 years. In the garden, plant *E. glutinosa* in a shrub bed or as a specimen shrub. *E. milliganii* makes a feature plant and flowers from a young age. *E. intermedia* and *E. nymansensis* make specimen trees or large upright shrubs.

Eucryphia can be raised from seed but cuttings are often the best method, using semi-hardwood cuttings taken in late summer. *E. glutinosa* will sucker and these can be removed and grown on.

All the forms prefer being shaded and kept cool at the roots, but with lots of light for the crown.

Eucryphia intermedia 'Rostrevor'

MOISTURE	Keep moist at all times
SITE/LIGHT	Position with shade in well-drained acid to neutral soil
GENERAL CARE	Protect from cold winds and mulch to protect roots
PESTS & DISEASES	Relatively trouble free

SHRUBS see also 213

COMPANION PLANTS see pages 184 358

Euonymus SPINDLE TREE

These make shrubs or small trees with capsule-like fruit in four or five segments, ripening to yellow-green or pink. *Euonymus europaeus* 'Red Cascade' is a deciduous species, providing excellent autumn colour.

In the wild they are to be found in scrubland, forest margins, hedges and wasteland areas. In the garden, plant Euonymus in shrub and mixed borders or as specimen plants in the lawn.

E. europaeus is found in hedgerows and makes a small tree, useful for screening.

Euonymus can be propagated by seeds sown as soon as ripe or from cuttings. Cuttings should be taken as semi-hardwood cuttings in early summer.

They thrive in full sun to moderate shade, although the more sun, the better the fruiting.

They like well-drained soils, and are especially good on shallow soils overlying chalk.

Euonymus used to be used to make spindles for the spinning industry, hence its common name.

Euonymus europaeus 'Red Cascade'

MOISTURE	Keep moist and water freely during hot spells
SITE/LIGHT	Sun or dappled shade in fertile, well-drained soils
GENERAL CARE	Mulch to maintain humus and moisture content
PESTS & DISEASES	Can be affected by caterpillars

TREES see also 139–40

COMPANION PLANTS see pages 344–5 427–8 437

Euphorbia SPURGE

These are mainly hardy herbaceous or evergreen perennials, although *Euphorbia characias* and *E. mellifera* are hardy, evergreen shrubby plants.

Euphorbia amygdaloides var. *robbiae*

All euphorbias are great character plants and suitable as single specimens. Most spurges can be used effectively in mixed borders. For example, *E. amygdaloides* looks good with grassy carex or sedges. Combine *E. dulcis* with alliums, geraniums and late tulips. *E. mellifera* has lovely, fragrant flowers.

Propagate perennials in spring, by division or from basal stem cuttings. Propagate shrubby types from stem-tip cuttings in spring or summer. Raise annuals from seed sown in flowering positions during spring.

Euphorbia characias

Euphorbia mellifera

MOISTURE	Water well to start with, then keep moist
SITE/LIGHT	Enjoys humus-rich soil in light dappled shade
GENERAL CARE	Leaves may irritate eyes and skin
PESTS & DISEASES	Prone to aphids, capsid bugs, grey mould and rust

FLOWERS see also 326

COMPANION PLANTS see pages 147 267 427–8

Fagus BEECH

Beech is widely grown for its shape, colour and texture, and can be used as a specimen tree in the garden or as hedging, especially *Fagus sylvatica*.

Mature beech trees usually form rounded, domed crowns. However, the Dawyck beech (*F. sylvatica* 'Dawyck Purple') has a narrow columnar crown. Apart from this variety's purple foliage, another attractive feature is its new foliage, which starts off a wonderful, fresh green colour, with the leaves turning russet colours in autumn.

The silvery grey bark of most forms is also quite stunning.

Propagate by seed sown as soon as it is ripe and keep the seed from mice. Selected forms can be grafted in spring.

As well as in a woodland garden, the other major use for beech, particularly *F. sylvatica*, is as a hedging plant, as it can be trimmed to almost any height. A beech hedge will retain the old dead leaves until they fall off in spring when the buds expand. Grow in sun to medium shade with good drainage.

Fagus sylvatica 'Dawyck Purple'

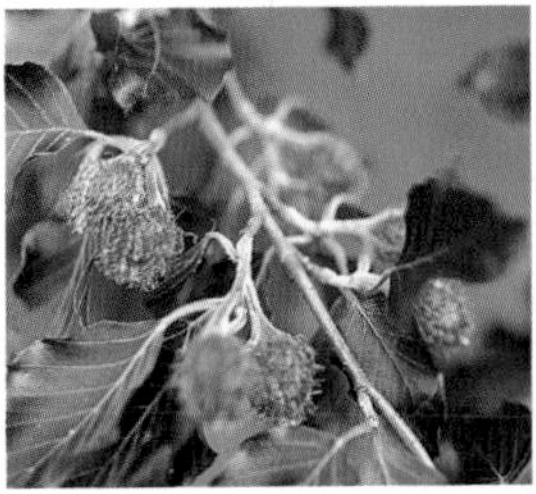

Fagus sylvatica 'Purple Fountain'

MOISTURE	Moist soil but not waterlogged
SITE/LIGHT	Prefers sun to medium shade in well-drained soil
GENERAL CARE	Surface rooting, so do not put other plants beneath it
PESTS & DISEASES	Prone to beech bark disease, aphids and powdery mildew

TREES
***see also* 418**

COMPANION PLANTS
***see pages* 139–40 196 219**

Fatsia

A genus of two or three evergreen shrubs or small trees, with leathery, palmate leaves and small, creamy white flowers, giving it an architectural form.

Fatsia japonica is an evergreen shrub, ideally situated in a shaded, sheltered courtyard, in a shrub border or indoors as a container plant in a cool conservatory. Milky white flowers are produced in the autumn and are followed by black pea-shaped berries.

F. japonica is native to Japan, Korea and Taiwan. *Fatshedera lizei* is a hybrid produced from *F. japonica* and *Hedera hibernica* (Irish ivy).

F. lizei is a smaller shrub with a scandent habit which benefits from staking.

Fatshedera lizei

F. japonica and *F. lizei* are best propagated by softwood cuttings in early summer.

Both species are fine architectural plants, valuable for their late flowering. They will grow in sun or shade, but *F. lizei* is especially useful for tolerating dry shade. Both have variegated forms which tend to be less vigorous, needing more sunlight.

Fatsia japonica

MOISTURE	Keep moist in full sun, but will tolerate drier soils in shade
SITE/LIGHT	Tolerant of sun and shade in fertile, well-drained soil
GENERAL CARE	Keep container plants slightly dry in winter
PESTS & DISEASES	Trouble free but leaves prone to frost damage

SHRUBS see also 139–40

COMPANION PLANTS see pages 251 285 290

Felicia BLUE DAISY

These half-hardy annuals and the tender sub-shrub grown as an annual, *Felicia amelloides*, are mat-forming and bushy plants respectively. They produce masses of daisy flowers in blue and other colours.

These plants are popular for summer bedding and containers in combination with other daisy-flowered bedding plants such as gazanias. They are most often grown for their mass of daisy-like, mainly blue flowerheads with yellow centres and lasting for prolonged periods over the summer.

Propagate annuals from seed in spring under cover, sub-shrubs from semi-ripe cuttings in late summer.

Try growing the low-growing forms, such as *F. bergeriana*, in a rock garden or raised bed. They particularly flourish at the base of a warm, sun-drenched wall. Blue daisies also make attractive container plants for a conservatory. Furthermore, they are not troubled by pests and diseases outdoors.

Felicia amelloides 'Santa Anita'

Felicia amelloides alba

MOISTURE	Water moderately during growth, sparingly during winter
SITE/LIGHT	Prefers full sun in fairly fertile, well-drained soil
GENERAL CARE	Pinch out young shoots to encourage bushiness
PESTS & DISEASES	Susceptible to aphids and red spider mites under glass

FLOWERS see also 163

COMPANION PLANTS see pages 239 264 309

Ficus FIG

This is a large genus of about 800 species containing mainly tropical evergreen species, as well as several indoor plants such as the rubber plant (*Ficus elastica*) and the Banyan fig (*F. benghalensis*).

For the garden, the common fig (*Ficus carica*) is a hardy species, more often grown for its foliage rather than its fruits. A deciduous shrub with large, deeply lobed leaves on stout shoots, it is usually grown against a sunny wall, which will help ripen the fruits. The fruits, however, can take longer than a year to ripen. The foliage can be aromatic on hot sunny days.

Ficus carica 'Brown Turkey'

Propagate by removing suckers, layering or by hardwood cuttings.

Hard pruning in the autumn will ensure the foliage grows to its optimum size the following season.

Figs are tolerant of any well drained soil, in sun or light shade. Water regularly until established and add manure or mulch annually to maintain the soil's richness.

MOISTURE	Prefers moist but not boggy conditions
SITE/LIGHT	Light shade in rich, well-drained soil
GENERAL CARE	Prune back hard each year in the autumn
PESTS & DISEASES	Prone to capsid bug and coral spot

TREES see also 319

COMPANION PLANTS see pages 137 353 438

Forsythia

This is a genus of about seven species of mainly deciduous, sometimes semi-evergreen shrubs. They are valued for their bright yellow bell-shaped flowers which are carried profusely on the bare branches in late winter or early spring, adding colour to the garden.

Grow Forsythia as isolated specimen shrubs, in mixed beds or as part of screening for different areas of the garden. They are also rather effective when grown as hedges. When pruning specimen shrubs, remove older shoots straight after flowering to maintain an open branch structure.

Propagate by cuttings, either semi-hardwood cuttings in summer, or long hardwood cuttings from mid-autumn to mid-winter, inserted in the ground outside.

F. 'Beatrix Farrand' is a particularly vigorous, bushy form for the garden, producing profuse deep yellow flowers from early spring.

Forsythia 'Beatrix Farrand'

MOISTURE	Keep moist but do not allow to get waterlogged
SITE/LIGHT	Sunny spot with light shade in well-drained soil
GENERAL CARE	Feed and mulch to maintain the soil's nutrients
PESTS & DISEASES	Generally trouble free

***SHRUBS* see also 227**

***COMPANION PLANTS* see pages 216 258 381**

Fothergilla WITCH ALDER

For autumn colour, these are among the best of all garden shrubs, turning crimson or orange-yellow, with white, bottle-brush flowers. The flowers come with the new leaves in *Fothergilla major*, so they develop while the leaves are still a glossy green with indented veins.

In *Fothergilla gardenii* the flowers are carried before the leaves on the bare shoots. The display is formed from the massed, spiky stamens. The flowers are also attractively fragrant.

Propagate by semi-hardwood cuttings taken in mid-summer, with bottom heat assisted rooting, by layering and by seed.

The genus requires a lime-free soil. They grow best on light, moist and rich but reasonably freely-drained soil. Site where the autumn colour will be best appreciated.

Fothergilla gardenii

MOISTURE	Keep moist but do not allow to get waterlogged
SITE/LIGHT	Full sun to light shade in lime-free, well-drained soil
GENERAL CARE	Mulch once or twice a year to add organic content
PESTS & DISEASES	Relatively trouble free

SHRUBS see also 216

COMPANION PLANTS see pages 243 252 374

Freesia

Normally thought of as half-hardy greenhouse pot plants in frost-prone climates, freesias can be obtained as heat-treated corms (to stimulate bloom production) for outdoor flowering in the summer.

Named cultivars with fragrantly scented flowers in a range of colours are available and their flowers are excellent for cutting. Plant in a sheltered position in border or patio tubs and window boxes. Discard corms after flowering in early spring.

Sow seed in the autumn or winter or remove small offsets in autumn.

Freesia 'Striped Jewel' is a particularly attractive white flowered cultivar with delicate, pinkish stripes.

In warmer areas, grow freesias in masses in a mixed border. Site in fairly fertile, moist but well-drained soil in the full sun. In frost-prone areas, grow under glass.

Freesia 'Striped Jewel'

Freesia 'Striped Jewel'

MOISTURE	Keep moist
SITE/LIGHT	Enjoys full sun in moderately fertile, well-drained soil
GENERAL CARE	Grow in drifts to really savour the sweet scents
PESTS & DISEASES	Prone to aphids and red spider mite

SHRUBS see also 335

COMPANION PLANTS see pages 143 161 214

Fremontodendron

This small genus is most often grown for its large and showy yellow flowers which are produced over a long period, usually from spring to autumn.

The first flush of flowers, in late spring, come from the buds on last summer's shoots, but later blooms are on the current season's growth.

One of the better forms is *Fremontodendron* 'California Glory'. This is a hybrid between the two species (*F. californicum* and *F. mexicanum*) but is hardier than either parent. 'Pacific Sunset' is very similar but has flowers of a brighter yellow. *F. californicum* has a more concentrated flush of flowers.

They can be propagated by seed or by softwood or semi-hardwood cuttings in the summer, rooting them in a freely drained, sandy substrate soil.

Fremontodendron 'California Glory'

They are best as wall shrubs, preferring all except mild gardens without the protection of a wall. Do not over-feed or plant on very fertile soils, as they will produce foliage at the expense of the flowers in these conditions.

MOISTURE	Requires only little moisture to thrive
SITE/LIGHT	A sunny, sheltered site in low to moderately fertile soil
GENERAL CARE	Tie in any wayward branches
PESTS & DISEASES	Phytophthora root rot may be a problem

***SHRUBS* see also 184**

***COMPANION PLANTS* see pages 187 283 409**

Fritillaria FRITILLARY

Fritillarias are hardy bulbs with nodding, bell-shaped flowers. *Fritillaria imperialis* (crown imperial) is suitable for a mixed border, while *F. meleagris* (snake's head fritillary) can be easily naturalized in grass.

The crown imperial combines well with shrubs, including rhododendrons, and must have exceedingly good drainage. However, one drawback is that the bulbs have a strange odour, akin to the smell of foxes.

Fritillaria imperialis 'Maxima Lutea'

Fritillaria meleagris

Propagate from offsets or bulbils when dormant or sow seed in autumn in a cold frame.

Prone to slugs and snails.

MOISTURE	Keep plants moist
SITE/LIGHT	Full sun to light shade with good drainage
GENERAL CARE	Smaller species should be grown under glass
PESTS & DISEASES	Prone to slugs, snails and lily beetles

FLOWERS
see also
310

COMPANION PLANTS
see pages
223
286
384–5

Fuchsia

Fuchsias are frost-tender to frost-hardy deciduous or evergreen shrubs, but the ones considered here are grown as summer bedding plants. They make bushy or, in some cultivars, trailing plants and flower profusely.

Fuchsia 'Harry Grey'

Fuchsias produce a succession of dangling, usually bell-shaped single or double flowers, often with swept-back petals, and mainly in combinations of blue, red, pink and white. They bloom over a long period. They make superb container plants, the trailing cultivars being especially suitable for hanging baskets. But the bush forms can also be grown in baskets as centrepieces.

Bush fuchsias also make good dot plants in summer bedding schemes and combine well with a wide range of summer bedding plants, including begonias and impatiens. They can also be used as fillers in a mixed border. In mild areas, they make excellent hedges.

Fuchsia magellanica

Propagate plants from semi-ripe cuttings in late summer, and winter the young plants in a cool, frost-free greenhouse or conservatory. Discard the old parent plants at the end of the season. Pinch out tips of young plants to encourage

FLOWERS
see also
224

COMPANION PLANTS
see pages
136
173

Fuchsia 'Marinka'

Fuchsia 'Swingtime'

pink coloured *F.* 'Harry Grey', the trailing shrub *F.* 'Marinka' and *F.* 'Swingtime' with its leaves with red veins, have been selected for their colourful flowers.

Fuchsias may be attacked by aphids, grey mould, red spider mites, rust and vine weevil grubs.

bushy growth, and also pinch out the resulting side shoots.

Species fuchsias, such as *Fuchsia magellanica,* generally have smaller flowers. *F. magellanica is* one of the hardiest species. Hybrids, such as *F.* 'Dark Eyes', with its medium, long-lasting double flowers, the

Fuchsia 'Dark Eyes'

MOISTURE	Keep all fuchsias moist
SITE/LIGHT	Fertile, well-drained soil in full sun or partial shade
GENERAL CARE	Protect plants with a generous mulch
PESTS & DISEASES	Prone to aphids, grey mould, rust and vine weevil grubs

FLOWERS
see also
236

COMPANION PLANTS
see pages
288
291

Gazania

Half-hardy evergreen perennials grown as annuals, gazanias are dwarf spreading plants generally with deep green leaves with white undersides, but they may also be grey in colour.

Large daisy-like flowers open mainly in direct sun, although cultivars are bred to perform better in cloudy weather. Grow in summer bedding schemes or patio tubs and window boxes with other daisy-flowered bedding plants such as blue felicias. Good for seaside gardens. Regularly remove dead flowers.

Raise from seed in spring under cover. Take semi-ripe cuttings in late summer and winter young plants in a cool, frost-free greenhouse.

The *Gazania* Daybreak Series has glossy leaves.

Gazania Daybreak 'Red Stripe'

MOISTURE	Water freely in growth but keep moist in winter
SITE/LIGHT	A sun-lover which likes light, sandy soil
GENERAL CARE	Dead-head to prolong flowering
PESTS & DISEASES	Watch out for grey mould

***FLOWERS* see also 276**

***COMPANION PLANTS* see pages 239 240 255**

Genista BROOM

Genista, closely related to Cytisus, is a group of mainly small to medium shrubs, as well as a few trees. Some brooms are spiny, especially *G. hispanica,* but are mostly grown for their pretty, pea-like flowers. They are rugged and reliable plants, which do not need much care.

Brooms are among the best flowering shrubs and trees, colourful at a time when most other woody plants have ceased flowering. They also provide light dappled shade – excellent for small gardens.

Propagate by seed or by semi-hardwood cuttings in summer.

G. aetnensis starts life as a bush, but will form a tree, making 6–12m (18–40ft) in height. *G. tenera* 'Golden Shower' is a spreading shrub with fragrant yellow flowers.

Genista aetnensis

Genista tenera 'Golden Shower'

MOISTURE	Does not need much watering
SITE/LIGHT	Enjoys full sun in well-drained but not too fertile soil
GENERAL CARE	Fairly tolerant of poor and dry conditions
PESTS & DISEASES	Generally trouble free

SHRUBS see also 227

COMPANION PLANTS see pages 194 379 398

Gentiana GENTIAN

A variable genus of hardy perennials generally valued for their brilliant blue flowers, the blooms being mainly trumpet-shaped.

There are low mat-forming forms of gentian for the rock or scree garden, including the evergreen *Gentiana acaulis* (trumpet gentian), the semi-evergreen *G. sino-ornata,* which needs acid soil, and the evergreen *G. verna* (spring gentian) which may be quite short-lived.

Gentiana 'Multiflora'

Propagate by division in spring or sow seed in containers in an open frame as soon as ripe.

Taller species for the mixed border or woodland garden include herbaceous *G. asclepiadea* (willow gentian). Most gentians need neutral to acid soil, with certain cultivars, such as *G.* 'Multiflora', requiring acid soil. They also need shade from the hottest sun.

Watch out for slugs and snails.

MOISTURE	Water well but do not allow to become soggy
SITE/LIGHT	Moderate sun in fertile, humus-rich, well-drained soil
GENERAL CARE	Provide shade in areas with warm, dry summers
PESTS & DISEASES	Prone to attacks by slugs and snails

FLOWERS see also 232

COMPANION PLANTS see pages 287 293 331

Geranium CRANESBILL

A large genus of hardy herbaceous and evergreen perennials, mainly low growing, bushy plants notable for their long display of bowl- or saucer-shaped flowers.

Geranium 'Johnson's Blue'

The leaves of some cranesbills are aromatic with brown or bronze markings, while others take on autumnal tints. Smaller geraniums, including *Geranium cinereum*, are great for rock or scree gardens. Others, such as *G.* x *oxonianum* and *G.* 'Johnson's Blue', are ideal for mixed borders.

Propagate by division or basal cuttings in spring.

Geraniums are especially at home in cottage-garden borders combined with old-fashioned annuals and perennials. Cranesbills need little attention apart from regularly removing flower stems, when blooms have finished, and old foliage.

Geranium x *oxonianum* 'Wargrave Pink'

MOISTURE	Water regularly during summer, sparingly in the winter
SITE/LIGHT	Enjoys full sun to light shade in any well-drained soil
GENERAL CARE	Grow small species in humus-rich, sharply drained soil
PESTS & DISEASES	Prone to caterpillars, powdery mildew, slugs and snails

FLOWERS see also 437

COMPANION PLANTS see pages 232 285 390–1

Geum AVENS

Geums are hardy herbaceous perennials with large pinnate leaves and bowl- or saucer-shaped, often brilliantly coloured flowers on thin wiry stems produced over a long period.

These are ideal plants for frontal positions in a mixed border and really look at home in cottage-garden borders. Avens combine well with other hardy perennials including achilleas, aquilegias and geraniums, and with old or modern shrub roses.

Propagate by division in spring.

Geum 'Lady Stratheden' produces rich yellow flowers all summer and *G. coccineum* bears brick-red blooms.

Geum coccineum

Geum 'Lady Stratheden'

MOISTURE	Keep moist; do not allow to get waterlogged in winter
SITE/LIGHT	Enjoys fertile, well-drained soil in the full sun
GENERAL CARE	Wet soils can cause the roots to rot
PESTS & DISEASES	Watch out for caterpillars

FLOWERS see also 141

COMPANION PLANTS see pages 155 267 390–1

Ginkgo GINKGO or MAIDENHAIR TREE

A genus of one species, originally found in southern China, the maidenhair tree is all but non-existent in the wild, even though it is now grown in gardens worldwide.

The main reason for planting *Ginkgo biloba* in the garden is its outstanding golden yellow autumnal colour. In addition, Ginkgo is remarkably tough and tolerant of all forms of pollution, which makes it an excellent plant to grow in the urban garden.

The leaves are fan-shaped and have an oily texture; an extract of the leaves is often used as a health tonic. The fleshy fruit is surrounded by a stinking oily layer, which smells even more unpleasant as they decay.

The habit of *G. biloba* is generally columnar in younger trees, and only really broadens out when the tree is around 100 years old.

Ginkgo can be propagated from seed sown in containers in an open frame as soon as they are ripe, as well as from semi-hardwood cuttings in summer.

Ginkgo will grow in a wide range of soils, provided they are well drained, but the more fertile the better. They are fairly pest and disease free.

Ginkgo biloba

MOISTURE	Keep moist but do not overwater
SITE/LIGHT	Likes fertile, well-drained soil in the full sun
GENERAL CARE	No pruning regime but will regrow if trimmed back
PESTS & DISEASES	Relatively trouble free

TREES see also 191

COMPANION PLANTS see pages 373 375

Gladiolus

These half-hardy plants grow from corms and produce widely flaring, funnel-shaped flowers in spikes in a wide colour range. The leaves are sword-like.

Various groups include the popular Grandiflorus or large-flowered gladioli, such as *Gladiolus* 'Early Yellow' and *G.* 'May Bride'. These are noted for substantial spikes, one per corm, and flower size ranging from giant to miniature. Butterfly gladioli have closely packed, flaring flowers, often with ruffled petals, blotched in the throat. Flowers are good for cutting. Grow in rows on the vegetable plot or plant in groups in a mixed border.

Gladiolus 'May Bride'

Gladiolus 'Early Yellow'

Propagate from cormlets removed when dormant and 'sow' them like seeds in spring outdoors. Feed fortnightly with a high-potash liquid fertilizer from the time the flower spikes are developing.

MOISTURE	Water moderately in growth
SITE/LIGHT	Enjoys fertile, well-drained soil in a sunny position
GENERAL CARE	In frost areas, lift corms in autumn and store over winter
PESTS & DISEASES	Prone to aphids, corm rot and slugs

FLOWERS
see also
238

COMPANION PLANTS
see pages
186
222
228–9

Grevillea SPIDER FLOWER

Grevillea have nectar-rich flowers, attracting nectar-feeding birds. The main characteristic is the combined calyx and corolla, giving flowers a spidery appearance.

This is a large genus of mainly tender trees and shrubs from Australia and nearby territories. As spider flowers can be frost tender, in temperate climates only a small selection can be grown.

The two plants mentioned here are among the hardiest of their kind and are extremely desirable in the garden for their evergreen needle-like leaves and terminal clusters of flowers – deep rosy-red in *Grevillea rosmarinifolia* and waxy reddish pink in *Grevillea* 'Canberra Gem'.

Sow seed, scarified or pre-soaked, in spring or take semi-ripe cuttings in summer.

Flowers can be produced at almost any time of year, but are usually carried in spring to summer.

Grevillea 'Canberra Gem'

Grevillea rosmarinifolia

MOISTURE	Keep moist but water sparingly in water
SITE/LIGHT	A sun-lover in acid to neutral, moderately fertile soil
GENERAL CARE	Clip after flowering to restrict size or shape
PESTS & DISEASES	Relatively trouble free

SHRUBS see also 323

COMPANION PLANTS see pages 184 287 384–5

Gypsophila

Gypsophila elegans is a hardy annual with clouds of tiny flowers. _G. paniculata_ (baby's breath) cultivars are hardy herbaceous perennials with similar blooms. _G. repens_, a partially evergreen perennial, forms mats of growth which become smothered with starry flowers.

G. repens is good for a rock or scree garden, but the others are ideal for mixed borders, combined with such plants as dianthus (pinks and carnations) and roses.

Raise annuals from seed in spring in flowering positions.

Propagate perennials in spring; cultivars from basal stem cuttings, species from seed under cover.

Flowers of larger species are excellent for cutting and adding to indoor floral arrangements.

Gypsophila paniculata 'Flamingo'

MOISTURE	Does not like overwatering
SITE/LIGHT	Full sun in light, mainly alkaline, sharply drained soil
GENERAL CARE	Most species dislike winter wet
PESTS & DISEASES	Stem rot may pose a problem

FLOWERS see also 165

COMPANION PLANTS see pages 234 390–1

Halesia SNOWDROP TREE

Snowdrop trees are ideal for the back of a border in its shrub forms or as a specimen plant in a woodland garden area. White, bell-shaped flowers hang beneath the previous summer's leaf growth.

A good, fairly small ornamental tree for the garden is *Halesia monticola* and its varieties. The largest growing of the species, it is likely to reach 10m (33ft) in thirty years. *H. caroliniana* is a smaller tree or spreading shrub up to 6m (20ft) high in thirty years but twice as wide.

The fruit is hard and woody, and is green in the beginning, but turns a light brown colour when ripe.

Germination can be slow, as the seeds need a warm period in autumn to break down the hard, woody coat, followed by a cold winter spell to stimulate germination. Softwood cuttings of the new growths with a heel taken in late spring should root in summer, but those plants will need over-winter protection to get them through to next year.

Halesia prefer moist soil, preferably neutral to acid and humus-rich, as long as it is well drained. They do not like chalk or limey soils. They thrive in either full sun or moderate shade. Provide shelter if they are likely to be affected by cold, dry winds.

Halesia monticola f. *vestita*

MOISTURE	Keep plants moist
SITE/LIGHT	Sun to moderate shade in well-drained, neutral/acidic soil
GENERAL CARE	Mulch to maintain humus content in the soil
PESTS & DISEASES	Relatively trouble free

TREES
see also
250

COMPANION
PLANTS
see pages
207
310

Hamamelis WITCH HAZEL

Witch hazels are the source of the preparation used in eye lotions, which is distilled from the twigs. In the garden, however, their use is as winter flowering shrubs.

The first form of Hamamelis intermedia can be in bloom well before early/mid-winter, and the season extends into early spring. The flowers of

Hamamelis intermedia 'Jelena'

Hamamelis intermedia and *H. mollis* are carried on the bare, leafless branches. The petals are long and very narrow, and tolerate extreme weather conditions. The flowers are also fragrant, especially in *H. mollis*. They are generally yellow, but in 'Jelena' the flowers seem to be a bright copper orange due to the base of the petal being red and the tip, yellow ochre.

They can be raised from seed, which often takes two years to germinate but the selected forms are grafted onto seedling rootstocks. They can also be layered.

Hamamelis make large shrubs, 4–6m (13–20ft) and as wide or wider in twenty or so years. Hamamelis like neutral to acidic well drained soils, but can be grown on deep soils overlying chalk.

Hamamelis intermedia 'Pallida'

MOISTURE	Requires only little moisture in order to thrive
SITE/LIGHT	A sun-lover which is happy in any type of soil
GENERAL CARE	Mulch to maintain a humus-rich soil
PESTS & DISEASES	Prone to phytophthora root rot and silver leaf

SHRUBS see also 435

COMPANION PLANTS see pages 217 290 331

Hebe SHRUBBY VERONICA

Hebes are grown for the flowers and evergreen foliage. Flowers are mainly white, especially the New Zealand varieties, but can include pink, blue, purple and red.

In the garden the smaller growing hebes, such as *Hebe* 'Red Edge', are useful on rockeries and at the front of shrub borders. The larger ones can also be used in borders or as specimen plants.

Some forms of Hebe have a purple colour to the leaves, while others appear to have blue-grey foliage (*H. recurva*).

Propagate from semi-hardwood cuttings taken at the end of the summer.

Hebes are tolerant of salt spray and coastal conditions, as well as a certain amount of atmospheric pollution.

Hebe 'Red Edge'

Hebe recurva

MOISTURE	Relatively unfussy but do not overwater
SITE/LIGHT	A sunny site in well-drained soil with shelter from wind
GENERAL CARE	Mulch and feed, especially if soil is poor
PESTS & DISEASES	Prone to phytophthora root rot

***SHRUBS* see also 247**

***COMPANION PLANTS* see pages 191 200 219**

Helenium SNEEZEWEED

These hardy herbaceous perennials have daisy-like flowers with conspicuous dome-like brown or yellow centres. The blooms are produced over a long period.

Heleniums are suitable for mixed borders in combination with perennials such as rudbeckias, helianthus, dahlias, asters, and ornamental grasses including miscanthus and stipa. The flowers are good for cutting.

Propagate in spring, by division every two years or from basal cuttings.

Tall cultivars, such as the copper-red *Helenium* 'Moerheim Beauty' and rich yellow *H.* 'Butterpat', need support with twiggy sticks.

Helenium 'Moerheim Beauty'

Helenium 'Butterpat'

MOISTURE	Do not allow to dry out
SITE/LIGHT	A sun-lover, happy in most well-drained soils
GENERAL CARE	Remove dead flowerheads regularly
PESTS & DISEASES	Prone to leaf spot

FLOWERS see also 159

COMPANION PLANTS see pages 228–9 278 336

Helianthemum ROCK ROSE

Hardy evergreen shrubs of prostrate, ground-covering habit, rock roses are spangled over a long period with brilliantly coloured flowers resembling small single roses. In some cultivars, the foliage is greyish.

Also known as sun roses, Helianthemum usually grows on rock gardens or screes with other rock plants such as *Iberis sempervirens*, sedums, saxifrages and *Euphorbia myrsinites.* They are also excellent plants for covering a bank or slope.

Although they seem to be continually in flower from late spring to early summer, most flowers open up in the morning and have withered by the end of one day.

Helianthemum 'Ben Macdhui'

Helianthemum 'Wisley Primrose'

Propagate from softwood cuttings in spring or early summer.

Two attractive forms are the yellow *Helianthemum* 'Wisley Primrose' and the red coloured *H.* 'Ben Macdhui'.

Rock roses thrive in chalky soils. When flowering is over, cut back all shoots to within 2.5cm (1in) of the old wood.

MOISTURE	Little moisture required
SITE/LIGHT	Neutral to alkaline, well-drained soil in the full sun
GENERAL CARE	Trim after flowering to restrict spread
PESTS & DISEASES	Generally trouble free

***FLOWERS* see also 352**

***COMPANION PLANTS* see pages 252 288 401**

Helianthus SUNFLOWER

Helianthus annuus and its cultivars is the popular hardy annual that can grow to great heights with huge flowers; other types are hardy herbaceous perennials. All produce large, daisy-like flowers with generally darker centres.

The main colour is yellow, such as *H.* 'Lemon Queen', but other colours are making an appearance, such as *H. annuus*

Helianthus 'Lemon Queen'

Helianthus annuus 'Double Shine'

'Double Shine' and *H. annuus* 'Ruby Sunset'. Sunflowers are suitable for mixed or prairie-style borders, especially combined with tall ornamental grasses such as miscanthus. Dwarf annual cultivars can be grown in patio tubs.

Propagate in spring by division or sown from seed. Perennials enjoy a permanent mulch of organic matter such as garden compost to prevent the soil rapidly drying out.

Helianthus annuus 'Giant Yellow'

MOISTURE	Requires only little moisture in order to thrive
SITE/LIGHT	Good for chalky, dry soils in a warm, sunny position
GENERAL CARE	Support tall sunflowers; flowers excellent for cutting
PESTS & DISEASES	Prone to powdery mildew, slugs and snails

FLOWERS
see also
276

COMPANION PLANTS
see pages
240
386
410

Heliotropium HELIOTROPE

This half-hardy deciduous shrub is generally grown as an annual summer bedding plant in frost-prone climates. Cultivars have fragrant, purple, violet-blue or white flowers and bloom continuously over a long period.

Heliotropes can be included as dot plants in summer bedding schemes, as well as grown in patio tubs and window boxes. They combine well with many other summer bedding plants, including pelargoniums, begonias, impatiens, petunias, tagetes (marigolds) and *Salvia splendens* (scarlet sage).

Propagate from semi-ripe cuttings in late summer, and winter young plants in a cool, frost-free greenhouse. Discard old plants at the end of the season.

Heliotropium 'Nagano', with its tiny, fragrant, tubular purple flowers, is a particularly good variety for use as a bedding plant.

The foliage may irritate the skin and eyes.

Heliotropium 'Nagano'

MOISTURE	Keep moist and water moderately during growing season
SITE/LIGHT	Enjoys any fertile, well-drained soil in a sunny position
GENERAL CARE	Apply a liquid fertilizer monthly during growing season
PESTS & DISEASES	Generally trouble free

FLOWERS see also 433

COMPANION PLANTS see pages 168 365 416

Helleborus HELLEBORE

Hardy evergreen or herbaceous perennials with lobed or divided leaves and heads of bowl-shaped flowers. The dwarf *Helleborus niger* or Christmas rose is the earliest hellebore to flower.

Other hellebores, such as *H.* x *hybridus* cultivars (Lenten roses) are taller plants. In a mixed border, plant around winter- or spring-flowering shrubs, with bergenias and dwarf bulbs such as snowdrops (galanthus) and early flowering narcissus.

Propagate by division in spring after flowering. *H. argutifolius* and *H. foetidus* should be grown on from seed when ripe in a garden frame.

Hellebores do not like extremes, so avoid dry or waterlogged soils. Provide a permanent mulch of bulky organic matter to maintain the humus-rich content and provide shelter from strong, cold winds.

Watch out for aphids, black root rot, leaf spot, slugs and snails.

Helleborus x hybridus

Helleborus niger

MOISTURE	Keep moist but avoid too dry or too wet soils
SITE/LIGHT	Most like neutral to alkaline soil in sun to dappled shade
GENERAL CARE	Maintain a humus-rich soil content by mulching
PESTS & DISEASES	Prone to aphids, black root rot, leaf spot, slugs and snails

FLOWERS see also 155

COMPANION PLANTS see pages 171 344–5

Hemerocallis DAYLILY

Hardy herbaceous or evergreen perennials with large, lily-like flowers, hemerocallis come in a wide range of colours and have broad, arching, grassy foliage. Each flower lasts for only one day but blooms are produced in succession over a long period.

Daylilies are essential plants for a mixed border, in combination with agapanthus, crocosmias, kniphofias, old or modern shrub roses, and ornamental grasses.

Flowers are produced in a number of forms: circular (*Hemerocallis* 'Ice Castles'), spider-shaped (*H.* 'Cat's Cradle'), star-shaped (*H.* 'Golden Chimes'), triangular (*H.* 'Millie Schlumpf'), trumpet-shaped (*H. fulva*) and double (*H.* 'Betty Woods').

Propagate daylilies by dividing plants every two years in spring or else sow seed in containers in a cold frame in autumn or spring.

Provide plants with a permanent mulch of bulky organic matter, which will also retain moisture. Liquid feed fortnightly during the flowering period.

Hemerocallis fulva

Hemerocallis 'Golden Chimes'

MOISTURE	Keep moist; water freely from spring until the first buds
SITE/LIGHT	Any fertile, well-drained soil in full sun
GENERAL CARE	Too much shade will reduce flowering
PESTS & DISEASES	Prone to aphids, rust, slugs and snails

FLOWERS see also 315

COMPANION PLANTS see pages 143 222 299

Heuchera CORAL FLOWER

Hardy evergreen or partially evergreen perennials, heucheras produce low mounds of fairly large lobed leaves, and heads of tiny flowers on upright, wiry stems. In recent years many cultivars with colourful foliage have become available.

Heuchera 'Palace Purple'

Heucheras, especially those with attractive leaves, make superb ground cover around shrubs in mixed borders or woodland gardens. The flowers are suitable for cutting.

Heuchera micrantha var. *diversifolia* 'Palace Purple' has metallic, bronze-red leaves with creamy-pink flowers, which are followed by attractive, rose coloured seed heads.

Coral flowers are best divided every few years in early autumn, but can be grown from seed.

Provide a permanent mulch of bulky organic matter, topping up annually. The roots can be attacked by vine weevil grubs.

MOISTURE	Keep moist all year round
SITE/LIGHT	Any fertile, well-drained neutral soil in sun or partial shade
GENERAL CARE	Mulch to cover the rootstock, which pushes upwards
PESTS & DISEASES	Prone to vine weevil grubs

FLOWERS see also 138

COMPANION PLANTS see pages 170 219 363

Hibiscus WOODY MALLOW

Woody mallows are found in the wild in a variety of habitats, including beside streams, in moist woodland and even rocky areas. Flowers are carried in late summer or early autumn in a warm, sunny garden site.

In general, the flowers can be various shades of blue, white, yellow or pink and typically have five petals forming a trumpet shape, but there are also semi-double or double flowering plants, such as *Hibiscus rosa-sinensis* 'Crown of Bohemia'.

Single-flowering forms include *H. syriacus* 'Hamabo', a white-flowered hibiscus with a tinge of pink in the petals, *H. syriacus* 'Meehani', with a low-growing habit and lilac-mauve coloured flowers and *H. syriacus* 'Pink Giant', with its clear pink blooms and dark red eyes.

Hibiscus syriacus 'Pink Giant'

Hibiscus syriacus 'Hamabo'

Propagate woody mallows by semi-hardwood cuttings in summer, dividing perennials in spring or sowing seed also in spring.

The *H. syriacus* flowers on the current season's growth, so will flourish if pruned back hard in spring to increase flower production.

MOISTURE	Keep soil moist, particularly in hot periods
SITE/LIGHT	Humus-rich, well-drained soil in the full sun
GENERAL CARE	Mulch in winter to protect the plant
PESTS & DISEASES	Prone to aphids, scale insects and whiteflies under glass

SHRUBS see also 278

COMPANION PLANTS see pages 139–40 438

Holboellia

These evergreen climbers are extremely useful in the garden for covering up unsightly walls or fences, which also provides them with the shelter they need to flourish.

Introduced from China (*Holboellia coriacea*) and the Himalayas (*H. latifolia*), these woody vine-like climbers are extremely vigorous growers, particularly *H. coriacea*, with masses of glossy, lance-shaped leaves. *H. latifolia* produces greenish-white flowers. *H. coriacea* has purple-white flowers. The flowers are extremely fragrant on both species.

Holboellia latifolia

Holboellia coriacea

Propagation is best from semi-ripe cuttings taken in late summer or autumn.

Keep holboellias moist and ensure the soil is well drained. As well as covering up drab surfaces, these plants can be trained on a support, grown through a small tree or over an arch in the garden.

MOISTURE	Keep moist
SITE/LIGHT	Happy in full sun or light shade in fertile, well-drained soil
GENERAL CARE	Apply a good measure of well-rotted manure each spring
PESTS & DISEASES	Aphids can be problematic but generally trouble free

SHRUBS
see also
294

COMPANION PLANTS
see pages
201–4
211

Hosta PLANTAIN LILY

These hardy herbaceous perennials are grown mainly for their large leaves and although most flower reasonably well, several produce particularly good displays of blooms, as well as having attractive foliage.

The leaves, which can be ovate to lance-shaped, vary from green, yellow, grey-blue to variegated. Flowers are bell-shaped, such as *Hosta* 'Regal Splendour', or tubular, such as *H.* 'Ground Master'.

Hostas are used mainly as ground cover among shrubs, in woodland gardens and around pools. They also grow quite well in patio tubs.

Easily propagated by division in spring. Ensure that the soil remains moist, as dry conditions are seldom tolerated. Mulch permanently with organic matter such as leafmould, garden compost or peat substitute. Very prone to slugs and snails, and vine weevil grubs.

Hosta fortunei 'Francee'

MOISTURE	Ensure plants are kept permanently moist
SITE/LIGHT	Site in partial shade is any well-drained soil
GENERAL CARE	Shelter from cold, drying winds; do not allow to dry out
PESTS & DISEASES	Prone to slugs and snails, as well as vine weevil grubs

FLOWERS see also 209

COMPANION PLANTS see pages 164 183 211

Hyacinthus HYACINTH

Cultivars of *Hyacinthus orientalis*, such as 'Pink Pearl', are hardy bulbs with short, thick, heavy spikes of fragrant flowers. They are generally planted for spring bedding in combination with *Bellis perennis* (double daisies), violas or pansies, and tulips.

Hyacinths grow well in patio tubs and window boxes, but the bulbs in these containers may be damaged by severe frosts. When the display is over, lift the bulbs to make way for summer bedding and replant in a mixed border. After flowering, feed with a liquid fertilizer weekly until the leaves die down.

Propagate by removing offsets when dormant. Grow in well-drained, fairly fertile soil in the sun or partial shade. Protect container-grown plants from excessive wet in the winter.

Hyacinthus orientalis 'Pink Pearl'

Hyacinthus orientalis

MOISTURE	Keep moist but do not allow to become waterlogged
SITE/LIGHT	Any well-drained soil in the sun or partial shade
GENERAL CARE	Can also be planted in containers indoors
PESTS & DISEASES	Generally trouble free

FLOWERS see also 293

COMPANION PLANTS see pages 329–30 427–8 437

Hydrangea

This large genus of shrubs, and a few climbers, is mainly grown for the large, showy blooms that actually consist of a mass of tiny flowers clustered together.

Hydrangeas are relatively easy to maintain and are useful in a range of sites as specimen plants or group plantings in shrub or mixed beds or in a woodland setting. *Hydrangea aspera* forms are well suited to a woodland or shady setting, as they do not perform well in full sun.

H. macrophylla forms are divided into 'Hortensias' or mopheads (such as *H.m.* 'Générale Vicomtesse de Vibraye') or 'Lacecaps' (such as *H.m.* 'Lilacina'). *H. quercifolia* forms are known as oak-leaved hydrangeas.

Hydrangea aspera Villosa Group

H.m. 'Générale Vicomtesse de Vibraye'

Hydrangea quercifolia 'Snow Flake'

Propagate by seed or root softwood cuttings in early summer or hardwood cuttings in winter. Acid soils less than 5.5pH will give blue flowers; more than 5.5pH, pink, due to the aluminium in the soil.

MOISTURE	Any moist soil – pH of soil may determine flower colour
SITE/LIGHT	Full sun for small forms; most prefer a semi-shaded site
GENERAL CARE	Keep soil moist and well mulched
PESTS & DISEASES	Prone to mildew, aphids and a lot of common diseases

SHRUBS see also 207

COMPANION PLANTS see pages 329–30 435 436

Hypericum ST JOHN'S WORT

This genus occurs worldwide in a range of habitats from woodland to rocky, mountainous regions. All have showy, yellow cup-shaped flowers, which can appear to take over and hide the foliage in some species.

Hypericum is excellent as a shrub in a mixed border, a specimen plant and also used as an informal hedge. Certain forms, such as *Hypericum calycinum*, make good ground cover plants. *H. moserianum* 'Tricolor', a hybrid of *H. calycinum*, is also a good spreader, grown especially for its variegated pink, white and green leaves.

Hypericum thrives on most soils, particularly chalky ones. They flourish in full sunlight with some light shade.

Propagate by rooting semi-hardwood cuttings in the summer or divide perennials in spring or autumn.

H. calycinum will appreciate partial to deep shade and *H. moserianum* 'Tricolor' prefers a sheltered position to prolong its summer to autumn flowering period.

Hypericum moserianum 'Tricolor'

MOISTURE	Keep fairly moist, depending on the species
SITE/LIGHT	Well-drained soil in full sun to partial shade
GENERAL CARE	Give smaller species and young plants shelter
PESTS & DISEASES	Prone to hypericum rust

***SHRUBS* see also 367**

***COMPANION PLANTS* see pages 177 262–3**

Iberis CANDYTUFT

This genus of annuals, perennials and evergreen shrubs can be grown at the front of mixed borders, among roses, in a rock or scree garden, or in patio containers. Annual candytufts will flower profusely over long periods.

Iberis amara

Iberis amara and *I. umbellata* (common candytuft) are hardy annuals with domed or flat heads of flowers. *I. sempervirens* is a hardy, dwarf, evergreen shrubby plant for the rock or scree garden, and looks good combined with such plants as helianthemums and saxifrages.

After flowering, lightly trim *I. sempervirens* to ensure a compact habit. Raise annuals, such as *I. amara*, from seed in spring or autumn, sowing in flowering positions.

Propagate *I. sempervirens* from semi-ripe cuttings in summer. Root them in a cold frame or with gentle bottom heat in a greenhouse.

Trim perennials and shrubs lightly after flowering to keep their shape. Watch out for caterpillars, slugs and snails.

MOISTURE	Keep moist but not too damp
SITE/LIGHT	Full sun in fairly fertile, well-drained soil
GENERAL CARE	Some species (*I. amara*) prefer alkaline soil
PESTS & DISEASES	Prone to caterpillars, slugs and snails

FLOWERS see also 166

COMPANION PLANTS see pages 277 300 401

Ilex HOLLY

Hollies are grown for their variously spiny or smoothed-margin foliage and colourful berries. Most make large shrubs or tall trees and can be deciduous or evergreen.

Hollies can be grown in a woodland garden, as specimen trees, such as *Ilex aquifolium* varieties, or as hedges or dense screens in garden perimeters. *I. crenata* is mainly grown for its small, dense foliage and makes a narrow, upright shrub with glossy green leaves and black fruits.

Ilex crenata 'Golden Gem'

I. meserveae produces bluish-green leaves and gives it the common name of the blue holly. Blue hollies are suited to hard, dry winters.

Ilex aquifolium 'Ferox Argentea'

Seed propagation may take two or more years to germinate. Hardwood cuttings will root readily in a cold frame.

Hollies are easy to grow as they are tolerant of deep shade as well as full sun.

Ilex meserveae 'Blue Angel'

MOISTURE	Keep reasonably moist
SITE/LIGHT	Thrives in sun or shade in any well-drained soil
GENERAL CARE	Plant out in late winter or early spring
PESTS & DISEASES	Can be prone to aphids, scale insects and leaf miners

SHRUBS
see also
181

COMPANION PLANTS
see pages
274
393
408

Impatiens BUSY LIZZIE

Impatiens walleriana cultivars (busy lizzie) and the New Guinea Group are frost-tender perennials generally grown as annuals. Busy lizzies are dwarf, bushy plants.

Impatiens are rated as major summer bedding plants, combining well with many other bedding subjects such as fuchsias, begonias, ageratum, lobelia and petunias. They are widely planted in patio containers and window boxes, and can also be used as centrepieces for hanging baskets.

They are particularly good for growing in partial shade, but will thrive in sun provided it is not excessively strong and the soil remains moist.

Impatiens walleriana Super Elfin Series

I. walleriana 'Mosaic Rose'

Impatiens New Guinea Group

Raise plants from seed in spring under glass. Impatiens can also be propagated from softwood cuttings in spring or summer. The buds and flowers may be affected by grey mould in damp summers.

MOISTURE	Keep well watered, particularly during hot summers
SITE/LIGHT	Partial shade to full sun in well-drained, humus-rich soil
GENERAL CARE	Liquid feed every three to four weeks; protect from wind
PESTS & DISEASES	Prone to grey mould and viruses

FLOWERS see also 350

COMPANION PLANTS see pages 262–3 321 362

Ipomoea MORNING GLORY

These fast growing, frost-tender twining climbers are grown as annuals. The large, flaring or trumpet-shaped flowers are produced against a background of large, often lobed or heart-shaped leaves.

Morning glories are found in a great range of diverse habitats, from open scrubland to dense woodland, seashores and cliffs. In a garden environment, grow ipomoeas up a pergola, wall or fence or, in a mixed border, through large shrubs. They look good combined with *Tropaeolum peregrinum* (canary creeper).

Ipomoea purpurea

Raise plants in spring under glass, first soaking the seeds for a day in tepid water to soften the hard seed coats.

Ipomoea tricolor 'Heavenly Blue'

These climbers need a sheltered position, as they dislike cold, drying winds.

Ipomoea tricolor 'Heavenly Blue' is an attractive form with its trumpet-shaped sky-blue to purple flowers. *I. purpurea* is another favourite, bearing pink, purple-blue, magenta or white flowers.

MOISTURE	Keep moist but water sparingly in winter
SITE/LIGHT	A sheltered site in the full sun in well-drained soil
GENERAL CARE	Give shelter from cold, drying winds
PESTS & DISEASES	Prone to viruses and powdery mildew

FLOWERS see also 201–4

COMPANION PLANTS see pages 211 425

Iris

This is a diverse group of plants whose flowers consist of three upright inner petals (the standards) and three outer reflexed or horizontal petals (the falls). Most popular are the hardy rhizomatous perennials.

Iris reticulata 'Harmony'

Bearded irises come in a wide range of colours and have a 'beard' of hairs on the falls. Beardless rhizomatous irises include the herbaceous *Iris sibirica* cultivars with grassy foliage. Rhizomatous crested irises, such as *I. confusa*, spread freely by rhizomes.

Irises also grow from bulbs, ranging from miniatures, such as *I. danfordiae* and *I. reticulata*, to tall Dutch irises whose flowers are particularly good for cutting.

Iris confusa

Rhizomatous irises are good for mixed borders. Miniature bulbs are generally grown on rock gardens, while Dutch irises can be grown in rows on the vegetable plot for cutting.

Lift and divide rhizomatous irises every three years in early summer after flowering. Propagate bulbous irises by dividing congested clumps of bulbs in autumn.

MOISTURE	Keep irises moist throughout the year
SITE/LIGHT	Most thrive in long, hot summers in well-drained soil
GENERAL CARE	Grow tender varieties under glass
PESTS & DISEASES	Prone to slugs, snails, grey mould, leaf spot and aphids

FLOWERS see also 270

COMPANION PLANTS see pages 326 359 390–1

Jasminum JASMINE

Jasminum is a genus of around 200 species of climbers and shrubs, all of which are easy to grow. Most jasmines tolerate shady positions in virtually any well-drained soil.

Jasmines are excellent subjects for the garden, often producing fragrant flowers, and come in a variety of colours and habits, from the shrubby, scandent forms, such as *Jasminum humile*, to the climbing varieties, such as *J. officinale*, with its trusses of white scented flowers.

Grow the climbers over pergolas or up pillars. The scented forms are effective trained next to gates and doors so the fragrance is really appreciated. Even shrub forms can be displayed against a wall.

Propagate by semi-hardwood cuttings in summer or by layering in autumn.

Jasmines enjoy a wide range of soil types provided it is well drained, but they thrive in moist, well-drained and fertile soil. Prune out old wood and any dead stems after flowering, and keep well watered during summer.

Jasminum officinale

Jasminum humile

MOISTURE	Keep moist, particularly during hot spells
SITE/LIGHT	Partial shade for climbers, sun for shrubs in fertile soil
GENERAL CARE	Mulch occasionally to maintain a humus-rich soil
PESTS & DISEASES	Prone to aphids and mealybugs

SHRUBS see also 201–4

COMPANION PLANTS see pages 134 184 429

Juglans WALNUT

Most of these deciduous trees are grown for their edible nuts, as well as their attractive habit. The nuts can be pickled before they are ripe or left to mature.

Juglans nigra

Walnuts are monoecious, producing male and female flowers on the same tree. As male and female flowers are not open at the same time, two or three trees should be planted near each other for pollination. *Juglans regia*, the English or Persian walnut, grows up to 30m (100ft) high.

J. nigra, the Black walnut, is hardier than *J. regia*, and is grown for its attractive, large leaves and can also reach 30m (100ft). In addition, the Black walnut is valued for its wood, which is a rich, dark brown colour.

Grow walnuts from seed, which will germinate in spring. Varieties and hybrids should be propagated by grafting.

Walnut trees will flourish in well-drained, loamy soil. *J. regia* should be grown on deep, fertile, light ground, which is free from alkali. It needs to be moist all the time.

MOISTURE	Water well until established
SITE/LIGHT	A sun-lover which is happy in any type of soil
GENERAL CARE	Prune young plants to encourage a central shoot
PESTS & DISEASES	Relatively trouble free

TREES see also 411

COMPANION PLANTS see pages 301

Juniperus JUNIPER

Junipers range from evergreen, coniferous shrubs to tall trees. The needle-like foliage can be blue-green, grey-green or golden. All forms are an ideal way of providing year-round colour in the garden.

As well as berries that can be used for flavouring, Junipers also produce fleshy cones, as opposed to the woody cone of Cupressus.

Juniperus scopulorum 'Skyrocket' has a narrow, upright habit making 6m (20ft) in height. Other forms make excellent ground cover, such as *J. horizontalis*, and forms such as *J. pfitzeriana* 'Gold Coast' are upright spreading bushes, offering spread as well as height.

Seeds are slow to germinate, taking up to five years, but they can also be grown on from cuttings, taken at most times of the year.

Most junipers thrive in full sun, but will grow on a wide range of soils.

Juniperus pfitzeriana 'Gold Coast'

Juniperus scopulorum 'Skyrocket'

MOISTURE	Tolerates drier conditions once established
SITE/LIGHT	Mostly in full sun in any well-drained soil
GENERAL CARE	Cut back only to restrict growth or reshape
PESTS & DISEASES	Prone to leaf fungi, aphids and honey fungus

TREES see also 196

COMPANION PLANTS see pages 135 139–40 275

Kalmia CALICO BUSH or MOUNTAIN LAUREL

Kalmias are from the same family as Rhododendron, with similar leathery leaves and cup- or saucer-shaped flowers. The flowers tend to be largely pink and bloom profusely from mid spring to late summer.

Kalmias look particularly attractive in a shrub border or woodland area in the garden, as a specimen plant and can even make informal hedging. Like rhododendrons, kalmias dislike lime in the soil.

Kalmia latifolia 'Pink Charm' produces red buds which open into pale pink flowers.

Propagate by seed scattered over damp compost. Selected forms can be grown on by semi-hardwood cuttings taken in summer.

These shrubs enjoy full sun to light shade for the upper parts, just as long as the roots have moist to boggy conditions.

Kalmia latifolia 'Pink Charm'

MOISTURE	Keep well watered throughout – even boggy
SITE/LIGHT	Loves the sun, along with boggy conditions
GENERAL CARE	Mulch occasionally with leaf mould to retain moisture
PESTS & DISEASES	Relatively trouble free

SHRUBS see also 384–5

COMPANION PLANTS see pages 329–30 431

Kerria JEW'S MALLOW

Kerria is a genus of one species of deciduous shrub, *Kerria japonica*, which is at home in thickets and woodland areas of the garden. They are most often grown for their foliage and golden yellow flowers.

The ovate, simple leaves of *Kerria japonica* have a double-serrated margin. The cup- or saucer-shaped yellow flowers bloom at the end of the branches in mid to late spring. They have five sepals and five petals. *K. japonica* 'Pleniflora' produces double flowers, similar to pom-poms.

Kerria japonica 'Picta'

The variegated *K. japonica* 'Picta' variety has grey-green leaves that are creamy white on the margins. The fruit is ovoid in shape and dark brown.

Jew's mallow is best propagated by taking soft greenwood cuttings in the summer or else by division in autumn. In summer, prune back the shoots that have flowered. Cut out any dead wood or broken branches.

This hardy ornamental shrub grows profusely but does not like excessive shade. Although it prefers the full sun, Jew's mallow will also thrive in partial shade. Any fertile, well-drained garden soil will be fine.

Even though it is fully hardy, it is best not to plant in wind-swept areas. Offer it shelter beside other shrubs or grow it against a wall.

MOISTURE	Keep moist and do not allow to dry out in the summer
SITE/LIGHT	Full sun to partial shade in most fertile, well-drained soils
GENERAL CARE	Prune back older stems after flowering
PESTS & DISEASES	Relatively trouble free

SHRUBS see also 213

COMPANION PLANTS see pages 220 251 382

Kniphofia RED HOT POKER or TORCH LILY

Kniphofias are distinctive evergreen or deciduous perennials with clumps of grassy foliage and thick spikes of tubular flowers in a variety of colours.

In a mixed border red hot pokers combine well with ornamental grasses such as cortaderia, miscanthus and stipa, and with hardy perennials including agapanthus, flat-headed achilleas and crocosmias. They also look good in gravel areas and in association with architecture and paving. Young plants are best mulched with dry straw in winter to protect roots from hard frost.

Propagate by division in spring. However, bear in mind that kniphofias do not like to be disturbed, so only lift plants when it is necessary to divide clumps.

Kniphofia 'Royal Standard' produces bright yellow flowers after red buds and can grow to 1m (3ft) high. As an added bonus, all kniphofias tend to attract bees to the garden.

Kniphofia 'Royal Standard'

MOISTURE	Keep moist but do not allow to become too wet
SITE/LIGHT	Enjoys full sun to partial shade in fertile, well-drained soil
GENERAL CARE	Mulch young plants with straw during the first winter
PESTS & DISEASES	Generally trouble free

***FLOWERS* see also 326**

***COMPANION PLANTS* see pages 143 227 281**

Kolkwitzia BEAUTY BUSH

Kolkwitzia is a genus of one species, *Kolkwitzia amabilis*, of deciduous shrub and is related to the honeysuckles (Lonicera). Its main asset is its large number of tubular bell-shaped flowers in late spring or early summer.

The beauty bush, which originates from the mountainous Hubei area in China, is a fast-growing shrub forming an arching habit with dark green, mainly oval-shaped leaves. The clear pink flowers with a yellowish throat, which are produced in abundance, are carried in pairs. Kolkwitzia makes an excellent specimen plant, as well as being the centrepiece to a mixed or shrub border.

The bark is light brown and tends to flake off in thin sheets, particularly on older stems. This shrub tends to become 'leggy' with age.

The beauty bush is easily propagated from semi-hardwood cuttings taken in summer or else from suckers, which can be removed and grown-on.

Kolkwitzia amabilis 'Pink Cloud'

Kolkwitzia enjoys a position in the full sun. *Kolkwitzia amabilis* 'Pink Cloud' can grow up to 3m (10ft) in height and spreads to a width of 4m (12ft). Prune out any old, dead stems after flowering.

MOISTURE	Fairly drought tolerant once established
SITE/LIGHT	Full sun in fertile, well-drained soil
GENERAL CARE	Cut back old stems after flowering
PESTS & DISEASES	Generally trouble free

SHRUBS see also 323

COMPANION PLANTS see pages 289 303 388

Laburnum

This is a genus of two species of deciduous trees that are at home in woodland and thicket areas. They are often grown for their pendulous, yellow racemes.

Laburnums are best used as specimen trees or trained over a pergola with the pea-like flowers hanging down. Flowers are produced profusely from late spring or early summer. The shiny green leaves are alternate and trifoliate, sometimes turning yellow in autumn, but forming a wonderful colour contrast with the yellow flowers. They can reach 5–8m (15–25ft) in height and spread almost as far. *Laburnum watereri* 'Vossii' produces hairy young shoots and long racemes of golden yellow flowers.

Propagate Laburnum by seed, which will germinate more quickly after scarifying. Hardwood cuttings in late winter should also root and these can be grafted onto seedling rootstocks.

Laburnum watereri 'Vossii'

MOISTURE	Keep moist but do not over water
SITE/LIGHT	Site in sun or partial shade in any well-drained, fertile soil
GENERAL CARE	Remove the seed pods after flowering
PESTS & DISEASES	Can be prone to black fly, powdery mildew and silver leaf

TREES
see also
137

COMPANION PLANTS
see pages
295
395

Lagurus HARE'S TAIL

This hardy annual grass has tufts of light green leaves and hairy, egg-shaped flowerheads on thin stems.

This plant's flowers are good for cutting and drying but should be gathered while still young. *Lagurus ovatus* can be grown in a mixed border with daisy flowered annuals such as cornflowers (centaurea),

Lagurus ovatus

Lagurus ovatus

English marigolds (calendulas), coreopsis and strawflowers (bracteantha), as well as other annuals like love-in-a-mist (nigella), limnanthes and cerinthe. Ideal for sandy soils and seaside gardens.

Raise plants from seed in spring, sown in the flowering position. They are not troubled by pests or diseases.

MOISTURE	Fairly tolerant of dry conditions
SITE/LIGHT	Enjoys light, sandy and well-drained soil in the full sun
GENERAL CARE	Flowerheads are good for dried flower arrangements
PESTS & DISEASES	Generally trouble free

FLOWERS see also 336

COMPANION PLANTS see pages 176 193 351

Lathyrus EVERLASTING PEA or SWEET PEA

The everlasting pea, *Lathyrus latifolius*, is a hardy herbaceous perennial while sweet peas, *L. odoratus* cultivars, are hardy annuals. They are mainly climbers, although dwarf bushy sweet peas have been bred. Many sweet pea cultivars are very fragrant.

The everlasting pea is a favourite cottage-garden plant and looks great scrambling through shrubs. Sweet peas can be grown up wigwams or obelisks in mixed borders. Dwarf sweet peas are ideal for patio containers. The flowers are excellent for cutting.

Sow sweet peas in autumn or early spring in a cold frame or in flowering positions in mid-spring. Propagate perennials by division in spring.

Feed sweet peas fortnightly with liquid fertilizer and dead-head regularly. Watch out for aphids, black root rot, foot rot, powdery mildew, slugs, snails and viruses.

Lathyrus latifolius

MOISTURE	Keep moist and do not allow to dry out
SITE/LIGHT	Fertile, humus-rich, well-drained soil in sun or light shade
GENERAL CARE	Dig in organic matter before planting and support climbers
PESTS & DISEASES	Prone to aphids, slugs, snails, powdery mildew and viruses

FLOWERS see also 154

COMPANION PLANTS see pages 245 264 425

Laurentia

Also known as Isotoma and Solenopsis, *Laurentia axillaris* is a small tender perennial with deeply cut leaves and star-shaped flowers which are produced in profusion over a very long period.

Laurentia is often used for summer bedding, especially in patio containers and window boxes. It is also a good subject for hanging baskets. Try combining this flower with *Bidens ferulifolia*, brachyscome, calceolarias, diascias and gazanias.

Remove dead flowerheads regularly to ensure continuous flowering. Propagate from seeds in spring under glass or from softwood cuttings in summer.

Winter young plants in a cool greenhouse but water sparingly. Plant out after the last frosts have finished.

Laurentia axillaris

MOISTURE	Water moderately
SITE/LIGHT	Enjoys fairly fertile, well-drained soil in the full sun
GENERAL CARE	Grow under glass in frost-prone areas
PESTS & DISEASES	Prone to aphids, especially in hot, dry conditions

FLOWERS
see also
198

COMPANION PLANTS
see pages
173
179
235

Laurus BAY LAUREL

Bay laurel is most often grown for its aromatic leaves, which are used in cooking but its flowers, which can be creamy-green to golden yellow, are also attractive.

The shrub or small tree can be clipped to shape or planted at the back of a border to make use of its dense, evergreen habit. *Laurus nobilis* f. *angustifolia* has more elongated leaves that are slightly serrated and is an excellent choice for coastal gardens, being much hardier to cold, salty winds than the more commonly grown *L. nobilis*.

All species grow equally well in pots where clipping into topiary should be carried out when the plant is young and continued every now and then during the growing season. Propagate by semi-hardwood cuttings in the summer or by seed, which germinates readily.

In the garden bay laurel thrives in a warm, sunny position on most well-drained soils, with protection from very strong winds.

Laurus nobilis

Laurus nobilis f. *angustifolia*

MOISTURE	Must be kept moist, especially in hot periods
SITE/LIGHT	Any fertile, well-drained soil in the full sun or partial shade
GENERAL CARE	Feed annually with a blood, fish and bone mix
PESTS & DISEASES	Apart from scale insects, fairly trouble free

TREES see also 314

COMPANION PLANTS see pages 201–4 254 441

Lavandula LAVENDER

Lavenders are most often grown both for the flowers, which are usually some shade of blue or purple, as well as for the aromatic foliage. The flowers in most species have a high nectar content which the bees love.

Lavenders have grey-green foliage and make excellent low hedges. Flowers are carried in erect spikes on long stalks above the foliage. Both the leaves and flowerheads can be cut and used dry as pot-pourri or in sachets.

Lavandula 'Marshwood'

The bushy shrubs can be compact, rounded or spreading, but all species need a clipping back in spring to keep them tidy. Older specimens tend to become leggy and are best replaced after ten years or so. Propagate new shrubs from softwood to semi-hardwood cuttings in summer and expect to replace them every few years.

Lavendula angustifolia 'Hidcote'

Lavendula angustifolia 'Hidcote' and *L.* 'Marshwood' are more compact varieties.

MOISTURE	Keep moist but avoid sites that get waterlogged in winter
SITE/LIGHT	Any well-drained soil in the full sun
GENERAL CARE	Clip regularly to shape or remove old flowerheads
PESTS & DISEASES	Generally trouble free

***SHRUBS* see also 364**

***COMPANION PLANTS* see pages 177 228–9 405**

Lavatera MALLOW

Mallow is grown for its showy flowers. *Lavatera trimestris* cultivars are hardy annuals with lobed leaves and trumpet-shaped flowers in shades of pink or white.

Lavatera is an excellent plant for a cottage garden or modern mixed border, particularly in association with shrub roses, mallows also mix well with other annuals such as clarkia and *Salvia viridis* (annual clary). These plants also look good with grey-leaved plants such as lavenders and artemisias. They are vigorous growers and produce profuse numbers of saucer- or funnel-shaped flowers throughout the summer.

Raise plants from seed in spring, under glass or in the flowering positions. Shrubs and perennial species, such as *Lavatera cachemiriana*, can be short lived, so propagate regularly.

The blooms last well when cut for flower arrangements. Protect plants from cold winds, preferably against a warm wall. Watch out for leaf spot, stem rot and rust.

Lavatera trimestris 'Silver Cup'

MOISTURE	Keep moist continually
SITE/LIGHT	Enjoys the full sun in fertile, well-drained soil
GENERAL CARE	Grow shrubby mallows in a shrub border
PESTS & DISEASES	Prone to leaf spot, stem rot and rust

SHRUBS
see also
213

COMPANION PLANTS
see pages
161
390–1
396

Leptospermum TEA TREE

The common name for these shrubs derive from early settlers in Australia and New Zealand soaking the leaves in boiling water to make a tea substitute, but nowadays Leptospermum makes a desirable garden plant.

Flowers are abundant and can completely hide the foliage, which is often glossy and aromatic. Forms vary in the size of their flowers, from the small, red double flowers of *Leptospermum scoparium* 'Red Damask', to the larger pale-pink flowers of *L. scoparium* 'Keatleyi'. Many tea trees make useful screen plants as most have a tight, compact growth, and are best planted up against a wall in colder areas. *L. scoparium* cultivars in particular are more spreading than tree-like.

Flowering stems can be cut and kept for some time in a vase of water.

Leptospermum is easy to propagate from seed, on top of damp compost, or softwood and semi-hardwood cuttings. Several cultivars have been established, originating mainly from *L. scoparium,* the New Zealand tea tree. However, most of the *L. scoparium* cultivars can be prone to scale insects.

Leptospermum scoparium 'Red Damask'

MOISTURE	Tolerates both wet and dry conditions
SITE/LIGHT	Site in the full sun in fertile, well-drained soil
GENERAL CARE	Do not disturb the roots when planting out
PESTS & DISEASES	Generally trouble free but can be prone to scale insects

***SHRUBS* see also 227**

***COMPANION PLANTS* see pages 143 275 354**

Leucanthemum SHASTA DAISY

Leucanthemum x _superbum_ cultivars are hardy herbaceous perennials, invaluable for their long display of white, single or double daisy flowers.

These are vigorous plants that are sometimes sold as Chrysanthemum, forming substantial clumps, which combine well in a herbaceous border or wild garden with many other hardy perennials, particularly those with strong colours. These include *Lychnis chalcedonica* (Maltese cross), and oriental poppies (*Papaver orientale*).

Propagate by division in spring or autumn. To keep plants young and vigorous, divide them every two to three years.

The flowers are extremely suitable for cutting. Provide supports for tall cultivars.

Leucanthemum x superbum 'Aglaia' produces semi-double, fringed flowers and *L. x superbum* 'Snowcap' has single, daisy-like flowerheads. Plants may be troubled by aphids, earwigs, leaf spot, slugs and snails.

Leucanthemum x superbum 'Aglaia'

Leucanthemum x superbum 'Snowcap'

MOISTURE	Keep moist but do not over water
SITE/LIGHT	Full sun or partial shade in fertile, well-drained soil
GENERAL CARE	Support taller plants because of the large flowerheads
PESTS & DISEASES	Prone to aphids, earwigs, slugs, snails and leaf spot

FLOWERS *see also* 199

COMPANION PLANTS *see pages* 163 327 359

Leucojom SNOWFLAKE

These hardy bulbs, which are rather similar to snowdrops (Galanthus), have bell-shaped flowers, mainly in white, and strap-shaped or grassy foliage.

Leucojum aestivum 'Gravetye Giant'

Snowflakes vary in size, the larger *Leucojom aestivum* and *L. vernum* being suited to mixed borders, where they look good drifted informally among shrubs or naturalized in grass, while the tiny *L. autumnale* is suitable for a rock garden. *L. aestivum*, also known as the summer snowflake, has a variety, 'Gravetye Giant', that is a particularly robust grower when it is planted near water.

Propagate by division of clumps, either in spring immediately after flowering or in autumn. *L. autumnale* should be divided while dormant in summer.

L. aestivum and *L. vernum* require rather moist, humus-rich soil, but other species will thrive in most moist, well-drained soils.

Leucojums may be attacked by narcissus bulb fly, slugs and snails.

MOISTURE	Keep well watered, especially *L. aestivum* and *L. vernum*
SITE/LIGHT	Generally happy in moist, well-drained soil in the full sun
GENERAL CARE	Ensure *L. aestivum* and *L. vernum* have humus content
PESTS & DISEASES	Prone to narcissus bulb fly, slugs and snails

***FLOWERS* see also 209**

***COMPANION PLANTS* see pages 165 166 226**

Leycesteria

Leycesteria is a genus of about six species of suckering, deciduous shrubs with hollow stems like canes. In the garden, they look great planted in light woodland, at the back of a border or beneath a large tree.

They are grown for their spiky racemes of yellow or white flowers. Berries follow the flowers and are either green (*Leycesteria crocothyrsos*) or shiny reddish purple in *L. formosa*, the Himalayan honeysuckle. The main colour in *L. formosa*, however, is provided by the claret red bracts. Both species have thick shoots, which are hollow in the centre, and greyish green leaves.

They can be propagated by seed, which birds can help with, and by semi-hardwood cuttings in summer.

The flowers and fruits develop stronger colours when the plants are grown in full sun. Leycesteria thrives on all soils, including chalky ones, except those of poor drainage.

Leycesteria formosa

MOISTURE	Keep reasonably moist
SITE/LIGHT	Best in the full sun in most well-drained soils
GENERAL CARE	Protect from cold winds and mulch deeply in autumn
PESTS & DISEASES	Generally trouble free

SHRUBS see also 323

COMPANION PLANTS see pages 220 290 382

Liatris GAYFEATHER

The hardy herbaceous perennial *Liatris spicata* is valued for substantial spikes of pink or white flowers produced late in the season among clumps of grassy foliage. Liatris grows from swollen stem-like corms.

The blooms of these plants, which attract bees, are suitable for cutting. Grow in mixed borders with ornamental grasses, especially *Stipa gigantea*, and with late-flowering perennials such as golden rod (solidago), asters, echinaceas and rudbeckias.

Propagate by dividing clumps in spring or sowing seed in a cold frame in the autumn.

Gayfeather dislikes wet soil in winter and is liable to rot in heavy, wet soil. Watch out for slugs and snails, which are partial to young foliage.

Liatris spicata

MOISTURE	Keep fairly moist but do not allow to become waterlogged
SITE/LIGHT	Enjoys full sun in moist, fertile, well-drained soil
GENERAL CARE	Flowers are good for cutting
PESTS & DISEASES	Prone to slugs and snails

FLOWERS
see also
313

COMPANION PLANTS
see pages
163
240
410

Ligularia

Hardy herbaceous perennials, ligularias are extremely vigorous plants with large, rounded or lobed leaves and erect, spiky stems of showy yellow or orange daisy-like flowerheads.

They are excellent for moist spots in the garden, including the edge of woodland gardens, and are especially at home planted around pools or on stream banks. Grow with shrubs in a mixed border, provided the soil is moist enough. Other good companions include rodgersias, hemerocallis, carex or sedges, waterside irises and ferns.

Propagate by division in spring or sow seed outdoors in containers in autumn or spring.

Ligularia przewalskii sends up purple-green stems up to 2m (6ft) high on which slender racemes of yellow flowerheads are produced.

Due to their height, protect ligularias from strong winds and keep moist. Slugs and snails are partial to the young foliage.

Ligularia przewalskii

MOISTURE	Keep well watered
SITE/LIGHT	Full sun with partial shade in deep, moist soil
GENERAL CARE	Shelter from strong, cold winds
PESTS & DISEASES	Prone to slugs and snails when young

FLOWERS
see also
312

COMPANION PLANTS
see pages
281
293
389

Ligustrum PRIVET

Privets are widely used as landscape shrubs, hedges and specimen trees. They are available in diverse leaf colours, leaf forms and growth habits. All are tolerant of heavy pruning which makes them suited as clipped hedges.

The white flowers are attractive during late spring and early summer. However, the pungent odour can be objectionable. *Ligustrum ovalifolium* forms are particularly useful as hedges, where their semi-evergreen foliage provides a dense screen in winter.

L. lucidum makes an excellent small to medium

Ligustrum lucidum

Ligustrum lucidum 'Excelsum Superbum'

specimen tree and has large, glossy leaves. It is also valuable for its early autumn flowering. 'Excelsum Superbum' is one of the best evergreen variegated forms.

Propagate by hardwood cuttings placed in a trench in winter (*L. ovalifolium* and *L.* 'Vicaryi') or by semi-hardwood cuttings in summer, or else by seed. They like any well-drained soil, preferably in a sunny spot.

MOISTURE	Water well, especially for the first two seasons
SITE/LIGHT	Enjoys any well-drained soil in the full sun
GENERAL CARE	Will tolerate frequent light clipping or trimming
PESTS & DISEASES	Honey fungus can be problematic

SHRUBS* *see also* *305

COMPANION PLANTS* *see pages* *178* *201–4

Lilium LILY

A large group of hardy bulbs of diverse habit, classified into nine divisions. The flowers may be shaped like a Turkscap (with reflexed petals), or trumpet-, funnel-, bowl- or star-shaped. Most have fragrant blooms.

Lilium 'Star Gazer'

Many species and hybrids are easy to grow, such as the ones listed here. Lilies are superb in woodland gardens or shrub borders. They prefer their roots shaded by low-growing shrubs and woodland perennials but like their heads in the sun. Lilies are also good for patio tubs, again with the root area shaded. The flowers are suitable for cutting.

Lilium 'Red Night'

Lilium 'Magic Pink'

Lilium 'Enchantment'

Propagate lilies from offsets or bulblets when dormant. They like humus-rich, acid to neutral soil, although some thrive in alkaline soils.

'Enchantment' and 'Star Gazer' both have star-shaped flowers. 'Magic Pink' has bowl-shaped, fragrant flowers, whereas 'Red Night' has unscented, cup-shaped blooms.

MOISTURE	Keep moist, particularly during hot spells
SITE/LIGHT	A sun-lover which prefers humus-rich soil
GENERAL CARE	Apply a mulch of leaf mould around its roots
PESTS & DISEASES	Prone to aphids, bulb rot, grey mould, slugs and snails

FLOWERS see also 149

COMPANION PLANTS see pages 139–40 374 384–5

Limanthes POACHED EGG PLANT

A hardy annual, *Limnanthes douglasii*, the best species, has flowers reminiscent of a poached egg (hence the common name) which attract bees.

Limnanthes douglasii is an attractive and cheerful plant for mixed borders from summer to autumn, and its sprawling informality makes a fine companion for nigella (love-in-a-mist), echiums (viper's bugloss), signet marigolds (tagetes), and dwarf grasses such as *Festuca glauca* (blue fescue). This is also a good annual for sowing in rock or scree gardens.

Propagate from seed sown in flowering positions during spring or autumn. Put cloches over autumn sowings in winter. Limnanthes also self sows prolifically.

Poached egg plants are ideal for exposed or windy gardens and are particularly at home in sandy soils.

They are not troubled by pests or diseases.

Limnanthes douglasii

MOISTURE	Keep fairly moist
SITE/LIGHT	A sunny position in well-drained, preferably sandy soil
GENERAL CARE	Usually takes care of itself
PESTS & DISEASES	Generally trouble free

FLOWERS see also 153

COMPANION PLANTS see pages 242 351 416

Limonium STATICE

Limonium sinuatum cultivars are frost-hardy, summer flowering perennials that are often grown as annuals. The heads of brightly coloured flowers, which are produced on winged stems, are suitable for cutting and drying.

Grow in a mixed border with eryngiums (sea holly), echinops (globe thistles), *Gypsophila paniculata* cultivars, osteospermums, gazanias and argyranthemums, or in rows on the vegetable plot, especially when used for cutting. Statice is particularly recommended for seaside gardens and it thrives in sandy soils.

Propagate from seed sown in early spring under glass. Transplant statice seedlings while fairly young as you may disturb the tap roots on older plants.

L. 'Sunset' varieties are especially attractive for their summer hues of apricot, peach, orange and pastel colours. *L. suworowii* is interesting for its long, curved spikes of bright pink blooms, which give rise to its other common name of pink pokers. Whichever your choice, statice is sure to brighten up any garden.

Limonium sinuatum cultivar

MOISTURE	Do not overwater
SITE/LIGHT	A sunny site in sandy, well-drained soil
GENERAL CARE	Pick flowers often to increase blooming season
PESTS & DISEASES	Prone to aphids and powdery mildew

FLOWERS
see also
166

COMPANION PLANTS
see pages
159
241
357

Linaria TOADFLAX

Linaria maroccana cultivars are dainty, hardy, summer flowering annuals with masses of small, two-lipped flowers in a wide range of bright colours. Grow toadflax at the front of mixed borders or in gravel areas.

Toadflax also looks good in gaps in paving. It is an excellent choice for cottage gardens and can look charming in window boxes and patio tubs. Suitable companions include border pinks and carnations (dianthus), and silver- or grey-foliage plants such as artemisias, catmints (nepeta) and lavenders. Especially suitable for sandy soils. Propagate from seed in spring, sowing in flowering positions. Toadflax also self sows prolifically.

L. maroccana 'Fairy Bouquet' is an excellent dwarf form, reaching 15cm (6in).

Linaria maroccana 'Fairy Bouquet'

MOISTURE	Do not overwater
SITE/LIGHT	Full sun in most well-drained soils, preferably sandy
GENERAL CARE	Avoid even partial shade as it produces poor blooms
PESTS & DISEASES	Prone to powdery mildew, aphids, slugs and snails

FLOWERS
see also
245

COMPANION PLANTS
see pages
234
306
348

Liquidambar SWEET GUM

In the garden, sweet gums are often grown for the maple-like leaves, which make a fantastic autumnal display, turning scarlet, red, crimson or orange and lasting for two or more weeks.

Liquidambar is an excellent choice as a specimen tree for large gardens with the space to allow it to grow to its full height of 25m (80ft), but that may take at least 100 years.

Liquidambar styraciflua 'Silver Icing'

Most sweet gums can be grafted onto seedling rootstocks, but softwood cuttings taken in summer from *Liquidambar styraciflua* forms may be more successful.

Liquidambar does not grow on shallow soils overlying chalk, where at best it is very chlorotic, but it will thrive in deeper soils.

Take care when transplanting these trees as they can be slow to reform their roots.

Liquidambar styraciflua 'Lane Roberts'

MOISTURE	Keep well watered, especially until established
SITE/LIGHT	Prefers a sunny position in heavy, wet soils
GENERAL CARE	Prune only if needed to reshape
PESTS & DISEASES	Generally trouble free

TREES see also 249

COMPANION PLANTS see pages 161 174

Liriope LILYTURF

A hardy evergreen perennial, lilyturf grows from tuberous roots. Spikes of pale violet or white flowers appear from clumps of grassy foliage late in the year.

An excellent plant for shady places in a woodland garden or shrub border. Planted in a large mass it also makes fine ground cover. Good companions include other ground cover plants such as ivies (hedera), *Pachysandra terminalis* and periwinkles (vinca). Winter and spring bulbs such as snowdrops (galanthus) and dwarf narcissus also look good growing through the foliage. Lilyturf prefers acid or lime-free soil.

Propagate Liriope by division in spring.

Liriope muscari varieties are great to add autumn and winter colour to the garden.

Liriope muscari

Liriope muscari 'John Burch'

MOISTURE	Likes to be kept moist
SITE/LIGHT	Good for shady areas in acid or lime free soil
GENERAL CARE	Gold-variegated leaves of 'John Birch' enliven winter beds
PESTS & DISEASES	Young leaves are prone to slugs and snails

FLOWERS see also 209

COMPANION PLANTS see pages 344–5 436

Lobelia

The most popular lobelias are *Lobelia erinus* cultivars, grown as half-hardy annuals. These low bushy or trailing plants are used for summer bedding, often edging beds, and are also good for containers – the trailing kinds being suitable for hanging baskets.

These plants produce masses of tiny two-lipped flowers over a long period and combine well with many other summer bedding plants. The traditional colour is blue, but various other colours are available.

Very different in habit are the hardy herbaceous perennials, ideal for planting at the edge of a pool, or in a mixed border if the soil is sufficiently moist, where they look best with shrubs and hostas. These include *L. cardinalis* (cardinal flower) and *L.* 'Queen Victoria'; *L.* x *speciosa* cultivars, often grown as annuals; and *L. siphilitica* (blue cardinal flower) which looks good in a woodland garden or shrub border.

Lobelia erinus 'Crystal Palace'

Lobelia erinus 'Cascade Mixed'

Raise annuals from seed under glass in late winter. Propagate perennials by division in spring, or from stem cuttings in summer.

MOISTURE	Keep soil sufficiently moist
SITE/LIGHT	Enjoys sun or shade in most damp soils
GENERAL CARE	Feed annuals fortnightly with low nitrogen liquid fertilizer
PESTS & DISEASES	Prone to attacks from slugs and snails

***FLOWERS* see also 165**

***COMPANION PLANTS* see pages 168 362 416**

Lobularia SWEET ALISON or SWEET ALYSSUM

Cultivars of *Lobularia maritima* are low, quick-growing, carpeting hardy annuals covered with heads of small, four-petalled, fragrant flowers. Mainly white, other colours are available, such as *L.* 'Purple Carpet'.

These plants are used for summer bedding, often for edging beds, and are good in containers, including hanging baskets. Traditionally combined with bedding lobelia, sweet alyssum associates well with many other summer bedding plants, and is especially useful as a foil for strong or 'hot' colours. They are excellent plants for seaside gardens.

Propagate from seed in spring, under glass or in flowering positions.

Plant in fertile, well-drained soil in a sunny position as even slight shade during the day will slow down flowering and eventually make the plants become spindly.

Lobularia maritima cultivar

MOISTURE	Keep moist but do not over water
SITE/LIGHT	Full sun in fertile, well-drained soil
GENERAL CARE	Regularly trim off dead flowerheads with shears
PESTS & DISEASES	Prone to slugs, snails, cabbage root fly and club beetle

FLOWERS see also 166

COMPANION PLANTS see pages 232 291 321

Lonicera HONEYSUCKLE

Honeysuckles are big, bold plants with a showy display of delicate, highly fragrant flowers and are among the easiest climbers to raise as they are very hardy and not particularly bothered by pests and diseases.

Lonicera fragrantissima

There are many places to grow honeysuckles, such as over a porch or arbour where the scents can be best appreciated. Alternatively, try up a pergola, or in a hedge, where it can grow unrestrained and mingle with other vegetation such as Clematis and Wisteria, perhaps popping out flowers 6m (20ft) up.

The stems of older honeysuckles become large, very woody and twisted around each other. Cut back the plant every few years, during the winter, to get rid of any knotted wood and branches, and to keep the plant within bounds.

Propagate either by seed or cuttings. Take off the leaves of a low stem in autumn, bend it to the ground and make an incision at ground level. Then bury the stem 3cm (1in) deep and detach the new plant a year later.

There are many species and varieties of honeysuckle to choose from. During the winter months the highly scented flowers of *Lonicera fragrantissima* burst from the stems in a great display. The cream flowers of *L. pileata* provides evergreen foliage all year round.

MOISTURE	Water regularly until established; check in drought periods
SITE/LIGHT	Full sun to partial shade in most, well-drained soils
GENERAL CARE	Avoid planting against a very hot wall; keep roots shaded
PESTS & DISEASES	Aphids may attack but the plant is usually not damaged

SHRUBS see also 311

COMPANION PLANTS see pages 275 288 369

Luma ORANGE-BARK MYRTLE

The orange-bark myrtle is, as its name suggests, most often grown for the amazing feature of its bark, as well as its waxy foliage. Orange or cinnamon in colour, the bark cracks to reveal stunning white streaks in older trees

The characteristic orange bark does not normally appear until the tree is around five years old. Its foliage consists of small, shiny green leaves with pointed tips and are aromatic if crushed. Fragrant white flowers appear in mid to late summer or early autumn, followed by round, fleshy fruit.

Unfortunately, this tree is not hardy in cold winters in inland sites, even with shelter. However, in milder areas, especially in woodland shelter, it is a really first-class, narrow-crowned tree or shrub.

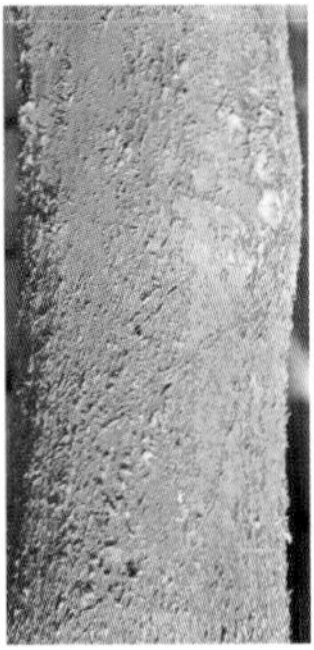

Luma apiculata

Luma apiculata

Grow on by taking semi-hardwood cuttings in summer or ripe cuttings with a heel of older wood in winter.

Luma apiculata enjoys lots of watering, particularly when young. Luma will thrive on all well-drained fertile soils and in full sun to moderate shade.

MOISTURE	Water often until established, then regularly
SITE/LIGHT	Full sun to partial shade in well-drained fertile soil
GENERAL CARE	Mulch to maintain a humus-rich soil and protect roots
PESTS & DISEASES	Generally trouble free

TREES
see also
247

COMPANION PLANTS
see pages
139–40
178

Lunaria HONESTY

Lunaria annua is grown as a hardy biennial, while _L. rediviva_ is a hardy herbaceous perennial. Both produce heads of four-petalled flowers above somewhat heart-shaped, saw-edged leaves.

The translucent silvery or buff seed pods that follow the flowers give off a shimmer effect in the late summer and are also suitable for drying.

Lunaria annua 'Variegata'

Lunaria rediviva

Both species are ideal for a wild or woodland garden but also look at home in a mixed border planted around shrubs, and among perennials such as hostas and astilbes. Lunaria is also a good choice for cottage gardens.

Raise plants from seed in late spring in a nursery bed and divide perennials in spring. Both species mentioned are self-seeders.

Plants showing symptoms of virus should be pulled up and discarded as there is no cure unfortunately.

MOISTURE	Keep moist, especially during summer
SITE/LIGHT	Full sun to partial shade in any well-drained soil
GENERAL CARE	Cut seed stalks to the ground for dried arrangements
PESTS & DISEASES	Virus can destroy plants

FLOWERS see also 379

COMPANION PLANTS see pages 155 240 341

Lupinus LUPIN

The lupins mentioned here are hardy herbaceous hybrid perennials, producing fat spikes of flowers above clumps of leaves, giving the garden a stunning vertical aspect.

These are virtually 'essential' plants for the mixed border, invaluable for combining with other early flowering perennials such as oriental poppies (*Papaver orientale*), peonies, bearded irises and delphiniums. Ornamental onions (allium) are also good companions, as are old and modern shrub roses.

Lupinus 'Polar Princess'

The perennial hybrid lupins are best propagated from basal cuttings in spring.

Lupinus arboreus (the tree lupin) is a shrubby form of the plant. *L.* 'Polar Princess' produces ice white flowers and *L.* 'The Page' adds a vivid red colour to the flower bed.

Lupins prefer acid, sandy soil. Problems include leaf spot, powdery mildew, slugs, snails and viruses.

Lupinus 'The Page'

Lupinus arboreus

MOISTURE	Keep moist
SITE/LIGHT	Flowers best in full sun in any well-drained soil
GENERAL CARE	Work in compost before planting
PESTS & DISEASES	Prone to leaf spot, powdery mildew, slugs and snails

FLOWERS
see also
299

COMPANION PLANTS
see pages
147
232
293

Lychnis

A diverse genus of hardy plants, lychnis often have strongly coloured, star-shaped or flat lobed flowers which produce a dazzling summer display.

Lychnis chalcedonica (Jerusalem or Maltese cross) is a popular herbaceous perennial and can be used to create dazzling combinations, particularly with flat-headed achilleas or day lilies (hemerocallis). *L. coronaria* (rose campion) is a short-lived perennial raised regularly from seed. It looks good with other silver-leaved perennials such as artemisias, and with shrub roses. *L. flos-cuculi* (ragged robin) is a herbaceous perennial for the woodland or wild garden.

Propagate in spring, from seed under cover, by division or from basal cuttings.

Plant in most well-drained garden soils in the full sun, although Lychnis does tolerate some shade in particularly hot areas. Keep the ground fairly moist and well fertilized, even though it can tolerate some dryness. Watch out for slugs and snails.

Lychnis coronaria

MOISTURE	Keep the soil evenly moist
SITE/LIGHT	Prefers full sun in any well-drained soil
GENERAL CARE	Apply a balanced fertilizer monthly and deadhead flowers
PESTS & DISEASES	Prone to attack from slugs and snails

***FLOWERS* see also 234**

***COMPANION PLANTS* see pages 161 281 289**

Lysimachia

Lysimachias are hardy herbaceous perennials, except for *Lysimachia nummularia* (creeping Jenny) which is an evergreen species.

L. nummularia is a prostrate ground-cover plant that can become invasive, but other species, such as *L. punctata*, are border plants with spikes of starry or cup-shaped flowers. Grow creeping Jenny

Lysimachia nummularia

among shrubs in a woodland garden or mixed border – it looks good combined with ajugas. The taller perennials, such as *L. punctata* and *L. clethroides*, are suitable for mixed borders, poolside planting or wild gardens, in combination with hemerocallis (day lilies), ligularias and rodgersias.

Propagate Lysimachia by division in spring.

All enjoy the full sun, but the creeping Jenny will perform better if it is given some shade. Do not allow plants to dry out.

Lysimachia punctata

MOISTURE	Keep moist at all times, especially during summer
SITE/LIGHT	Most species are sun lovers in any well-drained soil
GENERAL CARE	Trim back *L. nummularia* if it becomes too invasive
PESTS & DISEASES	Prone to attack from slugs and snails

FLOWERS see also 396

COMPANION PLANTS see pages 281 313 389

Magnolia

Magnolias are from a genus of trees or large shrubs. They are widely grown for their delicious fragrant and colourful flowers on grey-barked branches. They can be divided into two groups: those which flower early (or precociously) in early spring and those which flower later.

Whether early or late flowering, tree or shrub, magnolias produce large blooms in a range of vibrant colours. Magnolia is shown to its best effect planted against a backdrop of evergreens or positioned alongside a path where the perfume of its flowers can really be appreciated. The blooms tend not to last more than a few days each, but as they are produced copiously, this tends not to impede the overall beauty and impressiveness of the plant.

Magnolia grandiflora

Magnolia grandiflora

Precocious flowering forms, such as the shrubby star magnolia, *M. stellata*, herald the start of spring with its hues of white and pink covering the branches. *M. stellata* 'Royal Star' produces large, star-shaped flowers. Early flowering forms need protection from frost as this can damage the blooms. Train *M. stellata* up against a wall where it can be protected

***TREES* see also 283**

***COMPANION PLANTS* see pages 184 215**

Magnolia 'Iolanthe'

Magnolia loebneri 'Leonard Messell'

against strong sunshine, frost and the wind. *M. loebneri* is slightly later flowering, so is not as susceptible to damage.

M. sieboldii produces cup-shaped white flowers from late spring right through the summer. *M.* 'Iolanthe' has beautiful pale pink flowers. *M. grandiflora* or bull bay tree can be wall trained.

Magnolia sieboldii

Magnolia stellata 'Royal Star'

Most magnolias prefer all day sun and flower best in fertile, acid or neutral soil that is moisture retentive but that also has good drainage.

Where possible, give magnolias some shelter from strong winds, as not only do the flowers get blown off but branches can also snap.

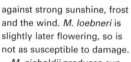

MOISTURE	Keep moist but do not allow to become waterlogged
SITE/LIGHT	A sunny and sheltered site in fertile, well-drained soil
GENERAL CARE	Apply a fertilizer or mulch in spring
PESTS & DISEASES	Prone to grey mould and scale insects

TREES see also 260

COMPANION PLANTS see pages 221

Mahonia

Mahonia is a close cousin to the Berberis, except that it has spineless stems. However, the pinnate leaves can be quite sharp. The larger growing Mahonia forms can make large shrubs or even excellent small flowering trees – given a few decades of growth.

Small, yellow-coloured, fragrant flowers are produced in clusters of long racemes. In *Mahonia japonica* and *M. aquifolium*, these are carried over the winter period. Blue-black fruits ripen in spring. Shrubby species such as *M. aquifolium* can be grown as ground cover and taller ones such as *M. lomariifolia* can be

Mahonia aquifolium

Mahonia japonica 'Bealei'

used as specimens in a shrub border or woodland garden. They also make thick hedges and screens.

Mahonia can be raised from seed or by cuttings from single nodes of a shoot taken in late winter.

Mahonia enjoys full sun or moderate shade and is quite happy on most well-drained soils. Pruning is only necessary to tidy up the plant or reshape it.

MOISTURE	Keep fairly moist, particularly if in full sun
SITE/LIGHT	A sunny site with some shade in most well-drained soils
GENERAL CARE	Remove stems damaged by winter frosts in spring
PESTS & DISEASES	Generally trouble free

SHRUBS see also 170

COMPANION PLANTS see pages 219 274

Malus CRAB APPLE

Crab apples are relatives of the domestic apple, and are grown for their usually fragrant flowers and their attractive, edible fruits. Some of the varieties, however, produce fruits which are inedible if uncooked. Masses of flowers engulf the tree in late spring, hiding the foliage.

Crab apples provide a focal point in the garden for much of the year. They are ideal specimen trees for the smaller garden or the larger shrub bed. They can also be trimmed and reshaped to make flowering hedges. The habit varies from conical, such as *Malus* 'Evereste', to open and rounded, such as *M.* 'Katherine'.

Malus 'Evereste'

Malus 'Katherine'

The fruits are often hard and only good to look at, except in *M.* 'John Downie' and *M. robusta* 'Red Sentinel' where they are used to make jelly.

Propagate by seed, by cuttings or grafting onto a rootstock.

Malus thrives on a wide range of soils and are excellent both for heavy clays and chalky sites. They tolerate light shade but flower, fruit and autumn colour are all much better when positioned in the full sun.

MOISTURE	Do not overwater or allow to dry out in summer
SITE/LIGHT	Prefers full sun on any soil type
GENERAL CARE	Remove defective branches and thin crowns
PESTS & DISEASES	Prone to honey fungus, canker, caterpillars and aphids

TREES see also 221

COMPANION PLANTS see pages 329–30

Matthiola STOCK

The hardy *Matthiola incana* cultivars, grown as annuals or biennials for bedding or containers, are valued for their spikes of fragrant flowers that are good for cutting. Ideal for mixed borders, these plants also look at home in cottage gardens.

Brompton stocks and the Legacy Series are grown as biennials; the Cinderella Series and Ten Week stocks are treated as annuals. *M. longipetala subsp. bicornis* (night-scented stock) is a hardy annual, useful for filling gaps in borders. All stocks prefer alkaline soil.

Sow annuals in early spring under glass. Biennials are sown in mid-summer in a cold frame or seed bed, planted out in autumn and protected with cloches, or wintered in a cold frame and planted out in spring. Sow night-scented stock in flowering positions in spring.

Watch out for aphids, club root, grey mould and virus.

Matthiola incana Brompton Mixed

MOISTURE	Do not allow to dry out – keep moist
SITE/LIGHT	Full sun to partial shade in fertile, well-drained soil
GENERAL CARE	Provide support for taller varieties
PESTS & DISEASES	Prone to aphids, club root, grey mould and virus

FLOWERS see also 245

COMPANION PLANTS see pages 171 358 437

Mespilus MEDLAR

Medlars are small, deciduous trees of the Rosaceae family, closely related to pear (Pyrus) and hawthorn (Crataegus). The trees have been grown since ancient times for their edible fruit and attractive spreading habit.

Quite attractive with its white flowers, it is well-known for its fruit, which is apple-shaped with a flat end. The flesh is hard and inedible until after-ripening, known as bletting. Bletted fruit has flesh with the consistency and taste of apple butter. The fruits are best left on the tree until mid autumn or even later. *Mespilus germanica* 'Nottingham' has more tasty fruits than other cultivars and is less thorny with larger leaves, flowers and fruits. In autumn the leaves turn russet. The medlar tree blooms and bears fruit when very young.

Mespilus germanica 'Nottingham'

Apart from being grown in an orchard setting, medlar is good as a specimen tree for a lawn area or wild garden.

It can be propagated by seed after the last frosts but is most often grafted onto an apple, quince or pear rootstock.

It requires full sun but can tolerate moderate shade. Mespilus thrives on a wide range of soil types, including clays and chalky soils, but must not be overwatered.

MOISTURE	Water regularly but do not overwater
SITE/LIGHT	Full sun on most garden soil types
GENERAL CARE	Prune only to resize or reshape
PESTS & DISEASES	Prone to leaf blotch fungus and mildew

TREES see also 332

COMPANION PLANTS see pages 221

Mimulus MONKEY FLOWER

Various hardy hybrids are generally grown as annuals for summer bedding or display in containers. They have brilliantly coloured, tubular, flaring flowers, often spotted with a contrasting colour.

These plants look good in the moist soil beside a pool, say with hostas and astilbes. *Mimulus cardinalis* (scarlet monkey flower) is a hardy herbaceous perennial for the poolside or bog garden. *M.* 'Puck' has attractive, apricot coloured blooms.

Raise annuals from seed in spring under glass. Propagate perennials in spring, by division or from softwood cuttings.

All mimulas like soil with a high humus content. Water well in dry weather. When growing in containers such as patio tubs and windowboxes, make sure that the compost does not dry out, as this will curtail growth and flowering.

Mimulus 'Puck'

MOISTURE	Keep well watered, particularly during summer
SITE/LIGHT	Full sun in moist, humus-rich soil
GENERAL CARE	Apply liquid fertilizer monthly
PESTS & DISEASES	Prone to powdery mildew, slugs and snails

FLOWERS see also 437

COMPANION PLANTS see pages 285 313 321

Miscanthus

These hardy, herbaceous, perennial grasses are valued as much for their foliage as for their airy panicles of flowers produced late in the season.

The dead foliage and flowers remain attractive through winter. The flowerheads are more numerous following long, dry summers. Miscanthus are great for combining with a wide range of hardy perennials in mixed borders, including late-flowering kinds, and with shrubs, especially those with autumn leaf tints or berries. They also look good in gravel areas and beside pools.

Propagate by division in spring or sow seed in containers in a cold frame.

Miscanthus sinensis 'Silberfeder' (silver feather) flowers freely with silvery to pale pink-brown panicles in early to mid autumn.

Miscanthus are not usually troubled by pests or diseases.

Miscanthus sinensis 'Silberfeder'

MOISTURE	Keep moist but protect from too much winter wet
SITE/LIGHT	Full sun in fairly fertile, well-drained soil
GENERAL CARE	Use flowerheads for cuttings
PESTS & DISEASES	Generally trouble free

FLOWERS
see also
302

COMPANION PLANTS
see pages
220
282
296

Monarda BERGAMOT

Hardy herbaceous perennials, monardas have aromatic foliage and whorled heads of tubular flowers attractive to bees, on stiff, upright stems.

These plants are particularly suited to prairie-style borders mixed with ornamental grasses such as miscanthus, and with later-flowering perennials including *Aster x frikartii* 'Mönch', rudbeckias, echinacea, helianthus and golden rods (solidago).

Propagate in spring, by division or from basal cuttings.

Monarda 'Violet Queen'

Monarda 'Beauty of Cobham'

Monarda 'Beauty of Cobham' is a nice form with pale pink flowers and purple-flashed leaves and *M.* 'Violet Queen' is a good modern cultivar.

Bergamot is not tolerant of excessively wet soil in winter nor of drought conditions during summer.

MOISTURE	Water moderately – not too wet and not too dry
SITE/LIGHT	Enjoys the full sun in humus-rich, well-drained soil
GENERAL CARE	Protect from too much water during winter
PESTS & DISEASES	Prone to powdery mildew, slugs and snails

FLOWERS see also 163

COMPANION PLANTS see pages 240 278 410

Morus MULBERRY

Most widely known, especially the white mulberry (*Morus alba*), as the food of the silkworm moth, Morus is a genus of about ten species of upright to rounded deciduous trees and shrubs.

Morus nigra

The foliage is attractive with its rounded, toothed, often lobed and heart-shaped green leaves. Oblong, raspberry-like fruits, which ripen to dark red or purple, follow pale green flower clusters. Plant mulberries as specimen trees. *M. alba* 'Pendula' is particularly good for small gardens, while *M. nigra* (black mulberry) is the best for edible fruit.

Morus alba 'Pendula'

Mulberries are easily propagated by semi-ripe cuttings in summer.

Morus needs full sun and a warm, well-drained soil, preferably a deep loam. Shallow soils such as those frequently found on chalk or gravel are not recommended.

MOISTURE	Fairly drought resistant, but needs watering in summer
SITE/LIGHT	Full sun in fairly fertile, well-drained soil
GENERAL CARE	Apply an annual balanced liquid fertilizer
PESTS & DISEASES	Prone to coral spot and mildew occasionally

TREES see also 221

COMPANION PLANTS see pages 395

Muehlenbeckia

Muehlenbeckia is mostly cultivated for its intricate habit and is a really versatile plant for screens, hedges and topiary work. Its moderate growth, tiny leaves and wiry stems are ideal for beginners at topiary.

These shrubs or climbers are excellent creepers over arches, pergolas and latticework. Species such as *Muehlenbeckia complexa* are also useful for ground cover. *M. adpressa* (climbing lignum) is a good coastal climber. It is an exceptional plant for coastal areas and is hardy in all but the most frost-affected areas. The minute flowers are cup-shaped and sweet-scented.

Propagate from seed, tip or root cuttings by using a gritty mix at any time of the year.

Muehlenbeckia tolerates shade or full sun and responds well to a rich soil and regular watering. They also tolerate occasional drought.

Muehlenbeckia complexa

Muehlenbeckia complexa

MOISTURE	In general, water regularly
SITE/LIGHT	Full sun or partial shade, in rich soil
GENERAL CARE	Prune to keep in shape
PESTS & DISEASES	Trouble free, but aphids could attack in hot summers

SHRUBS see also 178

COMPANION PLANTS see pages 144 441

Muscari GRAPE HYACINTH

Grape hyacinths are hardy dwarf bulbs. *Muscari armeniacum* has grassy foliage and short, stumpy spikes of tubular flowers. It is a particularly robust bulb and spreads quickly – an ideal plant for spring colour.

As muscari will take partial shade, plant it around shrubs in mixed borders, in bold groups or drifts, with other small spring bulbs such as miniature narcissus and erythroniums. Grape hyacinth is also suitable for a woodland garden, for naturalizing in grass and for planting on rock gardens.

Muscari also makes an excellent container plant as its spiky foliage spreads and quickly fills a large pot. Make sure it has good drainage though to prevent the bulbs from rotting.

Muscari armeniacum

Propagate by splitting up and replanting established clumps when dormant in summer or autumn.

Grape hyacinth prefers a rich, well-drained but moist soil. Add a few handfuls of sand or grit to the soil if the drainage is poor.

MOISTURE	Keep moist at all times, but not waterlogged
SITE/LIGHT	Partial shade or sun in rich, well-drained soil
GENERAL CARE	Buy bulbs in autumn, preferably loose and not packaged
PESTS & DISEASES	Apart from possible virus, generally trouble free

FLOWERS
see also
286

COMPANION PLANTS
see pages
246
344–5

Myosotis FORGET-ME-NOT

Myosotis sylvatica cultivars are hardy dwarf biennials producing a haze of tiny flowers, mainly in shades of blue, in spring. They can be planted in spring bedding schemes as a carpet for bedding tulips.

Forget-me-nots are delightful when planted in informal drifts around spring-flowering deciduous shrubs, such as Forsythia or Spiraea, or in woodland gardens. They also have a slight fragrance which can waft through the garden.

Raise plants from seed sown in an outdoor seed bed in early summer and plant out in autumn. Forget-me-nots will also self-sow freely.

M. sylvatica 'Royal Blue' is taller than most cultivars.

Myosotis sylvatiica 'Royal Blue'

Myosotis sylvatica 'Blue Ball'

MOISTURE	Requires only a little moisture in order to thrive
SITE/LIGHT	A sun-lover which is happy in any type of soil
GENERAL CARE	Plant young saplings from pots when small
PESTS & DISEASES	Prone to powdery mildew, slugs and snails

FLOWERS see also 279

COMPANION PLANTS see pages 169 245 427–8

Myrtus MYRTLE

Myrtle is widely grown for its white, fragrant flowers, which are carried mainly in mid- to late summer, as well as for its glossy and aromatic leaves.

Myrtle can be used as a hedging plant as it still flowers after trimming. It is also excellent in a shrub bed or an herbaceous border. It will flower much better in the full sun, not liking any amount of shade. As Myrtle is not fully hardy, it should be given the shelter of a sun-facing wall in colder districts.

Myrtus communis

Myrtus communis ssp. tarentina

Propagate myrtle from semi-hardwood cuttings in summer and hardwood cuttings in late autumn. It can also be grown from seed and by layering.

Myrtus communis forms are good for growing in the garden. They have an even spread in width and height, eventually reaching 2m (7ft) up and across.

Myrtles are tolerant of most soils, provided they are well drained, even those derived from chalk and limestone.

MOISTURE	Keep moist but not too wet
SITE/LIGHT	Full sun in any well-drained soil
GENERAL CARE	Protect myrtles in less temperate climates
PESTS & DISEASES	Generally trouble free

SHRUBS see also 308

COMPANION PLANTS see pages 170 294

Nandina HEAVENLY BAMBOO

Heavenly bamboo (*Nandina domestica*) is actually unrelated to bamboo. Its common name derives from its resemblance to bamboo due to the fine lacy foliage and the plant's habit, which is cane like.

What makes this plant special is the colour it provides in the garden throughout the year. New foliage emerges in spring as bright bronzed red, and is soon followed by large panicles of creamy white flowers. The foliage then becomes blue-green and clusters of green berries replace the flowers, ripening to a bright red. In autumn, the foliage changes to shades of pink and red, ending the year with bright red leaves and berries, which birds love.

Nandina is at its best when planted as a focal point, such as in a raised bed beside the front door or by an entrance path. It will thrive in containers and can make an interesting patio shrub.

Heavenly bamboos can be propagated with seeds, but germination may take several years, so it is best to take cuttings during spring or early summer.

Grow in full sun for intense foliage colours, with slight shade for the hottest part of the day. Give shelter from harsh winds. Nandina prefers fertile, well-drained soils.

Nandina domestica

MOISTURE	Keep moist at all times
SITE/LIGHT	Full sun with slight shade in fertile, well-drained soil
GENERAL CARE	Mulch regularly to maintain humus content
PESTS & DISEASES	Generally trouble free

SHRUBS *see also* 162

COMPANION PLANTS *see pages* 214 355 372

Narcissus DAFFODIL

One of the classic heralds of spring is swathes of golden daffodils, growing anywhere from coastal meadows to the foothills of mountains. There are now more than fifty species of narcissus and thousands of cultivars have been developed.

Daffodils are among the most popular of hardy bulbs. They range from miniature species (such as *Narcissus* 'Tête-à-tête') and hybrids to tall cultivars with large flowers. Leaves may be strap-shaped or, in miniature species, somewhat grassy. Basically, the flowers consist of a trumpet- or cup-shaped corona surrounded by flat or reflexed petals.

The Narcissus genus is classified into 12 divisions. The most popular are: the Trumpet daffodils with a large, trumpet-shaped corona; Large-cupped, with a large, cup-shaped corona; Double, with double flowers; Cyclamineus, with reflexed petals and long

Narcissus 'Tête-à-Tête'

FLOWERS
see also
427–8

COMPANION PLANTS
see pages
280
286
320

corona, such as the early flowering yellow *N.* 'February Gold' and the pure white *N.* 'Dove Wings'; Triandrus, Jonquilla and Tazetta with clusters of small flowers; and Split Corona, with a flat corona that is deeply split (often likened to a fried egg).

Daffodils generally look best when grown informally. For example, plant generous groups or drifts among shrubs in a mixed border or woodland garden. Daffodils are also suitable for containers and window boxes. They make excellent cut flowers.

Narcissus 'Dove Wings'

Narcissus 'February Gold'

Lift and divide congested clumps when dormant. Propagate by removing offsets also when dormant.

If the soil is light or you are planting in grass, set the bulbs slightly more deeply. Acid soil is best for Cyclamineus and Triandrus daffodils, and slightly alkaline for Jonquilla and Tazetta cultivars.

Daffodils are prone to bulb rot, narcissus bulb fly, slugs, snails and viruses.

MOISTURE	Keep fairly moist at all times
SITE/LIGHT	Partial shade to full sun in most well-drained soils
GENERAL CARE	Some shade will help the blooms last longer
PESTS & DISEASES	Prone to bulb rot, narcissus bulb fly, slugs and snails

FLOWERS *see also* 310

COMPANION PLANTS *see pages* 340 341

Nemesia

Nemesia strumosa **cultivars are half-hardy annuals with heads of small, two-lipped flowers in a wide range of bright colours, often bicoloured.**

Nemesia strumosa cultivar

Used for summer bedding, patio containers and window boxes, they should be mass planted for best effect. Try planting them with *Salvia farinacea* cultivars, *Nemophila menziesii* (baby blue-eyes) and *Scaevola aemula.*

Raise plants from seed in spring under glass.

Nemesias perform best in slightly acid soil and dislike hot dry conditions, so keep them cool and water as necessary.

Nemesia strumosa 'Sundrops Mixed'

MOISTURE	Keep well watered – do not allow to dry out
SITE/LIGHT	Likes the full sun in slightly acid soil
GENERAL CARE	Protect during extremely hot conditions
PESTS & DISEASES	May be prone to black root rot and foot rot

***FLOWERS* see also 291**

***COMPANION PLANTS* see pages 347 396 403**

Nemophila BABY BLUE-EYES

***Nemophila menziesii*, the best species, is a small, hardy annual with pinnate greyish-green leaves and shallow, bowl-shaped flowers in summer.**

Suitable for mixed borders, patio containers and window boxes, nemophila is ideal for combining with more strongly coloured annuals, such as nemesias.

Other effective companion plants are *Argyranthemum* 'Jamaica Primrose' and *Limnanthes douglasii* (poached egg plant).

To propagate, seeds can be sown in spring or autumn in flowering positions. Once introduced to a garden, plants will increase by self-sowing.

N. menziesii 'Snowstorm' is a particularly attractive variety with white dappled flowers.

Apart from aphids, there are no problems from pests or diseases.

Nemophila menziesii 'Snowstorm'

MOISTURE	Keep moist at all times
SITE/LIGHT	Full sun in most types of garden soil
GENERAL CARE	Vigorous self-seeder, so thin out if necessary
PESTS & DISEASES	Prone to aphids, but generally trouble free

FLOWERS *see also* 325

COMPANION PLANTS *see pages* 159 316 346

Nepeta CATMINT

Hardy herbaceous perennials, the catmints have aromatic foliage and spikes of two-lipped flowers, mainly in blue and purple shades, over a long period. The blooms attract bees. Grow nepeta in a mixed border, including cottage-garden borders.

Catmints combine particularly well with roses of all kinds (old and modern), and with geraniums, peonies and lupins. After flowering, trim plants lightly with shears to encourage more blooms to follow and compact growth.

Nepeta x faassenii

Nepeta 'Six Hills Giant'

Propagate by division in spring or autumn.

Nepeta 'Six Hills Giant' is a tall cultivar, reaching nearly 1m (3ft) in height. *N.* x *faassenii* is slightly more compact, only growing to about 45cm (18in) high. Both have aromatic, greyish-green foliage.

Watch out for powdery mildew, slugs and snails.

MOISTURE	Keep moist but do not overwater
SITE/LIGHT	Full sun is preferred in most garden soils
GENERAL CARE	Trim plants lightly after flowering to encourage blooms
PESTS & DISEASES	Prone to powdery mildew, slugs and snails

FLOWERS see also 306

COMPANION PLANTS see pages 267 326 358

Nerine

Nerines are bulbous perennials grown for their attractive umbels of colourful, lily-like flowers. The blooms, which appear in mid- to late autumn, are excellent for cutting. Plant in clumps for greater impact.

A hardy bulb valued for its late flowering, *Nerine bowdenii* produces heads of lily-like blooms with reflexed petals, the wide strap-like leaves appearing after the flowers. The best place to grow nerine is at the foot of a wall which receives plenty of sun, in combination with schizostylis and autumn-flowering sedums. Choose a spot that offers some protection from hard summer downpours and winter frosts.

Propagate by dividing clumps when dormant in summer.

Plant shallowly, with tips just below the surface.

In areas prone to hard frosts keep the root area covered with dry leaves or straw for the winter.

Good drainage is essential for nerines, as bulb rot occurs in wet soils. Apply a general-purpose fertilizer in spring.

Nerine bowdenii

MOISTURE	Keep moist but do not overwater
SITE/LIGHT	Likes the full sun in soil with good drainage
GENERAL CARE	Protect against frosts by adding straw or leaf mould
PESTS & DISEASES	Prone to slugs, snails and bulb rot

FLOWERS see also 315

COMPANION PLANTS see pages 404 405

Nicotiana TOBACCO PLANT

Nicotianas are grown as half-hardy annuals and produce a long display of tubular or widely flaring flowers which open mainly in the evening. However some, including the *Nicotiana* x *sanderae* cultivars and 'Lime Green', open during the daytime.

These are ideal for mass planting in summer bedding schemes where they combine well with many other bedders including verbenas, petunias, *Cosmos bipinnatus, Salvia farinacea* and pelargoniums. The larger *N. alata* and *N. sylvestris* are effective in sub-tropical bedding schemes, with foliage plants such as cannas.

Nicotiana alata

Nicotiana x *sanderae* Domino Series

Raise plants from seed under cover in spring.

Provide supports for taller plants, such as *N. langsdorffii*. Watch out for aphids, grey mould and viruses.

MOISTURE	Water regularly to keep soil moist
SITE/LIGHT	Full sun to partial shade in fertile, well-drained soil
GENERAL CARE	Mulch to maintain soil moisture and richness
PESTS & DISEASES	Prone to aphids, grey mould and viruses

FLOWERS see also 291

COMPANION PLANTS see pages 218 362 433

Nigella LOVE-IN-A-MIST

Nigella damascena is a hardy annual with feathery bright green foliage and flattish flowers, mainly in blue shades but also in other colours, with a ruff of foliage.

Grow love-in-a-mist in a mixed border with other annuals such as calendulas (English marigolds) and poppies (papaver), together with annual grasses. The flowers are excellent for cutting and the balloon-like seed pods can be dried for winter arrangements.

Raise plants from seed sown in their flowering positions, but plants do self-seed easily. Sown in autumn, they will flower earlier in the following year, but cover the young plants with cloches over the winter. Alternatively sow in spring for later flowering.

N. damascena 'Persian Jewels' is a popular variety of love-in-a-mist, producing flowers in hues of pink, white, purple or red.

Nigella is not troubled by pests or diseases, but slugs can nibble at the foliage.

Nigella damascena 'Persian Jewels'

MOISTURE	Keep fairly moist but do not overwater
SITE/LIGHT	Full sun with some shade in most well-drained soils
GENERAL CARE	Dead-head regularly to prolong flowering
PESTS & DISEASES	Generally trouble free, but slugs may cause problems

FLOWERS see also 193

COMPANION PLANTS see pages 180 359

Oenothera SUNDROPS

Hardy, herbaceous perennials, these sundrops have large, showy, bowl shaped, yellow flowers over a long period. Individual flowers last about one day.

A shrubby plant, *Oenothera fruticosa* is suitable for a mixed border, combined with shrubs such as cistus, lavenders and rosemary (rosmarinus), and ornamental grasses including *Stipa gigantea*. Cultivars of the white flowering *O. speciosa* also combine well with ornamental grasses in a border.

Propagate sundrops in spring, by division or from softwood cuttings.

Sundrops are suited to poor soils but are intolerant of especially wet soil in winter. They love a sunny site in the garden.

Watch out for black root rot, leaf spot, powdery mildew, and unwanted attention from slugs and snails.

Oenothera fruticosa 'Fireworks'

Oenothera speciosa 'Siskiyou'

MOISTURE	Keep moist but never over water
SITE/LIGHT	A sun-lover which is happy in any well-drained soil
GENERAL CARE	Too much shade causes plants to become straggly
PESTS & DISEASES	Prone to black root rot, leaf spot and powdery mildew

FLOWERS *see also* 437

COMPANION PLANTS *see pages* 200 306 392

Olea OLIVE

Although most often associated with Mediterranean climates, olives can adapt to more temperate areas if given the protection of a sun-drenched wall.

They can also be grown in sheltered coastal areas. Able to reach up to 6m (20ft) tall and 4m (16ft) across when mature, the light foliage consists of evergreen, grey-green leaves. The twisting, gnarled trunk makes the olive an attractive specimen tree for the garden. Fruits, which are the source for olive oil, are unlikely in cooler climates and would probably not ripen unless there was an exceptionally hot summer.

Olea europaea is very easy to cultivate. It will live quite happily in a large container, brought in to a conservatory or greenhouse for the winter.

It is fairly easy to propagate from cuttings.

Outdoors they perform best if planted in a rich, loamy soil, although as long as it is well-drained they can tolerate most soil types.

Watering once a day in hot weather is essential, particularly in conservatories, although once established, olives are extremely drought resistant. Never plant in boggy conditions, as this is likely to kill the tree.

Olea europaea

MOISTURE	Water regularly until established
SITE/LIGHT	Full sun in most well-drained soils
GENERAL CARE	Prune to restrict size, especially in a conservatory
PESTS & DISEASES	Can be affected by scale insects and verticillium wilt

TREES see also 249

COMPANION PLANTS see pages 190 306 392

Olearia DAISY BUSH

Olearia is a useful evergreen shrub that is grown for its daisy-like flowerheads, which can be fragrantly scented in late summer, and bushy habit.

Daisy bushes are excellent for sunny borders and *Olearia glutinosa* is especially good in coastal gardens. *O. macrodonta* is one of the species which has slightly spiky and coarse leaves that are aromatic when crushed.

Olearia macrodonta

Olearia responds well to trimming and old bushes can be cut down to near ground level. *O. macrodonta* is a very effective hedging plant, but Olearia's main use is for the shrub bed.

Propagate daisy bushes by semi-hardwood cuttings in summer. They can also be raised from seed, although seeds take a long time to germinate. As young plants are rather tender, grow over winter in a sheltered environment.

The hardiness of the many species differs and the more tender ones should be given a sheltered site. Daisy bushes need full sunlight, not really liking any shade (although they will tolerate just a light shade). They will grow in most types of garden soil, as long as they have good drainage, including even chalky soils.

MOISTURE	Keep moist but do not overwater
SITE/LIGHT	Prefers the full sun in most soils with good drainage
GENERAL CARE	Remove winter damage only after new growth in spring
PESTS & DISEASES	Generally trouble free

SHRUBS see also 382

COMPANION PLANTS see pages 275 287 308

Ophiopogon BLACK GRASS

These perennials are natives of Japan and are often grown for their architectural, grass-like foliage. They look very impressive planted in large drifts in beds.

Ophiopogon japonicus is a spreading plant that grows about 30cm (1ft) high. The evergreen, slender leaves are shiny dark green. This is good ground cover and it may also be grown in the edge of a pond, though it will not flower. *O. planiscapus* 'Nigrescens' (black grass) forms clumps of stunning black foliage, not as high as *O. japonicus*. In the summer, erect clusters of small, tubular, white or lilac flowers are produced, followed by small, berry-like, dull blue fruits.

Propagate simply by dividing the clumps that form.

Grow in fertile, moist, humus-rich soil with good drainage. Ophiopogons can be grown in both sun or light shade. They can also be grown successfully in containers for a patio.

Ophiopogon planiscapus 'Nigrescens'

MOISTURE	Fairly drought tolerant once established
SITE/LIGHT	Sun to partial shade in light, fertile, well-drained soil
GENERAL CARE	Plants lots of one variety together for best effect
PESTS & DISEASES	Generally trouble free

SHRUBS see also 219

COMPANION PLANTS see pages 252 441

Osmanthus

Osmanthus is one of the most delightful of all the fragrant shrubs for the late winter or early spring garden. It is also one of the most reliable evergreen shrubs for a wide range of soils and climates.

Osmanthus delavayi is a bushy shrub that will grow to a height of about 2m (7ft). It has small, sharply toothed, glossy, green leaves and clusters of perfumed, tubular, white flowers. Position it where its sweet perfume can be enjoyed, beside a pathway or near a garden seat. *O. burkwoodii* makes an excellent hedge if not exposed to strong, cold winds. *O. heterophyllus* flowers in the autumn but visually it is less showy than the other two species mentioned. Its variegated form, 'Variegatus', is particularly attractive.

It is best to propagate these shrubs by semi-hardwood cuttings in the summer, preferably with some bottom heat.

Osmanthus grows well in sun or partial shade and prefers well-drained soil that has been improved with a little homemade compost.

Osmanthus heterophyllus 'Variegatus'

MOISTURE	Keep moist
SITE/LIGHT	Sun or partial shade in well-drained neutral to acid soil
GENERAL CARE	Shelter from cold, drying winds
PESTS & DISEASES	Generally trouble free

SHRUBS see also 251

COMPANION PLANTS see pages 323 390–1 440

Osteospermum

Osteospermums are mainly evergreen, half-hardy to hardy sub-shrubs and perennials generally grown as annuals. They are dwarf, bushy plants producing masses of daisy-like flowers over a very long period.

Osteospermum 'Sunny Alex'

The flowers come in a range of colours, such as the pale pink *Osteospermum* 'Pink whirls' and the light yellow *O.* 'Sunny Alex'. Osteospermums are summer bedding plants and are excellent in patio containers and window boxes. Bold groups at the front of mixed borders are also effective. Attractive combinations can be created with many other summer bedding plants, including argyranthemums in contrasting colours, verbenas and foliage plants that are used for bedding such as *Aeonium* 'Zwartkop' and *Plectranthus argentatus*.

Osteospermum 'Pink whirls'

Propagate from semi-ripe cuttings in late summer, winter young plants under glass and plant out in the following spring when frosts are over. Sow seeds under glass in spring.

Dead-head regularly to ensure continuous flowering.

MOISTURE	Keep moist but do not overwater
SITE/LIGHT	Any well-drained soil in the full sun
GENERAL CARE	Dead-head on a regular basis
PESTS & DISEASES	Generally trouble free apart from aphids

***FLOWERS* see also 346**

***COMPANION PLANTS* see pages 175 235 255**

Paeonia PEONY

Paeonia lactiflora cultivars are hardy herbaceous perennials, as well as shrubs, producing large bowl- or cup-shaped flowers. Good for cottage gardens, peonies also look at home in modern mixed borders.

Peonies are superb with shrub roses, particularly old cultivars or the New English roses, and with silver- or grey-leaved shrubs such as lavenders and santolinas (cotton lavenders).

P. suffruticosa species make stiffly branched shrubs, which can produce white flowers up to 30cm (12in) across in some forms.

Peonies have a long life but once planted do not like to be disturbed, so lift them only if you want to propagate the plants by division in spring. Shrub forms can be propagated by removing suckers, grafting or by seed.

Peonies like a rich soil containing plenty of humus.

Paeonia lactiflora 'Bowl of Beauty'

Paeonia suffruticosa subsp. *rockii* (fruit)

Supports such as bamboo canes may be needed for the flower stems to prevent rain from flattening them.

Watch out for peony wilt and viruses.

MOISTURE	Keep moist but not too wet
SITE/LIGHT	Full sun in humus-rich, well-drained soil
GENERAL CARE	Cut out any plants affected by peony wilt
PESTS & DISEASES	Prone to peony wilt and viruses

FLOWERS see also 359

COMPANION PLANTS see pages 155 293 326

Papaver POPPY

Poppies form a large group of perennials, annuals and biennials with showy bowl-shaped flowers, often in brilliant colours, followed by attractive seed heads which can be dried for winter flower arrangements.

The best-known hardy biennial is *Papaver croceum* (Icelandic poppy). Hardy perennials include the flamboyant cultivars of *P. orientale* (oriental poppy).

Poppies combine beautifully with many plants. The annuals and biennials are especially lovely with ornamental annual grasses such as *Lagurus ovatus* (hare's tail), and with other ephemerals such as cornflowers (centaurea) and love-in-a-mist (nigella). The oriental poppies combine superbly with tall bearded irises, lupins, delphiniums and aquilegias (columbines). Dwarf perennials should be planted in front of oriental poppies to hide the foliage which becomes rather tatty after flowering.

Papaver orientale 'John Metcalf'

Raise annuals and biennials from seed in spring, sowing in flowering positions as they dislike disturbance. Propagate perennials from root cuttings in autumn or winter, rooting them in a cold frame and planting out in spring.

Papaver orientale 'Perry's White'

Papaver orientale 'Allegro'

MOISTURE	Keep moist but never over water
SITE/LIGHT	Loves full sun in well-drained soil
GENERAL CARE	Stake the taller oriental poppies
PESTS & DISEASES	Prone to aphids

FLOWERS see also 358

COMPANION PLANTS see pages 193 302 351

Passiflora PASSION FLOWER or GRANADILLA

Passion flowers are climbing vines bearing exotic, long-lasting blooms. They bring a touch of the tropics to the dullest of gardens with their unique, intricate flowers.

The flowers are intricate, having ten radiating petals, five stamens and three stigmas. Among the 400 species of passifloras, there are many different coloured ones to choose from to complement any colour scheme. For example, bright reds (*Passiflora coccinea*, *P. racemosa*), lovely pinks (*P. antioquiensis*), and whites and purples. One of the best examples must be *P. quadrangularis* (Giant granadilla) whose large filamented flowers are also scented. Passifloras are good screeners and will readily cover a wall, especially in warmer areas, with the added bonus of spectacular flowers. Many also produce fruits, most of which are edible.

Passion flowers can be grown from seed, from semi-ripe wood in the summer or from layering in summer or autumn.

Once established, plants can grow up to 4.6m (15ft) high. They do need support and possibly require controlling, depending on the area wanted for coverage. They can be grown outdoors in warm regions where they may even be evergreen, but in temperate climates they are really deciduous. Reasonably frost hardy, it is best to protect their roots by mulching during the coldest months.

Passiflora racemosa

MOISTURE	Water until established; only occasionally during winter
SITE/LIGHT	Partial shade in most well-drained soils
GENERAL CARE	Plant in a sheltered position against a warm wall
PESTS & DISEASES	Prone to red spider mite indoors, greenfly outdoors

SHRUBS see also 436

COMPANION PLANTS see pages 201–4 323 440

Paulownia FOXGLOVE TREE or EMPRESS TREE

These deciduous trees are most often grown for their habit, the usually large yellow-green leaves and their showy lilac-scented flowers which open in late spring.

The leaves can be up to 60cm (2ft) across on coppiced trees, are very thin and can be shredded by strong winds or frosts, so offer shelter in frost-prone areas. *Paulownia tomentosa* is a useful species as an over-storey tree above spring flowering shrubs. They are best as specimen trees or planted next to a path.

Paulownia tomentosa (flowers)

Paulownia tomentosa (coppiced)

Propagate from seeds sown on the surface of a pot, or root from softwood cuttings in summer or root cuttings.

Paulownia thrives in the full sun on all well-drained soils, including chalky ones, although for best results plant in more fertile soil.

Unripened growth and exposed flower buds could well be damaged by late frosts, so position this tree carefully in the garden.

MOISTURE	Water moderately until established
SITE/LIGHT	Full sun in fertile, well-drained soil
GENERAL CARE	Over-winter young plants in their first year
PESTS & DISEASES	Generally trouble free

TREES
see also
139–40

COMPANION PLANTS
see pages
185
213
238

Pelargonium

The seed-raised zonal pelargoniums listed here are tender, bushy, evergreen perennials grown as annuals. They produce large rounded heads of mainly single flowers over a very long period from spring onwards.

Ivy-leaved pelargoniums (*Pelargonium* 'Luna') are tender, trailing, evergreen perennials, also grown as annuals, with ivy-shaped leaves and rounded heads of single or double flowers. They include seed-raised strains and cultivars propagated from cuttings. Zonal pelargoniums (*P.* 'Sensation Scarlet' and *P.* 'Vista Deep Rose') are summer bedding plants and suitable for mass planting in formal beds. Also good in patio containers and window boxes.

Pelargonium 'Vista Deep Rose'

Pelargonium 'Sensation Scarlet'

Ivy-leaved pelargoniums are usually grown in containers for summer display, particularly hanging baskets and window boxes, along with trailing lobelias, ageratum, verbenas and petunias.

Sow seeds in late winter under glass. Propagate from semi-ripe cuttings in late summer, and winter young plants under glass.

MOISTURE	Keep moist but do not overwater
SITE/LIGHT	Full sun to partial shade in any well-drained soil
GENERAL CARE	Remove faded flowers and foliage regularly
PESTS & DISEASES	Prone to aphids, caterpillars, grey mould and rust

FLOWERS *see also* 267

COMPANION PLANTS *see pages* 321 322 365

Penstemon

Penstemons are frost-hardy to fully hardy herbaceous, partially evergreen or evergreen, perennials. They bear masses of tubular flowers, with two lobed lips, over a long period and most have narrow, spear-shaped leaves.

Penstemon 'Apple Blossom'

Grow penstemons in mixed borders, especially in cottage gardens, to show off the tall-stemmed flowers. Stems can reach 1m (3ft) high.

Suitable companions include silver- or grey-leaved plants such as artemisias, catmints (nepeta), lavenders and *Stachys byzantina*. They also look effective planted alongside shrub roses, especially old roses, and with alstroemerias, dianthus (border carnations and pinks) and ornamental grasses such as miscanthus. Nicotianas and verbenas are good annual companions.

Propagate from semi-ripe cuttings in summer or by division in spring. Cut back the stalks after the first flowering to encourage plants to bloom once more later on in the season.

Grow in the full sun in moist soil with good drainage – penstemons hate heavy, wet soils. Where frosts are hard protect plants with a thick mulch of dry straw, bracken or leaves over winter. Dead-head regularly.

MOISTURE	Keep moist at all times but never too wet
SITE/LIGHT	Full sun in any well-drained soil
GENERAL CARE	Feed perennials with slow-release fertilizer in spring
PESTS & DISEASES	Prone to powdery mildew, slugs and snails

FLOWERS
see also 238

COMPANION PLANTS
see pages 161 234 433

Perovskia

A hardy sub-shrub, *Perovskia atriplicifolia* 'Blue Spire' is grown for its spikes of blue flowers and ferny, grey foliage and stems. A good choice for dry parts of the garden, including gravel gardens and areas, it even grows well in poor or chalky soils.

It is an excellent plant for seaside gardens where it looks good with other maritime plants including tamarisk (tamarix), *Eryngium maritimum* (sea holly), *Limonium latifolium* (sea lavender) and *Crambe maritima* (sea kale). In other gardens suitable companions include shrub roses and late-flowering perennials such as rudbeckias.

Propagate from semi-ripe softwood cuttings in summer.

Perovskia requires a position in the hottest and sunniest part of the garden with good drainage. It is an excellent plant for coastal areas as it thrives on gravels and chalk, but dislikes waterlogged sites.

In spring cut back all last year's stems to a permanent, low, woody framework.

Perovskia atriplicifolia 'Blue Spire'

MOISTURE	Not tolerant of waterlogged soil
SITE/LIGHT	Full sun in any well-drained soil, including gravel
GENERAL CARE	Mulch annually to maintain humus-rich content
PESTS & DISEASES	Generally trouble free

SHRUBS
see also
190

COMPANION PLANTS
see pages
317
417

Petunia

Although correctly perennials, petunias are often grown as half-hardy annuals. They produce masses of flattish, five-lobed flowers over a very long period.

Petunias can be classified into Grandifloras, such as *Petunia* Surfinia Series, which bear large flowers, and Multifloras (Millifloras), such as *P.* Million Bells Series, which are bushier than Grandifloras with smaller flowers. Petunias are mainly used in summer bedding schemes and containers, where they combine effectively with many other summer bedders including pelargoniums, scarlet salvias, verbenas, bedding dahlias, osteospermums, tagetes (marigolds), fuchsias and impatiens.

Petunia Surfinia Series 'Blue Vein'

Raise plants from seed in spring under glass.

Petunias grow well in poor to moderately fertile soils and are good for coastal gardens. Dead-head regularly.

They are prone to aphids, foot rot, slugs, snails and viruses.

Petunia Million Bells Series 'Cherry'

MOISTURE	Keep moist but do not overwater
SITE/LIGHT	Full sun in most well-drained soils
GENERAL CARE	Avoid planting under trees, shrubs or in shady locations
PESTS & DISEASES	Prone to aphids, foot rot, slugs, snails and viruses

FLOWERS *see also* 437

COMPANION PLANTS *see pages* 362 396 433

Phacelia SCORPION WEED

A hardy annual, *Phacelia campanularia* is valued for its blue bell-shaped flowers, which are attractive to bees. Grow it in a sunny position in mixed borders and, as it thrives in dry soils, in gravel gardens.

For an attractive blue theme, combine phacelia with other blue-flowered annuals such as *Centaurea cyanus* (cornflower) and *Nemophila menziesii* (baby blue-eyes).

Phacelia tanacetifolia

Phacelia campanularia 'Ocean Waves'

Phacelia tanacetifolia is an upright, hairy annual, producing dense, curved racemes of blue or lavender-blue flowers. *P. sericea* is a short-lived perennial with hairy, silvery leaves and bears bell-shaped, indigo-blue flowers.

Raise plants from seed in spring or early autumn, sowing in flowering positions. Spring sowings quickly come into flower.

Where winters are wet or very cold, protect young plants with cloches over winter.

MOISTURE	Keep slightly moist
SITE/LIGHT	Enjoys the full sun in any fertile, well-drained soil
GENERAL CARE	Grow *P. sericea* in gritty, sharply drained soil
PESTS & DISEASES	Generally trouble free; *P. sericea* prone to aphids

FLOWERS *see also* 437

COMPANION PLANTS *see pages* 193 347

Philadelphus MOCK ORANGE

These deciduous shrubs have very attractive masses of fragrant white flowers, which smother the bushes in early to mid-summer.

Mock orange is a favourite of many gardeners for its sweet-scented blossoms. It is a fast-growing shrub with arching form and fits especially well in corners in the garden.

To propagate, take softwood cuttings in summer or hardwood cuttings in autumn or winter. Cut back shoots to a strong bud each year after flowering.

Give mock orange partial shade in the warmest areas. It tolerates most garden soils with good drainage.

Philadelphus 'Virginal'

Philadelphus 'Belle Etoile' has large, white flowers with purple centres; *P.* 'Virginal' bears white double flowers.

Philadelphus 'Belle Etoile'

MOISTURE	Keep reasonably moist
SITE/LIGHT	Sun with some shade on any well-drained soil
GENERAL CARE	Mulch poorer soils if necessary
PESTS & DISEASES	Generally trouble free

SHRUBS* *see also* *384–5

COMPANION PLANTS* *see pages* *275* *396

Phlomis JERUSALEM SAGE

Shrubby Phlomis are grown for their attractive flowers and foliage. Most species are herbs, but there are a few shrubby species, which are all evergreen, including *Phlomis fructicosa, P. chrysophylla* and *P. italica.*

They are excellent as part of a mixed border or at the front of a shrub border. Site in a dry, sun-drenched area beside the house, as they tolerate dry soils. In exposed gardens, position beside a wall for protection. In *Phlomis fruticosa* or Jerusalem sage, the nettle-like flowers are bright yellow and the foliage grey-green, making a shrub to 1m (3ft).

A similar sized shrub, *P. chrysophylla* also bears yellow flowers, with leaves of a golden-green tinge. *P. italica* is smaller, often not growing more than 0.3m (1ft) but with pink or pale lilac flowers.

Phlomis fruticosa

Phlomis is easily propagated from softwood cuttings taken in summer. They can also be raised from seed sown in spring.

These shrubs are suitable for a warm, sunny and sheltered spot in the garden with good drainage. They do not tolerate shade or cold dry winds in winter.

MOISTURE	Requires only a little moisture in order to thrive
SITE/LIGHT	Loves full sun in most soils with good drainage
GENERAL CARE	Roots will rot if soil gets waterlogged
PESTS & DISEASES	Can be prone to leafhoppers

SHRUBS see also 306

COMPANION PLANTS see pages 201–4 396

Phlox

Phlox grow both as annuals and perennials. *Phlox* x *drummondii* cultivars are frost-hardy annuals with flattish, lobed flowers. They are usually bedded out for summer display and are also suitable for containers.

Effective companions for annual phlox include *Salvia farinacea* cultivars, heliotrope and grey-foliage plants such as the half-hardy bedding shrub *Helichrysum petiolare*. Regular dead-heading adds several weeks or even months to the display. *P. paniculata* cultivars are hardy herbaceous perennials with heads of flattish, scented flowers on tall, erect stems, ideal for mixed borders. *P. subulata* (moss phlox) cultivars are hardy, evergreen, mat-forming perennials for the rock or scree garden, with masses of flattish flowers early in the season.

Phlox paniculata 'Spitfire'

Phlox paniculata 'Starfire'

Raise annuals from seed in early spring under glass. Propagate *P. paniculata* cultivars by division in spring or autumn, from root cuttings in winter or from basal cuttings in spring. Propagate *P. subulata* cultivars from softwood cuttings in spring.

MOISTURE	Keep moist but not overwatered
SITE/LIGHT	Enjoys full sun in most well-drained soils
GENERAL CARE	Stake tall cultivars for support
PESTS & DISEASES	Prone to leaf spot and powdery mildew

FLOWERS see also 350

COMPANION PLANTS see pages 279 396

Photinia

This genus of deciduous or evergreen shrubs is mostly grown for its attractive, colourful foliage, as well as its small, white hawthorn-like flowers. The leaves are matt green in *Photinia davidiana*, persisting through winter.

While *P. davidiana* does not have outstanding autumn colour, its display is protracted. *P. fraseri* 'Red Robin' has brilliant red foliage that contrasts with the dark glossy green of last year's leaves. *P. serrulatifolia* (*P. serrulata*) makes a large tree with time and is a high quality evergreen, although it is slightly tender when young.

Photinia can be grown from seed or from semi-hardwood cuttings in summer.

P. davidiana and *P. fraseri* 'Red Robin' are good in shrub beds and can be used as hedges, especially 'Red Robin'. Site *P. serrulatifolia* as a specimen tree.

Photinia all like full sun to light shade and tolerate a wide range of soils, including chalk, provided there is good drainage.

Photinia davidiana 'Palette'

MOISTURE	Keep moist until established
SITE/LIGHT	Full sun to light shade in any well-drained soil
GENERAL CARE	Prune only to restrict size or reshape
PESTS & DISEASES	Can be prone to fireblight

SHRUBS see also 374

COMPANION PLANTS see pages 155 177 379

Phygelius

Frost-hardy evergreen shrubs, Phygelius has a suckering habit and looks more like a perennial. Tubular flowers on upright stems are produced over a long period on these plants.

Grow in a mixed border with agapanthus and kniphofias or against a wall. Give them sufficient space as they have a spreading habit and do not look good when hemmed in by other plants.

In frosty areas Phygelius can be grown like herbaceous perennials by cutting down stems in spring. They can also be grown in a sheltered spot

Phygelius aequalis

Phygelius rectus 'Moonraker'

and mulched in winter with dry material such as straw.

Propagate from softwood cuttings in spring or sow seed in a cold frame in spring.

Remove dead flowerheads regularly and overwinter young plants under glass. *Phygelius rectus* 'Moonraker' has slightly curved, pale creamy-yellow flowers, whereas *P. aequalis* produces dusty pink flowers.

MOISTURE	Keep soil moist
SITE/LIGHT	Full sun in fertile, well-drained soil
GENERAL CARE	Shelter from cold, drying winds in frost-prone areas
PESTS & DISEASES	Generally trouble free but may be prone to capsid bug

SHRUBS see also 294

COMPANION PLANTS see pages 143 299

Phyllostachys

This is a genus of medium to large evergreen bamboos, grown for their elegant canes (culms), which range from green to black, and light foliage. The canes are hollow and grooved with nodes from where branches emerge.

The spaced culms make very effective plantings, even though some species can forms clumps. They make excellent garden screens. The culms can be a variety of colours. *Phyllostachys aurea* has stout green culms which turn a soft yellow in strong light. *P. nigra* has culms ageing to black. *P. viridi-glaucescens* has mid-green culms.

Propagate by division in spring. Water frequently until established, then only in drought conditions.

Phyllostachys nigra

Phyllostachys viridi-glaucescens

Phyllostachys aurea

MOISTURE	Water until established then only if really dry
SITE/LIGHT	Full sun or dappled shade in fertile, well-drained soil
GENERAL CARE	Shelter from harsh winds
PESTS & DISEASES	Check regularly for aphids, especially when young

SHRUBS see also 400

COMPANION PLANTS see pages 144 355

Picea SPRUCE

Spruces are conical, evergreen, coniferous trees. They have whorled branches and single, needle-like leaves varying from green to bluish-grey, with a single main stem and only light side branching.

Picea orientalis has short needles, brick-red male cones in mid-spring and red female cone flowers. 'Aurea' has golden yellow foliage which turns dark green. *P. pungens* has attractive blue-grey foliage. *P. abies*, although better known as the Christmas tree, is probably not ideal in this capacity as it drops its needles.

Grow spruces as shelter planting or as specimen trees in the middle of a lawn.

Propagate spruces by seed sown in spring. Forms can be grafted onto seedling rootstocks either in late summer or late winter, keeping the rootstock slightly dry to stop it bleeding and drowning the scion. Stake grafted plants to help them form an erect stem.

Aphids can attack the needles.

Picea orientalis 'Aurea'

Picea abies

Picea pungens 'Hoopsii'

MOISTURE	Keep the soil moist, particularly during its first year
SITE/LIGHT	Ideally neutral to acid, well-drained soil in the full sun
GENERAL CARE	Lightly trim to resize or reshape
PESTS & DISEASES	Prone to aphids

TREES
see also
196

COMPANION PLANTS
see pages
135
375

Pieris

An evergreen shrub with year round interest, bright foliage colour in spring and attractive flowers. With the bonus of being suitable for containers, it is surprising that Pieris is not grown in every garden.

Its habit is neat and compact, with rarely any need for pruning. Although the panicles of small flowers are

Pieris 'Flaming Silver'

attractive, it is really the foliage that gives the best display. In *Pieris* 'Firecrest', the new leaves burst forth in a vivid red, which become green via creamy-pink. *P.* 'Flaming Silver' has wonderful variegated leaves.

Propagate by taking greenwood cuttings in early summer or semi-ripe cuttings in mid- to late summer, with bottom heat.

As Pieris prefers an acidic soil, if your soil is too alkaline, a container grown specimen will thrive for many years if planted in an ericaceous compost, but do not allow it to become too dry for prolonged periods during the summer months.

Pieris 'Firecrest'

MOISTURE	Do not allow to dry out – always keep moist
SITE/LIGHT	Sun or light shade in acidic, humus-rich, well-drained soil
GENERAL CARE	Shelter from cold winds and winter frosts
PESTS & DISEASES	Generally trouble free

SHRUBS see also 297

COMPANION PLANTS see pages 184 384–5 408

Pinus PINE

Pines, as well as being useful for their evergreen foliage, come in many different sizes from tall trees to dwarf specimens. The leaves (needles) are in small groups of two, three or five – unlike spruces, which have sharp, single needles growing all around twigs.

Another difference between spruces and pines is with the cones. Pine cones are woody and rigid, whereas spruce cones have thinner and less rigid scales. Plant larger growing forms, such as *Pinus sylvestris* 'Fastigiata' as a specimen tree, and slow growing (*P. sylvestris* 'Watereri') or dwarf forms (*P. mugo*) together in groups in a bed.

Pinus sylvestris 'Watereri'

Pinus sylvestris 'Fastigiata'

Pines can be propagated by seed sown in spring, as well as grafted in late winter onto seedling rootstocks.

Position where there is full sun. Pines are not particularly fussy about the soil, as long as it has good drainage. If it is a particularly dry summer, give newly planted pines a thorough watering at regular intervals.

MOISTURE	Water regularly when first planted
SITE/LIGHT	Thrives in full sun in any soil with good drainage
GENERAL CARE	Restrict size by cutting back new growth candles
PESTS & DISEASES	Prone to aphids, honey fungus and various insects

TREES see also 373

COMPANION PLANTS see pages 296 418 420

Pittosporum

The plants in this genus are usually evergreen shrubs and trees. In more temperate regions, hard winters can damage them, but they are excellent for coastal areas.

Pittosporum is often grown for its fragrant flowers and attractive, glossy foliage. Flowers are chocolate-purple in *Pittosporum tenuifolium* but creamy white in *P. tobira*. *P. tenuifolium* has a number of forms with impressive foliage, ranging from bronze-purple in 'Purpureum', to variegated, creamy-white in 'Irene Paterson', to yellow-green in 'Abbotsbury Gold'. 'Tom Thumb' is a slow-growing form, perhaps the smallest of the species.

Pittosporum tenuifolium 'Tom Thumb'

In the garden, the smaller forms are excellent as part of shrub beds, with the larger ones at the back. They can be sited beside house walls, especially in colder areas, and make good hedges.

Pittosporum can be propagated by seeds sown in the spring. The coloured forms are propagated by semi-hardwood cuttings in summer, or by layering.

Pittosporum tenuifolium 'Abbotsbury Gold'

MOISTURE	Water regularly during growing period, less during winter
SITE/LIGHT	Full sun or partial shade in moist, fertile, well-drained soil
GENERAL CARE	Shelter from cold winds; trim hedges in spring
PESTS & DISEASES	Prone to mildew and tar spot fungi

SHRUBS see also 390–1

COMPANION PLANTS see pages 234 262–3 275

Polemonium JACOB'S LADDER

A hardy herbaceous perennial, *Polemonium caeruleum* has branching heads of bell-shaped flowers in the spring and summer and attractive pinnate foliage.

Grow Jacob's ladder in a mixed border, or in a more natural part of the garden, including long-grass areas. Taller species, such as *Polemonium caeruleum* and *P. foliosissimum*, are best in a border or wild garden. Good companions in a border include *Achillea* 'Moonshine', *Allium cristophii*, *Euphorbia characias* subsp. *wulfenii* and lupins. Smaller species, such as *P. eximium*, look good in rock gardens or scree beds.

Propagate by division in spring.

Remove dead flowers regularly and watch out for powdery mildew.

Polemonium caeruleum

MOISTURE	Keep moist, especially during the height of summer
SITE/LIGHT	Full sun or partial shade in any fertile, well-drained soil
GENERAL CARE	Dead-head regularly to prolong flowering
PESTS & DISEASES	Prone to powdery mildew

***FLOWERS* see also 238**

***COMPANION PLANTS* see pages 141 252 326**

Populus POPLAR

Populus is a large group of deciduous trees. They are among the easiest trees to propagate and grow, as they thrive on almost any soil and are rapid growers.

Poplars are excellent as specimen trees and can also be planted as windbreaks. *Populus alba* (white poplar) and *P.* x *canescens* (grey poplar) grow especially well in coastal sites. Most poplars are pretty in bloom, bearing tiny flowers in catkins of red, purple, green or yellow hues in late winter or spring before the leaves appear. *P. tremular* (aspen) has flat-stalked leaves which tremble and rattle in the slightest wind; *P. lasiocarpa* (Chinese necklace poplar) has large, heart-shaped leaves.

Seeds should be planted as soon as they are ripe, but it is more common to propagate by cuttings of well-ripened wood, in the autumn.

Although tolerant of most soils, poplars do not like constantly waterlogged conditions, so ensure the soil has good drainage. Choose a position in the full sun and do not plant too close to the house as the vigorous roots can damage foundations.

Populus lasiocarpa

MOISTURE	Keep fairly moist, especially during its first years
SITE/LIGHT	Full sun in most well-drained soils
GENERAL CARE	Beware of planting too close to drainage systems
PESTS & DISEASES	Prone to fungi and insect attack, particularly caterpillars

TREES see also 139–40

COMPANION PLANTS see pages 253 287

Potentilla SHRUBBY CINQUEFOILS

The shrubby cinquefoils are a small part of a genus of around 500 species of shrubs and perennials. Potentilla is one of the most reliable plants to suit most gardens.

They can be used in a variety of situations such as in mixed borders, rock gardens and for ground cover. Cinquefoils produce a display of small, bright flowers with five petals from mid-summer until mid-autumn. *Potentilla fruticosa* is the species from which many of the most popular varieties are derived. *P.* 'Abbotswood' has delicate white flowers with dark, blue-green leaves; *P.* 'Katherine Dykes' produces large numbers of canary-yellow flowers; and *P.* 'Princess' is a low-growing variety with pale pink blooms.

Propagate by sowing seed in containers in autumn or spring, by division in spring or by shrub cuttings in early summer.

Potentilla 'Abbotswood'

Potentilla prefers an open, sunny site where they will flower at their best – partial shade is acceptable but expect fewer flowers and a shorter flowering season.

Potentilla 'Katherine Dykes'

It is not too fussy about the soil type, but prefers soil that is not waterlogged, which can happen throughout the winter months.

Potentilla 'Princess'

MOISTURE	Keep evenly moist
SITE/LIGHT	Full sun to partial shade in most well-drained soils
GENERAL CARE	Prune only if resizing or reshaping is necessary
PESTS & DISEASES	Generally trouble free

SHRUBS see also 287

COMPANION PLANTS see pages 232 234 262–3

Primula

A diverse group of mainly hardy, herbaceous and evergreen perennials, grouped into border cultivars (*Primula auricula*), Candelabra, Polyanthus and Primose.

Border auriculas are ideal for the front of mixed borders and in cottage gardens. *P. denticulata* (drumstick primrose) is distinct with its ball-shaped flowers. Candelabra primulas, such as *P. japonica*, has whorls of blooms carried in tiers. The Primrose Group includes the wild primrose, *P. vulgaris*, and *P.* 'Wanda', ideal for the front of shady borders or woodland gardens. The Polyanthus Group includes perennials such as *P.* 'Guinevere'.

Propagate perennials by division in autumn. Raise biennials and perennials from seed in a cold frame in spring, grow on in a shady nursery bed and plant out in autumn.

Primulas are prone to grey mould, slugs, snails and vine weevil grubs.

Primula denticulata

Primula 'Wanda'

Primula vulgaris

MOISTURE	All groups like moist conditions
SITE/LIGHT	Mostly partial shade to full sun in well-drained, rich soil
GENERAL CARE	*P. japonica* looks good planted beside a pool
PESTS & DISEASES	Prone to grey mould, slugs, snails and vine weevil grubs

FLOWERS see also 350

COMPANION PLANTS see pages 344–5 427–8 437

Prunus CHERRIES, PLUMS

Prunus is a large genus of mainly small to large trees, with a few shrubs. As well as shrub varieties, and cherries and plums, also included in this group are the almond, apricot, nectarine and peach trees.

The tree forms are greatly valued for their often delicious, edible fruits, pretty spring blossoms and some for their colourful foliage. The shrubs, such as *Prunus cistena*, with its crimson, bronze-red foliage and *P. laurocerasus* (cherry laurel), an evergreen, are ideal for the smaller gardens. *P. lusitanica* (Portuguese laurel), an evergreen, makes a shrub or small tree and has fragrant flowers.

Prunus lusitanica

Prunus cistena

Prunus laurocerasus 'Otto Luyken'

Propagate by rooting greenwood cuttings in early summer or semi-ripe ones in mid-summer.

Deciduous prunus need a sunny location, but evergreens can tolerate partial shade. They can be grown in any good, moist, well-drained soil.

MOISTURE	Keep soil moist, increasing watering during dry periods
SITE/LIGHT	Full sun to partial shade in good, well-drained soil
GENERAL CARE	Mulch regularly throughout the year
PESTS & DISEASES	Prone to silver leaf, aphids, honey fungus and black fly

TREES see also 332

COMPANION PLANTS see pages 139–40 178 329–30

Pyracantha FIRETHORN

This dense shrub with stiff branches and bright orange berries is used as a hedge, screen, ground cover, barrier plant, or for espaliers on walls and fences. Do not plant near a path because of its sharp thorns.

Firethorns have two main seasons of display, producing clusters of white hawthorn-like flowers in the early summer, followed by yellow-orange to red berries in the autumn. In some forms, such as *Pyracantha* 'Teton', these last well into the winter.

They can be propagated from seed, but they are easier grown on from cuttings taken during the early summer or even into the autumn.

Pyracantha can be pruned frequently, particularly if used as hedging to protect the front of a property. They tolerate many soil conditions, from acidic sands to chalky soils, although they thrive on fertile loams.

They can be damaged by cold, dry winds in winter, so give some shelter in colder areas. They are also prone to scab and fireblight, as well as scale insects and aphids.

Pyracantha 'Teton'

MOISTURE	Keep moist but do not overwater
SITE/LIGHT	Full sun or partial shade in most well-drained soils
GENERAL CARE	Beware of the sharp thorns; cut out infected branches
PESTS & DISEASES	Prone to scab, fireblight, aphids and scale insects

SHRUBS see also 170

COMPANION PLANTS see pages 408 435

Ranunculus BUTTERCUP

A variable genus including hardy herbaceous perennials such as *Ranunculus aconitifolius* 'Flore Pleno' (batchelor's buttons), tuberous rooted *R. ficaria* (lesser celandine) cultivars and *R. gramineus* (grass-leaved buttercup).

Ranunculus flowers are generally saucer- or bowl-shaped but are fully double in some cultivars. These are good mixed-border plants, although *Ranunculus ficaria* cultivars are grown as ground cover in shady woodland gardens or shrub borders. *R. asiaticus* (Persian buttercup) cultivars are half-hardy tuberous perennials, planted in spring and wintered as dormant tubers in a frost-free place (store in dry peat substitute).

Ranunculus gramineus

Ranunculus asiaticus 'Accolade'

Propagate hardy perennials by division in autumn or spring.

Most prefer partial shade, although *R. asiaticus* 'Accolade' is one of the varieties that prefers the full sun. Keep Ranunculus moist at all times.

MOISTURE	Water regularly and do not allow to dry out
SITE/LIGHT	Partial shade to full sun in fertile, well-drained soil
GENERAL CARE	Contact with the sap may irritate the skin
PESTS & DISEASES	Prone to aphids, powdery mildew, slugs and snails

***FLOWERS* see also 380**

***COMPANION PLANTS* see pages 252 285**

Rhododendron

This is a very large genus of around 900 species and hybrids of evergreen and deciduous trees and shrubs. They vary greatly in habit from small shrubs to large trees and need acidic soil in which to thrive.

They are often divided into four main groups: evergreen rhododendrons, Vireya rhododendrons, azaleas and azaleodendrons. Evergreens have large leaves and flowers in a variety of shapes, sizes and colours. *Rhododendron* 'Pink Pearl', for example, has an open, erect habit with abundant soft pink flowers. Vireya rhododendrons, such as the evergreen *R. jasminiflorum*, are frost-tender and really need to be grown under glass in cooler climates. Azaleas generally have smaller sized leaves and can be either evergreen, such as *R.* 'Addy Wery', or deciduous, often with fragrant flowers, such as *R.* 'Daviesii'. Azaleodendrons are hybrids between deciduous azaleas

Rhododendron 'Daviesii'

Rhododendron 'Addy Wery'

Rhododendron 'Sapphire'

SHRUBS see also 184

COMPANION PLANTS see pages 261 267 285

and evergreen hybrid rhododendrons, such as *R.* 'Glory of Littleworth', a semi-evergreen with creamy white flowers.

Rhododendrons have a wide range of uses in the garden, such as in a woodland setting to brighten a shady setting, at the back of a shrub bed, as hedges or screens, as well as on shady patios in pots and containers.

Rhododendron 'Pink Pearl'

Rhododendron 'Morning Cloud'

Propagate rhododendrons by seed, layering, grafting or cuttings.

Rhododendron 'Golden Torch'

Most plants prefer light, dappled shade. As well as ensuring the soil is well-drained and acidic, mulch frequently with leafmould or peat to improve the organic content of the soil and add an ericaceous fertilizer mix.

MOISTURE	Keep moist but do not overwater
SITE/LIGHT	Partial shade in acidic, humus-rich, well-drained soil
GENERAL CARE	Do not plant too deep: rhododendrons are surface rooters
PESTS & DISEASES	Prone to vine weevil, whiteflies, aphids and silver leaf

SHRUBS
see also
287

COMPANION PLANTS
see pages
201–4
374
435

Rhus SUMACH

This genus of trees and large shrubs is most often grown for its glorious autumnal hues, which are normally red and yellow or orange.

In the wild, sumachs are found in woodland, bogs, dry sites and even rocky slopes. In the garden plant them in shrub beds towards the back or as specimen trees. The common Stag's horn sumach (*Rhus typhina*) has large red flowerheads, carried on separate male and female trees.

They are most easily raised from root cuttings, or by lifting a sucker.

Grow in moist soil which is reasonably fertile but which also has good drainage. The more sun it gets, the better the autumn colour. Sumachs have a thick sap which can irritate the skin and may produce an allergic reaction.

Rhus typhina

MOISTURE	Water regularly
SITE/LIGHT	Full sun for best results in fertile, well-drained soil
GENERAL CARE	Watch out for children because of its toxic qualities
PESTS & DISEASES	Prone to coral spot and verticillium wilt

TREES
see also
139–40

COMPANION
PLANTS
see pages
320
396
405

Ribes FLOWERING CURRANT

Some species of Ribes, including the blackcurrant (*Ribes nigrum*), redcurrant (*R. rubrum*) and the gooseberry (*R. uva-crispa*) are grown for the edible fruits, but these are used primarily for the beauty of their flowers.

Unlike their fruiting cousins, flowering currants tend not to have spines, except the semi-evergreen shrub *Ribes speciosum*, with its fuchsia-like red flowers hanging down in spring. It needs wall protection except in mild gardens. *R. sanguineum* flowers with the new foliage in spring, pendulous when they first open but turning up as they expand. This can be used as a hedging plant or in shrub beds.

Ribes sanguineum 'Pulborough Scarlet'

R. alpinum, and its yellow-green form 'Aureum', is one of the best shrubs for dry shady spots.

Ribes is easily propagated by softwood or semi-hardwood cuttings in summer or hardwood cuttings in autumn and then rooted outside.

Ribes speciosum

Flowering currants thrive on a wide range of soils and most forms enjoy the full sun.

MOISTURE	Once established needs only little water to thrive
SITE/LIGHT	Full sun to partial shade in most well-drained soils
GENERAL CARE	Trim *R. sanguineum* immediately after flowering
PESTS & DISEASES	Prone to aphids, leaf spot, powdery mildew and coral spot

***SHRUBS* see also 262–3**

***COMPANION PLANTS* see pages 170 220 301**

Robinia

This is a genus of deciduous trees or large shrubs with pinnate leaves and attractive, pea-like flowers. They can be bristly or thorny shrubs, such as *Robinia hispida*, or fast-growing, columnar trees, such as *R. pseudoacacia*.

R. pseudoacacia 'Lace Lady'

The bright foliage of *Robinia pseudoacacia* 'Frisia' is an excellent golden yellow tree for the garden, with white flowers that are hidden by the foliage. Other forms of *R. pseudoacacia* are good both for their flowers and the light open crowns. *R. pseudoacacia* 'Lace Lady' is interesting for its twisted habit. The rose acacia, *R. hispida*, has attractive, deep rose flowers, as well as its bristly stems.

Robinia pseudoacacia 'Frisia'

Robinia is easily propagated in the autumn either by seed or suckers. Graft forms onto a seedling rootstock.

Robinia branches tend to be rather brittle, so it is worth pruning young trees to prevent them from growing too dense and breaking in strong winds in autumn. Robinias prefer dry and sandy sites, with as much sun as possible. Root suckers from *R. pseudoacacia* can invade the garden, so remove from time to time.

MOISTURE	Keep reasonably moist, although does tolerate drought
SITE/LIGHT	Full sun in most well-drained soils, including sandy ones
GENERAL CARE	Remove root suckers to prevent it taking over the garden
PESTS & DISEASES	Generally trouble free

TREES see also 189

COMPANION PLANTS see pages 227 265 300

Rodgersia

This hardy herbaceous perennial produces large hand-shaped leaves and cone-shaped heads of flowers. Rodgersia should be grown at the edges of pools, in bog gardens and in moist borders.

In summer, the tall stems blossom with masses of tiny star-shaped white or pink flowers in large, pyramid-shaped panicles, which have an almost fluffy appearance. Flowers are followed by brown or dark red capsule-like fruits.

Effective companions for Rodgersia include hostas, astilibes, moisture-loving irises, lobelias such as *L. cardinalis*, *L.* 'Queen Victoria' and *L.* x *speciosa* cultivars, *Mimulus cardinalis*, and ferns, including the royal fern, *Osmunda regalis*.

Propagate by division in early spring before growth starts, or sow seed in containers in a cold frame.

Rodgersia likes sheltered conditions and plenty of humus in the soil. *Rodgersia pinnata* 'Superba' has bronze leaves when young.

Rodgersia pinnata 'Superba'

MOISTURE	Moist conditions at all times
SITE/LIGHT	Full sun or partial shade in fertile, humus-rich soil
GENERAL CARE	Shelter from cold winds and do not allow to dry out
PESTS & DISEASES	Prone to attack from slugs and snails

FLOWERS see also 293

COMPANION PLANTS see pages 237 321 335

Rosa ROSE

The genus Rosa includes around 150 species of shrubs and climbers. Highlighted here are two groups that are often grown in the garden, which feature old-fashioned shrub roses and a selection of species roses.

Shrub roses usually produce one period of bloom from summer to autumn, although some do occasionally bear a few late flowers. *Rosa* 'Golden Wings' is a dense, spreading shrub rose with prickly stems, light green leaves and wonderfully scented, single yellow flowers. *R.* 'Buff Beauty' is a shrub rose with a rounded habit, with dark green leaves and large clusters of double, lightly scented apricot flowers.

Rosa 'Golden Wings'

Old fashioned roses look great mingled in shrub beds or sited in a bed dedicated to just shrub roses.

Species roses usually have single, fragrant flowers, as well as attractive fruits. Most of the roses here are hybrids of *R. rugosa*, which has violet-red flowers followed by red to orange-red hips (fruits). *R.* 'Rosarie de l'Hay' is a

Rosa rugosa

SHRUBS see also 201–4

OMPANION PLANTS see pages 200 287 358

Rosa xanthina 'Canary Bird'

Rosa 'Rosarie de l'Hay'

vigorous Rugosa form, bearing strongly scented, purple-red blooms.

R. xanthina 'Canary Bird' is a species rose with attractive yellow flowers in late spring, followed by fairly insignificant black hips.

Propagation can be carried out by grafting or, more easily, from rooted semi-hardwood cuttings that are taken in summer or autumn.

Roses generally tolerate a wide range of conditions, but most prefer an open position in the full sun. The soil should be fairly fertile and humus-rich with good drainage. They will not thrive in very wet or acidic soils. Adding mulch or manure regularly will improve flowering.

Prune only to keep the shape or to remove old, woody stems.

Species roses can easily be trained to form hedges or act as barrier plants.

Rosa 'Buff Beauty'

MOISTURE	Keep fairly moist and do not allow to dry out
SITE/LIGHT	Full sun in any moderately fertile, well-drained soil
GENERAL CARE	Mulch or manure to maintain a good soil content
PESTS & DISEASES	Prone to aphids, scale insects, black spot and rust

SHRUBS see also 262–3

COMPANION PLANTS see page 199 278 435

Rosmarinus ROSEMARY

This herb is worth growing as an excellent spring flowering shrub, as well as for its culinary uses. The narrow leaves are wonderfully aromatic and the delicate flowers range from pale blue and pink to white.

Rosmarinus officinalis 'Sissinghurst Blue'

As well as its use in a kitchen garden, Rosmarinus can be grown in shrub or mixed borders, or even as a hedge (*Rosmarinus officinalis* 'Sissinghurst Blue'). Prostrate forms, such as 'Prostratus', are ideal for a rock garden, or tumbling over a container on a patio.

Propagate by semi-hardwood cuttings taken in the summer.

Rosmarinus officinalis

Rosemary needs a sunny site with good drainage, and is happy (once established) on dry sites, including chalky soils, and those of low fertility. It dislikes wet and heavy soils.

MOISTURE	Keep moist until established, then only in hot spells
SITE/LIGHT	Full sun in most well-drained soils
GENERAL CARE	Trim back plants used as hedging after flowering
PESTS & DISEASES	Generally trouble free

SHRUBS
see also
306

COMPANION
PLANTS
see pages
396
398

Rubus

This group consists of erect, arching or trailing deciduous and evergreen shrubs. Most are grown for their edible fruits but the ones here are ornamental.

Most people would think of Rubus as brambles and are best in a wild garden. *Rubus fruticosa* (blackberry) and *R. idaeus* (raspberry) are grown for their edible fruit. *R. cockburnianus* is a thicket-forming shrub, with prickly shoots and purple flowers which are followed by black, unpalatable fruit. *R. tricolor* is an evergreen shrub with creeping and arching shoots, covered in red bristles. Being prostrate, it is an excellent ground cover plant, good for filling corners in a shrub bed.

Ornamental varieties can be propagated by sowing seeds, as well as by cuttings or layering the branches.

Rubus thrive in the full sun on most types of garden soils, preferably in ground with good drainage.

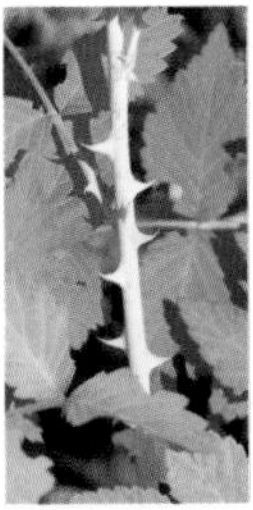

Rubus cockburnianus 'Goldenvale'

Rubus tricolor

MOISTURE	Not too fussy about watering regularly
SITE/LIGHT	A sun-lover which is happy in any type of soil
GENERAL CARE	Prune back two-year-old stems after flowering
PESTS & DISEASES	Generally trouble free

***SHRUBS* see also 382**

***COMPANION PLANTS* see pages 219 251 331**

Rudbeckia CONEFLOWER

Rudbeckias are mainly hardy herbaceous perennials producing large, showy, daisy-like flowers, each with a conspicuous central cone, over a long period.

Coneflowers are essential plants for mixed borders and staples of prairie-style borders. Effective companions are asters (including Michaelmas daisies), achilleas, sunflowers (helianthus), monardas, golden rod (solidago), *Echinacea purpurea* and ornamental grasses such as miscanthus and stipa.

Rudbeckia hirta (black-eyed Susan) cultivars are short-lived and usually grown as annuals. *R. fulgida* (also commonly known as black-eyed Susan) cultivars are long-lived perennials.

Rudbeckia fulgida var. *deamii*

Rudbeckia fulgida var. *sullivantii* 'Goldsturm'

Raise annuals from seed in spring under glass. Propagate perennials by division in spring or autumn.

The flowers are excellent for taking cuttings. Rudbeckias are suitable for most soil, including heavy ones if well drained, and are best if grown in the full sun. If drainage is poor, add gravel and sand to the soil for improved results.

Rudbeckias are prone to slug and snail damage, so keep a regular check for these.

MOISTURE	Not too much watering
SITE/LIGHT	Full sun in most garden soils with good drainage
GENERAL CARE	Stake taller plants to prevent damage
PESTS & DISEASES	Prone to slugs and snails

FLOWERS
see also
163

COMPANION PLANTS
see pages
141
240
278

Salix WILLOW

Salix consists of hundreds of species ranging from small shrubs to large trees. Often associated with water, the weeping willow, *Salix sepulcralis* 'Chrysocoma', is particularly impressive in the reflection of a pond.

Catkins of the two sexes occur on different trees; the male ones are usually more showy, especially at the silky hairy stage, than the green female catkins. *Salix gracillistyla* 'Melanostachys' male catkins are almost black with brick-red anthers and yellow pollen. *Salix fargesii* is a smaller species with very attractive glossy foliage.

Salix only need damp conditions to germinate seeds, and can grow quite happily in normal or even dry soils. Willows are easy to propagate from hardwood cuttings, best taken in late winter. They can be rooted in a jam jar of water on the kitchen window sill.

As willows demand lots of water, they can cause problems on clay subsoils if put too near foundations.

Salix gracillistyla 'Melanostachys'

Salix fargesii

MOISTURE	Lots of moisture, but does not like it too waterlogged
SITE/LIGHT	Enjoys a sunny spot in any type of well-drained soil
GENERAL CARE	Tolerant of being cut back to keep shape manageable
PESTS & DISEASES	Prone to anthracnose, aphids and honey fungus

TREES
see also
139–40

COMPANION PLANTS
see pages
293
344–5
427–8

Salvia SAGE

The salvias here range from hardy and half-hardy perennials to hardy annuals but all have tubular spikes of two-lipped flowers, the upper lip shaped like a hood.

Salvia farinacea looks good with other summer bedding plants, while the hot colours of *S. splendens* look good with silver-foliage plants such as *Senecio cineraria* 'Silver Dust'. The hardy perennials *S. nemorosa* and *S.* x *sylvestris* are ideal for mixed borders. The common sage (*S. officinalis*) is used as a culinary herb as well as a low shrub. And the shrub *S. microphylla* 'Maraschino' has attractive, cherry-red flowers.

Propagate salvias in spring, half-hardy annuals from seed under glass, hardy annuals in flowering positions and hardy perennials by division or from basal cuttings.

Salvia nemorosa 'Ostfriesland'

Salvia officinalis 'Tricolor'

Salvia microphylla 'Maraschino'

MOISTURE	Not too much water; winter wet will kill off the plant
SITE/LIGHT	Full sun in most well-drained soils
GENERAL CARE	Remove damaged leaves or pick those for culinary use
PESTS & DISEASES	Prone to aphids, black root rot, slugs and snails

FLOWERS see also 406

COMPANION PLANTS see pages 159 357 362

Sambucus ELDER

The elders are fully hardy trees and mostly grown for their foliage, flowers and fruit. Fruit, which follows pannicles of small white-ivory flowers, can be red, black or white.

The foliage is pinnate, but does not give any autumnal colour. There are certain forms which have golden-yellow foliage, including *Sambucus nigra* 'Aurea', *S. racemosa* 'Plumosa Aurea' and *S. racemosa* 'Sutherland Gold'. *S. nigra* 'Guincho Purple' and *S. nigra* 'Black Beauty' have blackish-purple leaves and pinkish flowers. Use in shrub borders or as specimen trees. They tolerate shade and the golden foliage forms can cheer up dark corners.

Raise from seed, hardwood cuttings or softwood cuttings in summer.

Sambucus racemosa 'Sutherland Gold'

Sambucus racemosa 'Plumosa Aurea'

Sambucus nigra 'Black Beauty'

Elders flourish in fairly barren conditions, tolerating acidic or chalky soils.

MOISTURE	Keep moist but do not overwater
SITE/LIGHT	Sun or shade in any well-drained soil
GENERAL CARE	Can be pruned back to restrict size and spread
PESTS & DISEASES	Generally trouble free

TREES
see also
388

COMPANION PLANTS
see pages
183
288
379

Santolina HOLY FLAX

Santolinas are mainly grown for their ornamental and aromatic foliage, as well as for their tiny, button-like flowers which are carried above the foliage on long stalks in mid- to late summer.

Santolinas make small evergreen shrubs and can be effectively used as small hedges, in a rock garden or to divide areas. Try trimming them to form a foliage carpet, or add colour in a border.

They are easily propagated from semi-hardwood cuttings in summer and it is wise to take cuttings each summer in case of damage over winter.

These are shrubs originating from hot, dry and sunny sites in the Mediterranean, and need good drainage.

S. chamaecyparissus 'Lemon Queen'

Santolina chamaecyparissus, also known as cotton lavender, is a compact rounded shrub, performing better on poorer soils than highly fertile ones.

All forms will benefit from being lightly trimmed in autumn.

Santolina chamaecyparissus

MOISTURE	Requires only a little moisture in order to thrive
SITE/LIGHT	A sun-lover which is happy in any type of soil
GENERAL CARE	Lightly trim during summer for the best foliage results
PESTS & DISEASES	Generally trouble free

SHRUBS
see also
306

COMPANION PLANTS
see pages
200
265
392

Sarcococca SWEET BOX

These evergreen shrubs, valued for their fragrant winter flowers, are related to the true box (Buxus). They are found in moist, shady woods and thickets in the wild.

Fleshy drupes (fruit), ripening to red, purple or black, follows the creamy flowers. *Sarcococca ruscifolia* is a suckering shrub to 1m (3ft) with red fruits that are almost lost among the foliage. *S. hookeriana* var. *digyna* has black fruits, but this suckering shrub spreads to 1m (3ft).

Propagate by semi-hardwood cuttings in summer, by removing suckers in late winter and by seed.

Sweet boxes grow on a wide range of soils, with good drainage, including acidic sands to chalky soils. Also good in polluted atmospheres. They will grow in full sun but need adequate soil moisture.

Sarcococca hookeriana var. *digyna*

Sarcococca ruscifolia

MOISTURE	If sited in sun, ensure ground is kept moist
SITE/LIGHT	Prefers shade in any well-drained soil
GENERAL CARE	*S. hookeriana* var. *humilis* is useful as ground cover
PESTS & DISEASES	Prone to slugs and snails

SHRUBS see also 178

COMPANION PLANTS see pages 266 287 293

Sasa

This is a group of low-growing bamboos which is extremely hardy in sheltered locations and can become quite invasive planted outdoors in the garden.

Choose your planting site with care, with ample space around it; once Sasa is established, it is hard to control. In particular, *Sasa palmata nebulosa* is a vigorous spreader and not very suitable for small gardens, unless grown in a large container. The smooth, cylindrical canes can reach 3m (9ft), with extremely large leaves up to 30cm (1ft) long.

Sasa palmata nebulosa

Sasa can be increased by division in spring, replanting the divided clumps.

Grow in moist, rich soil. They are great for planting in wetlands, and near streams and riverbanks. Plants flourish in light or moderately heavy loam and will benefit from a top dressing of manure every now and again. They can be grown in full sun but will do much better in light shade.

Sasa palmata nebulosa

MOISTURE	Water regularly, especially during dry weather
SITE/LIGHT	Prefers shade but tolerates sun in fertile, well-drained soil
GENERAL CARE	Divide and replant clumps if grown in a pot
PESTS & DISEASES	Generally trouble free

SHRUBS see also 372

COMPANION PLANTS see pages 237 285 293

Saxifraga SAXIFRAGE

Hardy, mainly evergreen perennials that grow as mats or low cushions and mounds, saxifrages have small bowl- or star-shaped flowers.

These plants are grown mainly in rock and scree gardens in combination with other alpines such as sempervivums (houseleeks) and sedums (stonecrops), and with miniature spring bulbs.

Saxifraga fortunei is an herbaceous or partially evergreen species with rounded, lobed leaves and heads of starry flowers, an excellent choice for a woodland garden or shady shrub border. *S.* x *urbium* (London pride) with rosettes of spoon-shaped leaves produces sprays of minute starry flowers. A vigorous mat former, it is used as ground cover in shady places. *S. cochlearis* is a cushion-forming saxifrage with rounded, white flowers.

Propagate saxifrages in spring, by division or removing rosettes and treating them as cuttings.

Saxifraga cochlearis

Saxifraga x *urbium*

MOISTURE	Keep fairly moist, especially if located in the sun
SITE/LIGHT	Mostly partial shade in humus-rich, well-drained soil
GENERAL CARE	Protect from strong sun
PESTS & DISEASES	Prone to aphids, slugs, snails and vine weevil grubs

FLOWERS see also 405

COMPANION PLANTS see pages 282 285 289

Scabiosa SCABIOUS

Mainly hardy, herbaceous perennials, scabious are essential plants for cottage gardens and mixed borders. The flowerheads have a dome-shaped centre of tiny flowers surrounded by broad petal-like flowers.

The flowers, which are excellent for cutting, are attractive to butterflies and bees. *Scabiosa atropurpurea* (sweet scabious) is a short-lived plant grown as a hardy annual. All scabious are suitable for sunny herbaceous or mixed borders, combined with shrub roses, artemisias, gypsophilas and eryngiums.

Divide perennials every three years in spring.

Propagate from basal cuttings and raise annuals from seed in early spring under glass or mid-spring in flowering positions.

S. 'Butterfly Blue' (syn. *S. columbaris* 'Butterfly Blue') has grey-green leaves and produces lavender-blue flowerheads in mid- to late summer.

Scabious are good plants for chalky soils but dislike excessive winter wet. Remove dead flowers regularly to prolong the flowering season and give support to annuals by propping them up with twiggy sticks.

Scabiosa 'Butterfly Blue'

MOISTURE	Keep moist but do not overwater
SITE/LIGHT	Likes a sunny site in most well-drained soil
GENERAL CARE	Support taller annuals with sticks
PESTS & DISEASES	Generally trouble free

FLOWERS see also 390–1

COMPANION PLANTS see pages 161 272

Scaevola FAIRY FAN FLOWER

A tender evergreen perennial of trailing habit, *Scaevola aemula* 'Blue Wonder', the best of the scaevolas, has small blooms in the shape of a fan over a long period.

The fairy fan flower is generally grown as an annual in patio tubs, window boxes and hanging baskets and combines effectively with diascias, *Lobelia erinus* cultivars, osteospermums, ivy-leaved pelargoniums, petunias (especially the Million Bells Series), and the grey-foliage plant *Helichrysum petiolare*.

Propagate from softwood cuttings in summer, and winter young plants in a cool greenhouse, planting out when frosts are over.

Several other cultivars are available, such as *S. aemula* 'Blue Wonder', with lilac-blue flowers, and *S.* 'Mauve Clusters', with its lilac-mauve flowers. Scaevola is not troubled by pests or diseases.

Scaevola aemula 'Blue Wonder'

MOISTURE	Water moderately
SITE/LIGHT	Full sun or dappled shade in humus-rich, well-drained soil
GENERAL CARE	Be careful of late frosts – only plant out when mild
PESTS & DISEASES	Generally trouble free

FLOWERS
see also
235

COMPANION PLANTS
see pages
321
357
362

Schizostylis KAFFIR LILY

Schizostylis coccinea and its cultivars are moderately hardy perennials growing from fleshy rhizomes and with narrow, upright, sword-like leaves that remain virtually all year round. Star-shaped blooms are carried in spikes.

These late flowerers are excellent for cutting. Grow schizostylis in a sheltered position, in a mixed border or at the base of a warm wall that receives plenty of sun the year round. Combine with other late-flowering plants, such as dwarf Michaelmas daisies (aster), dwarf hardy chrysanthemums, colchicums, *Crocus speciosus, Nerine bowdenii* and autumn-flowering sedums. Dwarf ornamental grasses can be included in the planting scheme, such as the dainty *Stipa tenuissima.*

Schizostylis coccinea 'Major'

Propagate schizostylis in spring by dividing established clumps. In any case, plants are best divided every three years or so.

Mulch the root area in winter with bulky organic matter such as well-rotted garden compost or leafmould, to serve as frost protection. Although schizostylis needs well-drained conditions, the soil should remain moist at all times as the fleshy rhizomes must not be allowed to dry out. Remove dead foliage as necessary. Slugs and snails like the shoots and hard frosts may damage the flowers.

MOISTURE	Water regularly to keep soil moist at all times
SITE/LIGHT	Full sun in fertile, humus-rich, well-drained soil
GENERAL CARE	Remove dead flowers regularly to prolong flowering
PESTS & DISEASES	Slugs and snails enjoy the young shoots

FLOWERS see also 163

COMPANION PLANTS see pages 199 208 349

Sedum STONECROP

A variable group of succulent perennials, *Sedum spectabile* cultivars are fully hardy and herbaceous in habit, with flattish heads of small star-shaped flowers.

Grow stonecrops at the front of a mixed border, combining the late-flowering kinds with such plants as *Anemone* x *hybrida* and *Anemone hupehensis* cultivars, schizostylis, Michaelmas daisies (aster), hardy chrysanthemums, *Nerine bowdenii*, ornamental grasses, and autumn-colouring shrubs such as berberis, rhus and cotinus.

Propagate in spring, by division or from basal stem cuttings. Regular division of clumps every three years improves performance.

Sedums are especially suitable for slightly chalky soils. Watch out for black root rot, foot rot, slugs and snails.

Sedum spectabile 'Brilliant'

MOISTURE	Keep moist but do not allow to become waterlogged
SITE/LIGHT	Full sun to light shade in most well-drained soils
GENERAL CARE	Cut back spreading species after flowering
PESTS & DISEASES	Prone to black root rot, foot rot, slugs and snails

FLOWERS see also 401

COMPANION PLANTS see pages 152 386 404

Sidalcea CHECKERBLOOM

Hardy herbaceous perennials, sidalceas have lobed leaves and spikes of widely flaring, five-petalled flowers in shades of pink. They look great in cottage gardens, but are also suitable for modern mixed borders.

When the summer flowering is over, reducing stems by half to two-thirds encourages another flush of flowers. This plant's flowers are excellent for cutting.

Propagate by division in spring or by seed.

For best results, grow in slightly acid, sandy soil containing plenty of humus. Very wet soil is anathema to sidalceas. A dry organic winter mulch (for example, straw) protects roots from severe frosts.

Sidalcea 'Elsie Heugh' has interesting fringed petals, while *S.* 'Wine Red' has stunning red flowers.

Sidalcea 'Wine Red'

Sidalcea 'Elsie Heugh'

MOISTURE	Water to keep moist but never too wet
SITE/LIGHT	Sun in any well-drained soil; prefers acid, humus-rich soil
GENERAL CARE	Cut stems back after flowering for another flush of blooms
PESTS & DISEASES	Prone to rust, slugs and snails

FLOWERS see also 396

COMPANION PLANTS see pages 232 270 359

Sisyrinchium

A hardy perennial with erect, evergreen, iris-like leaves, *Sisyrinchium striatum* produces spikes of small bowl-shaped flowers. A popular cultivar, 'Aunt May', has cream and green striped leaves.

Sisyrinchium striatum

The flowers are produced over a fairly long period, from early to mid-summer. Height is up to 90cm (36in), although the cultivar is shorter, at only 45cm (18in) in height, and spread is about 20cm (8in). Grow in a mixed border or gravel garden with other early summer perennials such as oriental poppies (*Papaver orientale*) and *Kniphofia* 'Royal Standard'.

Propagate by division in spring. Sisyrinchiums can also self-seed freely, so seedlings may be a source of new plants.

Suitable for chalky and poor soils, sisyrinchiums, however, hate very wet soil in winter where its roots are liable to rot. In extremely wet winters support a pane of glass over the plants, or use a cloche, to keep off the rain.

Prone to black root rot.

MOISTURE	Keep slightly moist; hates lots of water during winter
SITE/LIGHT	Full sun in any well-drained soil
GENERAL CARE	Protect plants from too much rain over winter
PESTS & DISEASES	Prone to black root rot

FLOWERS *see also* 270

COMPANION PLANTS *see pages* 299 359

Skimmia

A small genus of evergreen shrubs, skimmias have very fragrant flowers. Both male and female forms are needed to produce the fruit, which can be white, such as in *Skimmia japonica* 'Kew White', or most often red, such as *S. japonica* 'Veitchii'.

The handsome dark, green leaves, showy white spring flowers and attractive berries make Skimmia an ideal plant for the winter shade garden. Skimmias are especially good for borders, foundation plantings, spot colour or used as container plants.

Skimmia confusa 'Kew Green' and *S. japonica* 'Fragrans' are good male forms. *S. reevesiana* 'Robert Fortune' (also listed as a form of *S. japonica*) is good if there is only room for one plant as this is an hermaphrodite and produces crimson-red fruits (not good on chalky soil). Apart from this form, Skimmia grows on any well-drained soils, including chalk.

Propagate by semi-hardwood cuttings, with some bottom heat, in late summer, as well as by seed in spring.

Skimmia japonica

An evergreen, the plant should be grown in full shade or part sun and shade. In full sun the foliage turns yellow-green, which destroys the beauty of this plant. In the garden, they are useful to fill space beneath established trees or in other shady spots, as well as in shaded borders.

MOISTURE	Do not over water – keep fairly moist
SITE/LIGHT	Prefers a shady position in any well-drained soil
GENERAL CARE	Cut branches with berries are used as winter decorations
PESTS & DISEASES	Generally trouble free

SHRUBS see also 435

COMPANION PLANTS see pages 364 390–1 396

Solanum CLIMBING POTATO

This large genus contains a number of vegetables, including the potato (*Solanum tuberosum*), as well as the ornamental plants mentioned here.

Climbing potatoes are usually vigorous and need support for them to clamber up or have other plants through which to ramble. Among the most popular of the solanums is *S. crispin* 'Glasnevin', which bears trusses of deep-purple flowers from summer to autumn. *S. jasminoides* is a white-flowered climbing potato with fragrant blossoms and yellowish-white fruit. The fruits of climbing solanums are usually poisonous.

They can be grown from seed, cuttings or from layering a stem.

They thrive in full sun and are ideal against a wall, over a pergola, arbour or arch. Grow in fertile soil and keep well watered during the summer months.

Solanum ambosinum

Solanum rantonnetii

MOISTURE	Water regularly, especially during the summer
SITE/LIGHT	Full sun in fertile, well-drained soil
GENERAL CARE	In frost-prone regions, grow tender species indoors
PESTS & DISEASES	Prone to aphids and red spider mite under glass

FLOWERS see also 360

COMPANION PLANTS see pages 201–4 390–1

Solidago GOLDEN ROD

Hardy herbaceous perennials of vigorous habit, the golden rods are valued for their late colour, provided by sprays of small, daisy like, yellow flowers that are suitable for cutting.

Grow in a mixed or prairie-style border with asters (including Michaelmas daisies), hardy chrysanthemums, rudbeckias, late-flowering heleniums, helianthus, monardas, *Echinacea purpurea* and ornamental grasses such as *Miscanthus sinensis* cultivars.

Solidago also looks good with shrubs noted for autumn leaf colour, particularly rhus (sumachs).

Propagate by division in spring or autumn, or from basal stem cuttings in spring.

These perennials are suitable for poor and sandy soils in the full sun.

Solidago 'Goldenmosa' bears delicate, yellow-stalked, bright yellow flowerheads in late summer and early autumn. Solidagos are prone to powdery mildew.

Solidago 'Goldenmosa'

MOISTURE	Requires only little moisture in order to thrive
SITE/LIGHT	Enjoys the full sun in relatively poor, but well-drained soil
GENERAL CARE	Can be invasive in the garden
PESTS & DISEASES	Prone to powdery mildew

FLOWERS see also 163

COMPANION PLANTS see pages 199 276 386

Sorbus ROWAN AND WHITEBEAM

This is a large group of mostly hardy, deciduous trees, as well as shrubs. They are among the most decorative trees and large shrubs, providing an attractive display for more than one season. In essence, there are two types of Sorbus: the rowans and the whitebeams.

Sorbus cashmiriana

Whitebeams have simple leaves, silvery-white beneath, often with serrated margins. They have clusters of brown to red fruits in the autumn with vivid foliage colour. *Sorbus intermedia* (Swedish whitebeam) is a small to medium-sized tree with a dense, rounded head of branches. Compact heads of white flowers are borne in spring, followed by bunches of reddish-orange berries.

Rowans have pinnate, fern-like leaves; the foliage turns to shades of red and yellow in autumn. Cream-coloured flowers are followed by bunches of brilliant red (*S. aucuparia*), orange, pink or white (*S. cashmiriana*) berries in spring.

Sorbus aucuparia

Propagate by seed, by grafting or root from semi-hardwood cuttings.

Grow in any good, fertile soil that is well-drained and slightly acidic. They need full sun but do not like intense heat. Water well and mulch during periods of dry weather.

MOISTURE	Keep well watered, especially during dry periods
SITE/LIGHT	Full sun in any fertile, well-drained soil
GENERAL CARE	Prune in winter or early spring if necessary
PESTS & DISEASES	Generally trouble free apart from fireblight

TREES see also 220

COMPANION PLANTS see pages 332 435

Spiraea

With its numerous clusters of tiny flowers lasting all summer long, Spiraea makes quite a show. The effect continues into autumn as the foliage ends the growing season by turning a blaze of yellow, orange or red.

Spiraea japonica (Japanese spiraea) has larger leaves than most species and is swamped during the flowering period with profuse sprays of tiny pink blooms. Certain forms are selected for the colour of the foliage alone, such as *S. japonica* 'Fire Light', with its orange-coloured new leaves maturing to green and then turning red in autumn. Some cultivars of *S. japonica* can reach 1.5m (5ft) or higher, but most forms are shorter.

Spiraeas can be propagated by seed (which should be sown directly onto damp compost), or softwood or semi-hardwood cuttings in early summer.

In the garden, spiraeas are useful among a variety of sun-loving shrubs, perennials and annuals, but can also be used as informal hedges or low screens. They thrive on all types of well-drained soil and should be located in the full sun, although it does tolerate dappled shade at the heat of the day. Water during exceptionally dry periods up until the autumn.

Spiraea japonica 'Fire Light'

MOISTURE	Water regularly and do not allow to dry out
SITE/LIGHT	Full sun to dappled shade in fertile, well-drained soil
GENERAL CARE	Prune back to ground level in early spring to rejuvenate
PESTS & DISEASES	Can be prone to spiraea sawfly

SHRUBS
see also
374

COMPANION PLANTS
see pages
329–30
384–5
435

Stachys BETONY

These hardy herbaceous perennials have spikes of tubular, often hooded flowers arising from rosettes of wrinkled leaves. All stachys have square as opposed to rounded stems. The flowers attract insects, including butterflies and bees.

Stachys is suitable for a mixed border, where it combines effectively with old shrub roses, lavenders, cistus and rosemary (rosmarinus). *Stachys macrantha* and *S. officialis* species will tolerate a position in partial shade.

Stachys densiflora

Stachys macrantha 'Superba'

Propagate by division in spring just as plants are starting into growth.

Low-growing Stachys, such as *S. byzantina*, is suitable as an edging plant or for ground cover.

MOISTURE	Keep moist but avoid excessive winter wet
SITE/LIGHT	Enjoys full sun in fairly fertile, well-drained soil
GENERAL CARE	Protect plants from being waterlogged over winter
PESTS & DISEASES	Prone to slugs and snails; (*S. byzantium*: powdery mildew)

FLOWERS see also 396

COMPANION PLANTS see pages 161 306 392

Stipa GIANT FEATHER GRASS or GOLDEN OATS

This hardy perennial grass forms tufts of narrow, evergreen or partially evergreen leaves. However, it is mostly grown for its impressive heads of oat-like flowers, which are dried and used in flower arrangements.

Stipa gigantea, generally acknowledged as the best species, is usually used as an effective contrast with many hardy perennials. This plant looks particularly good with flat-headed achilleas, or with the bold spikes of kniphofias, or with the rounded heads of agapanthus, or with the brilliant flowers of crocosmias. It also contrasts well with many shrubs.

Stipa gigantea

Stipa gigantea

Giant feather grass is good, too, for a gravel garden or set against a backdrop of dark green conifers.

Propagate by division in mid-spring to early summer.

Cut back deciduous species in early winter and remove dead leaves on evergreens in early spring.

MOISTURE	Does not require much watering once established
SITE/LIGHT	Grow in full sun in fairly fertile, light, well-drained soil
GENERAL CARE	Cut back deciduous species in early winter
PESTS & DISEASES	Generally trouble free

FLOWERS see also 336

COMPANION PLANTS see pages 141 222 299

Syringa LILAC

Syringa is a genus of around 20 species of deciduous shrubs and trees that are grown for their conical or pyramid-shaped panicles of tiny, fragrant flowers which bloom in late spring or early summer.

Most garden cultivated lilacs are grouped under the *Syringa vulgaris* (common lilac) species which produces predominantly lilac-coloured flowers, but there are hybrids of many other colours, especially whites and purples. As they tend to lack much beauty out of flower, try growing summer climbers such as Clematis through them or plant spring bulbs underneath for added interest. Grow smaller lilacs in shrub beds.

Syringa vulgaris

Propagate from softwood cuttings taken in early summer, or by grafting or layering.

Lilacs prefer fertile, well-drained soils but can sometimes tolerate chalky sites. Avoid planting in areas of heavy frosts, as late spring frosts can destroy the flower buds. If lilacs are used as informal hedging, trim after flowering.

MOISTURE	Keep moist especially during hot summers
SITE/LIGHT	Sun or light shade on fertile, well-drained soil
GENERAL CARE	Mulch regularly and deadhead newly planted lilacs
PESTS & DISEASES	Prone to lilac blight and honey fungus

SHRUBS see also 364

COMPANION PLANTS see pages 201–4 344–5 427–8

Tagetes MARIGOLD

Marigolds are half-hardy annuals with ferny, strongly aromatic foliage and single to fully double flowers in a range of bright colours – shades of yellow, orange and red. They vary in size from dwarf-bushy to tall plants.

There are four groups of hybrids. African marigolds – large, fully double flowers, and an upright habit; French marigolds (*Tagetes* 'Safari Series') – dwarf-bushy plants with double or single flowers; Afro-French marigolds – dwarf and bushy in habit with small single or double flowers; and Signet marigolds – dwarf, very bushy plants bearing masses of small single flowers. African marigolds are best suited to formal bedding schemes and are often used as dot plants in other bedding plants. Remove dead flowerheads regularly to ensure continuous flowering.

Tagetes 'Safari Tangerine'

Tagetes Gem Series

Raise plants from seed in early to mid-spring under glass. The flowers of all marigolds are good for cutting, but especially African marigolds with their long stems. During dry weather, water regularly to keep the plants growing and flowering.

MOISTURE	Water regularly during dry weather to ensure flowering
SITE/LIGHT	Fairly fertile, well-drained soil in the full sun
GENERAL CARE	Dead-head regularly to prolong flowering
PESTS & DISEASES	Prone to grey mould (African marigolds), slugs and snails

FLOWERS see also 350

COMPANION PLANTS see pages 186 279 433

Tamarix TAMARISK

Although these shrubs seem to thrive in windy, coastal areas, Tamarix is just as suitable for cultivating away from the coast with its delicate, feathery foliage.

The foliage is complemented by the equally small but prolifically carried pink-coloured flowers. They are excellent for planting in shrub borders or as specimen shrubs, and can also be used to make hedges. *Tamarix ramosissima* flowers in late summer on the current season's shoots, while *T. gallica* flowers in early spring.

Propagate from hardwood cuttings in winter or semi-hardwood cuttings in summer, as well as from seed sown as soon as it is ripe.

Tamarix tolerates salt in the ground and thrives on poor soils, apart from shallow soil overlying chalk.

Tamarix ramosissima

Tamarix gallica

MOISTURE	Requires only little moisture in order to thrive
SITE/LIGHT	Full sun in most light, well-drained soils
GENERAL CARE	Prune regularly or they become unstable and straggly
PESTS & DISEASES	Generally trouble free

SHRUBS see also 247

COMPANION PLANTS see pages 170 183 288

Taxus YEW

Yew is one of the best evergreen, coniferous large shrubs or trees to grow as a hedging or topiary plant. It also has attractive peeling bark and ornamental, often reddish, stems.

The dark green leaves or needles are arched and often arranged in two rows. Taxus can be reshaped for renovation at any age and, unlike Leyland cypress (*Cupressus leylandii*), will not romp out of control. Even the columnar forms such as *Taxus baccata* 'Fastigiata' will eventually grow no taller than 10m (33ft) high. Prostrate forms, such as *T. baccata* 'Repandens', make excellent ground cover.

Taxus baccata 'Fastigiata'

Yew can be propagated from seed, which may take a few years to germinate, or better still from cuttings, preferably taken in late summer.

The foliage and bark is poisonous, so bear this in mind if there are grazing animals such as cattle, horses or goats around.

Grow yew in any well-drained, fertile soil, even chalky or acid soils, in either full sun or deep shade. Trim yews used for hedging in summer or early autumn.

MOISTURE	Keep reasonably moist but can withstand drought
SITE/LIGHT	Sun or deep shade in any well-drained, fertile soil
GENERAL CARE	All parts are highly toxic if eaten
PESTS & DISEASES	Prone to phytophthora root rot

TREES see also 420

COMPANION PLANTS see pages 178 196 381

Teucrium SHRUBBY GERMANDER

Many teucriums are herbaceous perennials, but there are a few shrubby species which are reliably evergreen if sheltered from cold winds. In the wild they are found in woodland and dry, rocky places.

The only woody species commonly cultivated is *Teucrium fruticans*, the shrubby germander. Expect a brilliant show of silvery, evergreen foliage joined in summer by beautifully contrasting pale blue flowers. In mild gardens it can be grown as a formal, clipped hedge, although regular trimming removes the fine spikes of two-lipped rosemary-like flowers. In cooler settings, plant in a sheltered spot as a border in a shrub bed or train it against a wall.

Teucrium can be propagated by seeds or by softwood or semi-hardwood cuttings in summer.

Shrubby germanders appreciate a sunny position in the garden and in soil with very good drainage, preferably light, sandy soil. It needs moderate to little watering and is quite hardy.

Another favourable feature is that they are generally not prone to pests and diseases.

Teucrium fruticans

MOISTURE	Requires little to moderate watering
SITE/LIGHT	Full sun in most light, well-drained soils
GENERAL CARE	Smaller species stay more compact on poor, gritty soil
PESTS & DISEASES	Generally trouble free

SHRUBS see also 190

COMPANION PLANTS see pages 358 381 398

Thuja RED CEDAR

This genus of evergreen, coniferous trees has delightfully scented, scale-like spreading foliage. As well as specimen trees, most forms are also suitable for hedging in the garden.

Red cedars are capable of reaching up to 12–15m (40–50ft), such as the conical, yellow-leaved *Thuja plicata* 'Zebrina'. But there are dwarf species which do not tend to reach above 1m (3ft), such as *T. occidentalis* 'Hetz Midget' and *T. occidentalis* 'Tiny Tim'.

Thuja plicata 'Zebrina'

The female cones are small and erect, and the male cones small and ovoid. Thujas are generally wider at the base and becoming more conical at the top as they grow.

Thuja occidentalis 'Tiny Tim'

Propagate from seed or from semi-ripe cuttings taken in the late summer.

Thuja is best grown on deep, moist but well-drained soils, but tolerates poor drainage better than other cypress-like conifers. It prefers the full sun.

MOISTURE	Likes to be kept moist
SITE/LIGHT	Full sun in deep but well-drained soil
GENERAL CARE	Contact with the foliage may aggravate skin allergies
PESTS & DISEASES	Prone to scale insects, canker and aphids

TREES
see also
418

COMPANION PLANTS
see pages
196
296
373

Thunbergia BLACK-EYED SUSAN

A tender, perennial, evergreen climber, *Thunbergia alata,* the best species, is grown outdoors as an annual. With leaves like arrow heads, it produces five-lobed flowers with black eyes (hence the common name).

Combine black-eyed Susan with other annual climbers such as *Tropaeolum peregrinum* (canary creeper) and ipomoea (morning glory), or even with hardy climbers such as clematis.

Grow thunbergia in a very warm, sheltered position and provide supports for it to climb, such as an obelisk, trellis or pergola. It can even clamber up through a small tree or large, open shrub.

Raise plants from seed in spring under glass or insert greenwood cuttings in early summer.

Black-eyed Susans prefer moist conditions in fertile, well-drained soil in a sunny position.

Thunbergia alata Suzie Hybrids

MOISTURE	Keep moist but water regularly when in growth
SITE/LIGHT	Full sun in fertile, well-drained soil
GENERAL CARE	Tropical climbers (*T. gregorii*) prefer partial shade
PESTS & DISEASES	Prone to red spider mites and scale insects under glass

FLOWERS see also 425

COMPANION PLANTS see pages 201–4 292 323

Trachelospermum STAR JASMINE

Grown for its attractive foliage and fragrant flowers, Trachelospermum is ideal for a courtyard garden. It can also be grown as ground cover, so long as the upright shoots are cut off regularly. In temperate climates, Trachelospermum can also be grown in a conservatory.

Trachelospermum jasminoides

Star jasmine is a popular and widespread climber grown for its pure white and scented flowers. A well-established plant will produce abundant flowers and fragrance, though the plant can take a while to get to this stage.

Its star-like flowers are borne in tiny clusters, and its tough and slightly glossy leaves are evergreen and ovate shaped.

To propagate, insert semi-ripe cuttings with bottom heat in summer.

The best place to grow star jasmines is in full sun, up against a warm wall, with some shade in a really hot climate.

Plant in fertile, well-drained soil and make sure that the plant is well watered. However, water sparingly during the winter months.

MOISTURE	Water well during the summer, sparingly in the winter
SITE/LIGHT	Loves a sunny site in fertile soil with good drainage
GENERAL CARE	Provide shelter from cold, drying winds
PESTS & DISEASES	Generally trouble free

FLOWERS see also 294

COMPANION PLANTS see pages 201–4 323 360

Trachycarpus

Trachycarpus fortunei is the species most commonly cultivated for the garden. They are grown for their attractive habit and fan-shaped, palmate leaves. It is an ideal plant for the courtyard garden.

This is a magnificent palm, originating from the sub-tropical forests in Asia, which is quite a slow grower; in colder climates, especially, it may only reach around 8m (25ft). The trunk is solid and hairy, out of which sprouts the enormous fan-shaped leaves. Mature plants will bear small yellow flowers close to the leaf bases in large, pendant panicles in early summer.

Propagation is by sowing seed in spring or autumn.

Trachycarpus enjoys lots of watering – a spot by a pond would be ideal– and will thrive with a regular feed of manure or blood, fish and bone during the spring and early summer.

A sunny spot is best but it can tolerate a shady site. Protect this palm from wind to prevent its large leaves from getting a battering.

Trachycarpus fortunei

MOISTURE	Needs plenty of moisture
SITE/LIGHT	Sun or shade in fertile, loamy soil
GENERAL CARE	Remove brown leaves and do not allow to dry out
PESTS & DISEASES	Generally trouble free

***SHRUBS* see also 197**

***COMPANION PLANTS* see pages 237 285**

Tradescantia

As well as growing among other plants in a mixed border, Tradescantia is also at home in hanging baskets in a cool greenhouse or conservatory.

T. Andersoniana Group 'Osprey'

Some good effects can be achieved if planted in a mixed border by combining tradescantias with ornamental grasses of similar stature, particularly grasses with white- or cream-variegated foliage. They also go well with hemerocallis (day lilies) and crocosmias.

The Andersonian Group of cultivars are hardy, herbaceous perennials with clumps of broad, grassy foliage and a long succession of three-petalled flowers.

Propagate by division in spring or autumn.

When flowering is over, cut back the stems to ensure more blooms follow and to prevent seeding.

Tradescantia Andersoniana Group 'Purple Dome'

MOISTURE	Water regularly, especially during growth
SITE/LIGHT	Full sun or partial shade in moist, fertile soil
GENERAL CARE	Under glass, water sparingly during winter
PESTS & DISEASES	Prone to aphids, slugs and snails

FLOWERS *see also* 321

COMPANION PLANTS *see pages* 222 281

Tropaeolum

This is a large and varied genus. The most popular are the half-hardy annuals derived from *Tropaeolum majus*, popularly known as nasturtiums, with either a dwarf bushy or trailing habit.

Use tropaeolums in patio containers and hanging baskets, or at the front of mixed borders. These plants rarely need companions to enhance their effect, but if you want a contrast mix in some blue *Lobelia erinus*.

Tropaeolum peregrinum, the canary creeper, is a tender annual climber with attractive lobed leaves and masses of small, spurred flowers over a long period. It is a vigorous grower and can be combined with other annual climbers such as ipomoea (morning glory) and *Thunbergia alata* (black-eyed Susan). Provide suitable supports such as an obelisk, trellis, garden arch or pergola. A good perennial climber is *T. speciosum*, the flame creeper.

Raise annuals from seed in early spring under glass, or in flowering positions during mid-spring.

Nasturtiums (*T. majus*) flower best in poor soils.

Tropaeolum speciosum

MOISTURE	Keep moist but do not overwater
SITE/LIGHT	Likes full sun in fertile, humus-rich soil
GENERAL CARE	Support the climbing stems; give roots shade if possible
PESTS & DISEASES	Prone to black aphids, caterpillars, slugs, snails and viruses

FLOWERS *see also* 321

COMPANION PLANTS *see pages* 292 421

Tsuga HEMLOCK

Tsuga heterophylla is one of the most beautiful of all evergreen trees, not only for its conical habit and glossy leaves, but also for its cracked, purple-brown bark.

As a specimen tree, it is hard to beat. One feature is its tolerance of shade, so it can be grown in dark, shady corners, offering a brighter hue than *Taxus baccata*.

Slightly pendent branches carry the dense green foliage with silvery undersides. The leading shoot bends with the wind, giving the tree a graceful aspect.

Tsuga heterophylla

Tsuga can be raised from seed sown in spring or from cuttings taken in late summer.

T. heterophylla can also be used to form very attractive hedges. *T. mertensiana* 'Glauca' is a dwarf form with glaucous, silver-grey foliage.

Tsuga grows on a wide range of soils, in sun or shade, and is especially suited to dry, acidic sands. When the plant is young, provide shelter from strong, cold winds.

MOISTURE	Keep moist, particularly when young
SITE/LIGHT	Sun or shade in most well-drained soils
GENERAL CARE	Trim back hedges from early to late summer
PESTS & DISEASES	Generally trouble free

TREES see also 418

COMPANION PLANTS see pages 135 296 373

Tulipa TULIP

Tulips are hardy spring-flowering bulbs with six-petalled flowers, which are generally produced singly or in clusters in some species. The cultivars of hybrid tulips have mainly single flowers, although some are double, and most are wine glass- or bowl-shaped.

Tulips are split, according to flower type, into 15 groups. For example, *Tulipa* 'Burgundy Lace' (Fringed Group); *T.* 'Clara Butt' and *T.* 'Queen of Night' (Single Late Group); *T.* 'Golden Apeldoorn' and *T.* 'Apeldoorn' (Darwin Hybrid) and *T.* 'Spring Green' (Viridiflora Group).

Tulipa 'Queen of Night'

Tulips have various uses in the garden. Smaller species like *T. tarda* (Miscellaneous Group) are suitable for rock gardens or the front of mixed borders. Small hybrids such as the Kaufmanniana and Greigii tulips are excellent in patio tubs or window boxes. The taller hybrid tulips are favourites for formal spring bedding schemes, planted through carpets of forget-me-nots (*Myosotis sylvatica*), double daisies (*Bellis perennis* cultivars) or wallflowers (erysimum). However, tulips can also be used in mixed borders,

Tulipa 'Burgundy Lace'

FLOWERS
see also
344–5

COMPANION PLANTS
see pages
151
257
329–30

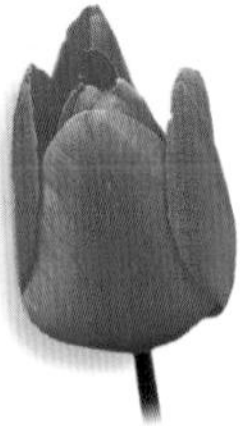

Tulipa 'Apeldoorn'

Tulipa 'Spring Green'

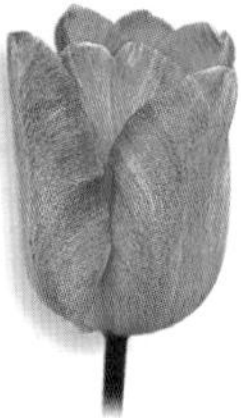

Tulipa 'Clara Butt'

planting them in irregular groups or drifts. Always grow tulips in a sheltered position. Remove dead flowerheads.

Species tulips (*T. tarda*) are generally left in the ground for a number of years, but hybrid tulips are lifted every year when the foliage has died down and the bulbs stored for the summer in an airy place after drying off and ripening under glass. Large bulbs can then be planted for flowering again, smaller ones planted in a nursery bed to grow to a larger size. Propagate by removing offsets in summer.

Tulip fire is a fungal disease, leaving bleached spots on the petals, which can make some plants wither badly. Remove and burn all affected plants.

Tulipa tarda

Tulipa 'Golden Apeldoorn'

MOISTURE	Keep moist but do not allow to become excessively wet
SITE/LIGHT	Full sun in fertile, well-drained soil
GENERAL CARE	Dig up and destroy plants displaying tulip fire
PESTS & DISEASES	Prone to tulip fire, bulb aphids, bulb rot, slugs and snails

FLOWERS ***see also 286***

COMPANION PLANTS see pages 301 332 381

Ulex GORSE

Gorse is a genus of around 20 species of spiny, evergreen shrubs common to lowland heath and waste ground. The spines are quite ferocious but it is often grown for its clusters of pea-like yellow flowers.

Although often viewed as a wasteland plant, the quality and quantity of the gorse's blooms is outstanding, with open, bright-yellow flowers present at all times of the year in milder climates. The common gorse or furze, *Ulex europaeus*, is an upright to rounded, dense bush producing dark brown seed pods in summer. A form of *U. europaeus*, 'Flore Pleno', is a sterile double-flowered form, which makes a smaller and more compact bush and holds on to its flowers for longer.

To propagate, take semi-ripe cuttings in summer.

Gorse will grow on any neutral to acidic soil but is best on the most barren sands and gravels; on fertile sites it becomes lank and dismal. Grow in full sunlight, or no more than light shade.

Ulex europaeus

MOISTURE	Requires only little moisture in order to thrive
SITE/LIGHT	Full sun or partial shade in poor, sandy, well-drained soil
GENERAL CARE	Grow in a shrub border or use as a barrier hedge
PESTS & DISEASES	Generally trouble free

SHRUBS see also 265

COMPANION PLANTS see pages 306 392 398

Ulmus ELM

An aggressive strain of Dutch elm disease in the late 1960s has significantly reduced the number of elms, particularly the American (*Ulmus americana*) and European (*U. procera* and *U. minor*) species.

The tiny, bell-shaped flowers of the elm are usually a purplish colour. The seeds are in a flat, papery disk which ripens during early summer.

Ulmus minor 'Jaqueline Hillier'

Ulmus minor 'Dampieri Aurea'

U. americana grows into a large tree 30m (100ft) high, with glossy, dark green leaves on top, and paler and downy ones underneath. *U. minor* 'Jacqueline Hillier' is a compact shrub form, only reaching around 2.5m (8ft) in height.

For the Wych elm (*U. glabra*), seeds should be used whenever possible in propagation, but most other elms will grow from root cuttings.

Elms will thrive in soil that is acidic or alkaline, although loamy soil is the best. They also like a position in the full sun or light shade.

MOISTURE	Keep just moist
SITE/LIGHT	Full sun to partial shade in loamy, well-drained soil
GENERAL CARE	Choose cultivars that are disease (or partially) resistant
PESTS & DISEASES	Prone to Dutch elm disease, honey fungus and aphids

TREES
see also
388

COMPANION PLANTS
see pages
358
384–5

Vaccinium BLUEBERRY

This is a large group of species of evergreen and deciduous shrubs. Most are grown for their attractive flowers, autumnal hues and edible fruits.

In the garden, grow *Vaccinium arctostaphylos* in the shrub border for its colourful, pink-white flowers and attractive red-brown leathery leaves in the autumn. *Vaccinium cylindraceum* bears cylindrical, red-tinged flowers in early autumn. Vacciniums produce edible, usually spherical, berries after the flowers.

Take semi-ripe cuttings of evergreens in summer.

Vaccinium arctostaphylos

Vaccinium cylindraceum

All vacciniums prefer fertile, acidic, peaty or sandy and generally moist soil with good drainage. They usually perform better in light shade.

Keep a look out for root rot, particularly after a very wet winter.

MOISTURE	Keep moist at all times
SITE/LIGHT	Partial shade in fertile, acidic, well-drained soil
GENERAL CARE	Fine in full sun so long as there is sufficient moisture
PESTS & DISEASES	May be prone to phytophthora crown and root rot

SHRUBS see also 435

COMPANION PLANTS see pages 287 384–5

Verbascum MULLEIN

A variable genus, *Verbascum* 'Helen Johnson' is a hardy, evergreen perennial, although it is rather short lived. From rosettes of large greyish-green leaves (or deep purple-green in some cultivars) bold spikes of saucer-shaped flowers arise.

Verbascum 'Helen Johnson'

Used in mixed borders, these plants combine well with old shrub roses, and with perennials such as flat-headed achilleas, artemisias and ornamental grasses.

Mulleins are also suitable for gravel gardens, as well as naturalizing in a wild or woodland garden setting.

Propagate Verbascum by division in spring or from root cuttings in winter. Regular propagation is advised due to the rather short lives of these plants.

For best results, grow in chalky soils, which should not be too fertile.

V. 'Cotswold Queen' and *V.* 'Gainsborough' are both partial evergreens, with grey-green foliage.

Watch out for caterpillars and powdery mildew.

MOISTURE	Keep moist but do not allow to become too wet
SITE/LIGHT	Full sun in not too fertile, well-drained soil
GENERAL CARE	Protect alpine species from winter wet
PESTS & DISEASES	Prone to caterpillars and powdery mildew

***FLOWERS* see also 238**

***COMPANION PLANTS* see pages 141 161 390–1**

Verbena VERVAIN

Verbena x _hybrida_ cultivars are half-hardy perennials grown as annuals. Plants may be bushy and upright or spreading in habit, and produce rounded heads of small five-petalled flowers. Mass plant in beds or grow in containers, including hanging baskets.

Verbena x hybrida Blue Series

These plants mix well with many other summer bedders, including petunias, salvias, dwarf dahlias and pelargoniums (zonal and ivy-leaved). *Verbena bonariensis*, a frost-hardy perennial with a delightful branching habit, can be used as a dot plant in summer bedding schemes and in mixed borders. This plant looks great with cannas, tall dahlias or tall ornamental grasses.

Verbena x hybrida

Raise *V.* x *hybrida* cultivars from seed sown in spring under glass, or buy plug plants. Propagate *V. bonariensis* by division in spring or semi-ripe stem-tip cuttings in summer.

Grow in full sun in moderately fertile soil for best results and watch out for aphids, powdery mildew, slugs and snails.

MOISTURE	Keep fairly moist
SITE/LIGHT	Full sun in moderately fertile, well-drained soil
GENERAL CARE	Protect with a dry mulch in winter in frost-prone areas
PESTS & DISEASES	Prone to aphids, powdery mildew, and slugs and snails

FLOWERS see also 416

COMPANION PLANTS see pages 186 228–9 365

Veronica SPEEDWELL

This is a large genus of plants, only a few of which are described here. These hardy perennials produce spikes of small saucer- or star-shaped flowers over a long period.

Grow veronicas, such as the popular *Veronica gentianoides* and the newer *V. kiusiana* from Japan, in a mixed border, using the low-growing kinds at the front. Veronicas combine effectively with many plants, including shrub roses and hardy

Veronica gentianoides

Veronica kiusiana

perennials such as Paeonia, geraniums and sidalceas. *V. peduncularis* 'Georgia Blue' and *V. spicata* subsp. *incana* can also be grown in a rock or scree garden.

Propagate by division or from basal stem cuttings in the spring.

Grow Veronica in fairly fertile, loamy, well-drained soil in sun or partial shade.

MOISTURE	Keep fairly moist
SITE/LIGHT	Sun or partial shade in loamy, well-drained soil
GENERAL CARE	Grow alpines or rock garden veronicas in poorer soil
PESTS & DISEASES	Prone to leaf spot and powdery mildew

FLOWERS see also 232

COMPANION PLANTS see pages 234 267 406

Viburnum GUELDER ROSE

This genus contains around 150 different species of evergreen to deciduous shrubs plus many garden forms. They are grown for their attractive foliage, tiny, often fragrant, flowers and ornamental fruits.

Viburnum can be used in shrub beds and in woodland gardens. As an evergreen shrub, *Viburnum burkwoodii* has very attractive flowers.

Viburnum plicatum 'Pink Beauty'

Use *V. davidii* as ground cover to smother weeds. *V. bodnantense, V. farreri* and *V. tinus* are excellent for the flowers which are carried during the winter period. Use *V. plicatum* and its forms as specimen shrubs or in a prominent bed.

Viburnums can be raised from seed, cuttings or by layering.

Viburnum thrive on well-drained soils, including chalky and acidic ones. They perform better on fertile sites, and like full sun to moderate shade.

Viburnum burkwoodii

MOISTURE	Needs to be kept moist
SITE/LIGHT	Sun or partial shade in fairly fertile, well-drained soil
GENERAL CARE	Prune after flowering to remove damaged branches
PESTS & DISEASES	Prone to aphids and honey fungus

SHRUBS see also 384–5

COMPANION PLANTS see pages 251 329–30 358

Vinca PERIWINKLE

Periwinkles are evergreen trailing shrubs or sub-shrubs and make useful ground cover. However, unless kept under control they can become invasive.

Vincas can be quite showy and their spreading, star-like flowers with five petals come in a variety of colours. They are usually bright blue, but are dark plum-purple in *Vinca minor* 'Atropurpurea', lavender-blue in *V. minor* 'La Grave', and white in *V. minor forma alba* and 'Gertrude Jekyll'. Flowering lasts a long time, usually from late spring into the autumn. The lance-shaped opposite leaves are often variegated and complement the flowers.

Propagate either by division or separating the wandering shoots that have rooted, which should be carried out either in autumn or spring, or by taking cuttings in summer.

Periwinkles are much happier in full sun as flowering can be rather spasmodic in shade. Vincas thrive on almost all soils, except those which are too dry.

Vinca minor 'La Grave'

MOISTURE	Keep watering regularly, especially over summer
SITE/LIGHT	Prefers full sun in most well-drained soils
GENERAL CARE	Cut back hard in spring to prevent vincas taking over!
PESTS & DISEASES	Prone to rust fungi but generally trouble free

SHRUBS see also 243

COMPANION PLANTS see pages 252 280 293

Viola PANSY or VIOLET

Hardy, short-lived perennials grown as annuals or biennials, pansies and violas have flat, five-petalled flowers which are held vertically.

Pansies have the largest flowers, violas have masses of smaller blooms. Pansies are generally larger plants, violas are smaller and more compact. Violas have an incredibly long flowering period and, with suitable cultivars, can be found in flower all year round. Pansies and violas are used for bedding and also make good container plants for patio tubs and window boxes. They do not really need other plants – mass plant them on their own. Grow them in mixed borders, the winter- and spring-flowering kinds positioned around shrubs that flower during these seasons.

Viola 'Sorbet Supreme Mix'

Raise from seed sown under glass in cool conditions. Sow summer-flowering kinds in early to mid-spring and plant out the young plants in late spring. Biennials for flowering in winter and spring are sown in early summer. Grow on the young plants in a nursery bed and plant them out in the autumn.

Viola Joker Series

Viola Penny Series

MOISTURE	Keep fairly moist particularly during summer
SITE/LIGHT	Sun or partial shade in humus-rich, well-drained soil
GENERAL CARE	Deadhead regularly to prolong flowering
PESTS & DISEASES	Prone to aphids, powdery mildew, rust, slugs and snails

***FLOWERS* see also 380**

***COMPANION PLANTS* see pages 286 344–5 427–8**

Vitis VINE

Vines are reliably good in the garden. They can be grown up walls or alternatively there are forms that are compact and suited to container growth.

The gardening interest with vines lies not only in adorning conservatories with garlands of grapes, or decorating a pergola with fruit, but also in dark leaved varieties such as *Vitis vinifera* 'Purpurea', that offer different effects. There are other Vitis species available that are decorative and not edible.

Vitis vinifera 'Purpurea'

The most popular species of vine is the deciduous *V. coignetiae* that has large green leaves that turn a maroon colour in the autumn, providing plenty of colourful foliage during summer and autumn months.

They can be propagated without too much difficulty from cuttings made from hard wood, or from grafting. They can even be grown from seed.

Grape vines demand well-drained, preferably neutral to alkaline, humus-rich soil in the full sun or partial shade. Keep this plant well watered until established. Prune it back to restrict the growth, particularly if more formal training up a pergola is required.

Vines may be troubled by powdery mildew or fungus.

MOISTURE	Keep well watered, especially when first planted
SITE/LIGHT	Full sun or partial shade in humus-rich, well-drained soil
GENERAL CARE	Prune it to restrict growth or to train up a structure
PESTS & DISEASES	Prone to powdery mildew and honey fungus

SHRUBS* *see also* *409

COMPANION PLANTS* *see pages* *201–4* *323

Weigela

Weigela is a genus of twelve species of mainly spreading to upright deciduous shrubs. They are excellent shrubs for adding colour to an open woodland area, as well as a mixed or shrub border.

In the garden, Weigela is useful for the spring or early summer flowers, adding colour to shrub beds. The flowers are bell- to funnel-shaped, usually varying from pink to red, such as *Weigela* 'Eva Rathke' with its dark crimson flowers, but sometimes white or yellow. The spreading shrub *Weigela* 'Snowflake' bears delicate, pure white flowers. The more compact *W. florida* 'Variegata' is one of the best variegated types of Weigela.

To propagate, root greenwood cuttings in early summer.

Weigelas require good drainage and fertile soils for the best results.

Weigela 'Eva Rathke'

MOISTURE	Keep reasonably moist
SITE/LIGHT	Sun to light shade in fertile soils with good drainage
GENERAL CARE	After flowering, cut back heavily to ground level
PESTS & DISEASES	Prone to leaf worm and honey fungus

***SHRUBS* see also 435**

***COMPANION PLANTS* see pages 344–5 380 437**

Wisteria

This genus is a quick-growing climber, and capable of making 6m (20ft) in a year. Train it to grow into and through tall trees to add a touch of early spring colour.

Wisteria is often grown for its showy, pea-like, fragrant flowers that are borne profusely in long, pendent trusses in shades of purple-blue to white. The stems will wind themselves, vine-like, around any supports and its twisting habit make it ideal to be trained to grow anywhere in the garden.

Wisteria floribunda

Regular pruning will keep it within the space required and also encourage flowering. The Japanese wisteria, *Wisteria floribunda*, is a particularly vigorous, twining climber which produces an abundance of scented, blue-violet to pink or white flowers.

Wisteria can be raised from seed but such plants are slow and rather erratic to flower. A much better idea is either grafted plants (grafted in winter) or to layer a long shoot. Basal cuttings in early summer should also root.

Wisteria grows in most soil types, in either full sun or shade. Give it plenty of water to start, then leave it more or less to its own devices. The plant needs support if not growing into a tree shape, but check that stems do not grow into any supporting wires, as this could kill the shrub.

MOISTURE	Keep moist until well established
SITE/LIGHT	Sun or shade in most well-drained soils
GENERAL CARE	Prune back to resize or reshape
PESTS & DISEASES	Generally trouble free

SHRUBS see also 201–4

COMPANION PLANTS see pages 292 294 323

Yucca

This group consists of about forty rosette-forming perennials and evergreen shrubs and trees which are found in hot, dry areas such as deserts and plains.

Grown for their stunning architectural habit, Yuccas also produce rosettes of rigid, slender, sword-shaped leaves and tall panicles of large, drooping, waxy, bell-shaped flowers. *Yucca glauca* (Soapweed) is a low-growing, hardy plant with a round head of thin, greyish-green leaves that are edged with white and curly threads. *Y. gloriosa* (Spanish dagger) forms a fairly hardy shrub with green, sharp-tipped leaves. 'Variegata' has leaves with bright yellow edges, producing a splash of colour to a spiky border. *Y. aloifolia* (Spanish bayonet) is perhaps the most dangerous, with its large, sharp spines on each leaf.

Propagate by sowing seeds or removing suckers in spring, or taking root cuttings in winter.

Grow hardy yuccas outdoors in a hot, dry site in well-drained soil in full sun. They are excellent for gardens in coastal areas. Cut off dead leaves once or twice a year.

Yucca aloifolia 'Variegata'

MOISTURE	Requires little moisture to thrive once established
SITE/LIGHT	Grow in any well-drained soil in the full sun
GENERAL CARE	Remove dead leaves once or twice a year
PESTS & DISEASES	Prone to black aphids in the summer

SHRUBS see also 144

COMPANIO PLANTS see pages 211 423 429

Zantedeschia ARUM LILY

Zantedeschia aethiopica is a frost-hardy perennial. Depending on the climate it may be evergreen or herbaceous, but its best cultivar 'Crowborough' is more or less fully hardy.

The arum lily is one of the more exotic-looking plants for the garden with its broad, arrow-shaped leaves and tubular, flaring flowers (correctly called spathes). Grow where a bold accent plant is called for in the garden – even when it is not in bloom, the arum lily's glossy foliage is desirable.

This plant can be grown as an aquatic in a pool in the shallow water at the edge – up to 30cm (12in) in depth. Plant in an aquatic basket filled with heavy loam. Otherwise, grow in a border with moist soil, well enriched with humus. In this situation, a winter mulch of dry straw or leaves will protect the roots in frosty climates.

Zantedeschia aethiopica 'Crowborough'

Propagate by division in spring.

Although they thrive in full sun, arum lilies tolerate partial shade. They are prone to aphids and various fungal root rots.

MOISTURE	Give plenty of water but rots in soil that is waterlogged
SITE/LIGHT	Full sun to partial shade in humus-rich, well-drained soil
GENERAL CARE	Deadhead regularly for best results
PESTS & DISEASES	Prone to aphids and various fungal root rot

FLOWERS see also 186

'OMPANION PLANTS see pages 293 335 380

Zenobia

There is only one species in this genus – *Zenobia pulverulenta,* also known as dusty Zenobia. It is a spreading deciduous or semi-evergreen shrub.

A native of the coastal plains in south-eastern USA, Zenobia makes a shrub to about 2m (6ft). Its flowers are bell-shaped, like large lily-of-the-valley flowers, and are delicately scented. The new foliage is dusty blue on top and silvery-looking underneath.

It can be propagated by sowing the small seeds onto the top of damp compost, but semi-hardwood cuttings in mid-summer allow the best forms to be grown.

Zenobia pulverulenta

Zenobia pulverulenta

Site Zenobia in either full sun or light shade. It is best positioned in a certain amount of shade, if it is not possible to water adequately in summer.

MOISTURE	Likes permanently moist soil; hates drought
SITE/LIGHT	Full sun to partial shade in acidic, humus-rich soil
GENERAL CARE	Excellent shrub for a woodland garden
PESTS & DISEASES	Generally trouble free

SHRUBS
see also
435

COMPANION PLANTS
see pages
227
252
280

Zinnia

Half-hardy to frost-tender bushy annuals, zinnias have rounded, daisy-like heads of double or single flowers in a wide range of colours.

The blooms of zinnias are good for cutting. These plants perform best in hot summers. Grow in a mixed border, particularly with other daisy-flowered plants such as *Rudbeckia hirta* cultivars and tagetes (marigolds) and with ornamental grasses of appropriate stature. Also grow in patio containers, particularly the dwarf *Zinnia haageana* 'Persian Carpet' (Mexican zinnia).

Raise plants from seed, under glass in early spring, in flowering positions during late spring. To ensure a long display, sow seeds in succession.

Remove dead flowerheads regularly. Few pests and diseases are troublesome but watch out for grey mould, particularly with large, double-flowered cultivars.

Zinnia haageana 'Persian Carpet'

MOISTURE	Keep moist but never waterlogged
SITE/LIGHT	Enjoys full sun in fertile, humus-rich, well-drained soil
GENERAL CARE	Remove dead flowerheads regularly
PESTS & DISEASES	Prone to grey mould, but otherwise trouble free

FLOWERS see also 416

COMPANION PLANTS see pages 163 336 394

Index of Common Plant Names